P9-AOT-641

Modern European History

A Garland Series of Outstanding Dissertations

General Editor
William H. McNeill
University of Chicago

Associate Editors

Eastern Europe
Charles Jelavich
Indiana University

Great Britain
Peter Stansky
Stanford University

France
David H. Pinkney
University of Washington

Russia
Barbara Jelavich
Indiana University

Germany
Enno E. Kraehe
University of Virginia

MODERN EUROPEAN HISTORY

The British Catholic Press and the Educational Controversy, 1847–1865

Mary Griset Holland

Garland Publishing, Inc.
New York and London 1987

Library of Congress Cataloging-in-Publication Data

Holland, Mary Griset, 1939–
    The British Catholic press and the educational
controversy, 1847–1865 / Mary Griset Holland.
    p.   cm.—(Modern European history)
    Thesis (Ph.D.)—Catholic University of America,
1975.
    Bibliography: p.
    Includes index.
    ISBN 0-8240-7817-9 (alk. paper)
    1. Catholic Church—Education—England—
History—19th century.   2. Education and state—
England—History—19th century.   3. Church and
state—England—History—19th century.   4. Church
and state—Catholic Church—History—19th century.
5. Catholics—England—History—19th century.
6. Press, Catholic—England—History—19th
century.   I. Title.   II. Series.
LC506.G72E544   1987
377'.8242—dc19   87-26021

All volumes in this series are printed on acid-
free, 250-year-life paper.

Printed in the United States of America

THE CATHOLIC UNIVERSITY OF AMERICA

THE BRITISH CATHOLIC PRESS AND THE

EDUCATIONAL CONTROVERSY, 1847-1865

A DISSERTATION
Submitted to the Faculty of
The Graduate School of Arts and Sciences
Of The Catholic University of America
For the Degree
Doctor of Philosophy

by
Mary Griset Holland

Washington, D.C.
1975

TABLE OF CONTENTS

LIST OF TABLES

PREFACE

Every society is, to some extent, a mystery to outsiders. The older the society, the more difficult it is to fathom its mysteries unless one is born or trained into it. Sometimes societies exist side by side, each little known to the other though seemingly a part of the same social fabric. Such is the case with the Roman Catholic Church and the English nation in the nineteenth century. In a very real sense these were two different worlds, each with its own long-established institutions and traditions. As a student of Victorian Catholicism and Victorian England seeking to focus a doctoral dissertation, I sought to understand the ways in which these two very different societies interacted.

It seemed to me then, as it does today, that the interactions are played out in two developments that clearly reflect the values of the Victorian age: the evolution of the popular press and the rise of popular education. In studying the English Catholic press´s coverage of the latter, I sought answers to several questions: What perspectives concerning English politics shaped the way Catholics worked with the state? How did Catholics view the larger church-state struggles of this period? What was the Catholic understanding of the education movement? How important was the poor school movement to the historical development of

English Catholicism? What can the Catholic poor school movement tell us about the tensions within the Catholic community? And, what can we learn about that community by studying its press?

The study that follows demonstrates that Catholics were deeply divided over church-state-education issues and suggests that the Catholic poor school movement had a much more important role in the evolution of Victorian Catholicism than is indicated by the attention scholars have given this subject. The Catholic press coverage of educational questions also reveals a great deal about how Catholics perceived English politics, society, and religion.

Since 1975, when my dissertation was completed, an extraordinary number of books and articles has been published concerning the topics examined here: Victorian Catholicism, its press, popular education, and the Catholic poor school movement. A famous lawyer once said of the prison population that 99 percent of the convicts are not guilty exactly as charged. I might argue that very few of the works published since 1975 have an exact bearing on my subject. But all too many have some bearing upon the themes my study developed, shedding light upon this or that issue or controversy, correcting specific facts or approaches, and suggesting methodologies that might be profitably applied to questions raised but not resolved.

In this brief preface I cannot list all of the changes I would make if I were writing the work now: such a list would be long, and it would be dull. Nor can I discuss all the implications of recent scholarship. But I do wish to express my great admiration for those scholars who have described events more clearly or more accurately than I and whose originality in asking the right questions has produced delightful debates, especially with regard to the larger history of popular education in Victorian England. The scholarship of the past decade has confirmed my conviction that the church-state-education debates were at the very heart of Victorian politics.

One work towers above them all. John Bossy's The English Catholic Community, 1570-1850[1] is historian's history at its best, confirming the scholar's intuition that many nagging questions would be resolved if only one could see more of the total picture. Bossy's broad synthesis presents old facts in a new light and provides much new evidence about the English Catholic community. Above all, it brings to life the members of the community--the lay people who are so frequently neglected in histories of Catholicism and whose role is often seen as a mere function of the role of bishops, clergy, and religious.

Bossy develops what might be termed a national case study of the rise of "clerical absolutism." In tracing the replacement of "aristocratic supremacy" by "clerical supremacy,"[2] he transcends the traditional political and theological polemics. Leaving aside the language of grand ideas, he examines more ordinary tensions over day-to-day questions: How are affairs to be managed? Who has what role? And what are the practical ramifications of this or that policy? My own experience in administration has taught me

---

[1]John Bossy, The English Catholic Community, 1570-1850 (London: Darton, Longman & Todd, 1975).

[2]Ibid., p. 337.

that when participants in a quarrel say that great truths are at stake, a more credible explanation may often be found by looking at issues of turf or money or conflicts of personal style. When scholars examine tensions within the English Catholic community, they often find it difficult to understand what, in fact, was at issue. Bossy's study helps us look at such questions with greater insight.

It is Bossy's thesis that there was an organic unity within the Catholic community during the period from 1570 to 1850 and that after 1850 the community became something very different. In describing the historical developments that explain the dissolution of the old and the emergence of the new, he tells a story of particular significance to the student of the Victorian Catholic poor school movement.

It is a fascinating story concerning four basic developments: the emergence of Catholic congregationalism as a possible alternative to aristocratic supremacy in the community; the revival of clerical claims that challenged both aristocratic and middle-class leadership; the decline of mutual understanding between Catholics and Dissenters; and the imposition of new patterns of public worship and prayer that rejected the use of the English language, curtailed congregational involvement, and introduced "the unadorned Latin Mass" and "Latin evening services of vespers and Benediction."[3]

My own work shows that there were intense controversies in the

---

[3]Ibid., p. 385.

Catholic press about the education of the poor and raises important questions about problems underlying them. Bossy makes it clear that the problems hinted at in the press were attendant on fundamental changes taking place within the community. His chapters "Hierarchy Restored" and "The Heart of the Matter"[4] depict the conditions that help explain the controversies and are essential background reading to the present work. And I believe that the developments he portrays--especially congregationalism--underscore the importance of educational controversies to Victorian Catholic history.

The congregationalism he describes as emerging in the latter half of the eighteenth century is similar in many respects to the lay trusteeism that developed in the United States. It is not possible here to do justice to the subject except to say that congregationalism was the creation of a rising middle class and farming interest and was strongest in the industrial towns that most needed Catholic poor schools. Bossy shows that as bishops and clergy moved to restrict lay involvement in church management, the fight for lay participation in church affairs came to center on chapel building and elementary education.[5]

It appears that the rise and fall of the Catholic Institute, 1838-47, was perhaps the closing chapter of the history of congregationalism within the English Catholic community. The institute's central committee in London was aristocratic in its membership, but its provincial branches were dominated by middle-class Catholics.

---

[4]Ibid., pp. 322-363, 364-390.

[5]Ibid., p. 349.

According to Bossy, none of the bishops was enamored of the institute,[6] but Bishop Brown of the newly created Lancashire district-- where congregationalism was strongest--manifested the greatest hostility. Brown issued a pastoral abolishing lay fund-raising efforts for churches and schools and establishing a new board--with no lay board members--for this purpose. Tensions came to a head in 1843 when the institute's committee supported the government's factory bill which would have given control over factory education to Anglicans. Because the institute failed to get a quid pro quo in the form of a government grant for Catholic schools, it was discredited in the provincial branches and fell into disarray. In 1847, says Bossy, "the bishops had little difficulty replacing it with a Poor School Committee consisting of two laymen and eight representatives of themselves; the local school-committees seem to have been got rid of at the same time."[7]

Bossy's narrative shows that the struggles resulting in the demise of congregationalism were closely linked to the controversies over the Catholic poor school movement. One of the problems often referred to in the Catholic press was the lack of adequate lay support for poor schools. I had tended to view this problem in relation to what I conceived to be a general lack of

---

[6]This counters information provided on p. 56 of my work. Further examination of bishops' correspondence should help clarify this issue.

[7]Ibid., p. 350. See pp. 187 and 255 of my study. H. C. Maxwell complained about the lay domination of the Catholic Poor School Committee; this raises important questions. Further investigation is needed to clarify the extent of lay participation on the Catholic Poor School Committee.

wealth and inept fund-raising methods. Looked at in relation to the situation Bossy describes, however, this lack of financial support for the Catholic Poor School Committee's work must be viewed in an entirely different light. The question that now needs to be asked is whether the lack of lay financial support reflected resistance to the bishops' control over the poor schools as much as it reflected concern about government policy.

Another point Bossy makes is equally relevant. In explaining the factors that contributed to the demise of congregationalism he mentions the role of converts who brought to the Catholic community a different kind of hostility to Protestantism and a submission to authority that was at odds with lay attitudes within the community.[8] As many of the Catholic newspapers and periodicals examined in my dissertation were controlled by converts, another question that now must be asked is how well the Catholic press reflected the attitudes of the more seasoned members of the community.

Bossy's treatment of liturgical developments of the decades prior to 1850 is also illuminating. Anyone associated with the intricacies of parish life knows that the slightest change in liturgy can cause a great stir among parishioners. Surely the elimination of English and the curtailment of lay involvement in public worship must have generated serious problems. Further study is needed to determine the impact of such tensions upon the poor schools controversies.

These are just a few examples of how Bossy's work calls for a reexamination of some of the controversies described in my disser-

---

[8]Ibid., p. 387.

tation. Insofar as his work calls generally for further investigation of the major changes in the Catholic community at mid-century,
I hope my study will prove instructive.

Two other categories of works on Victorian Catholicism must be
acknowledged: specific articles on Catholicism that have a direct
bearing on educational issues, and works that deal with the Irish
in England. John P. Marmion and J. M. Feheney[9] have written
articles that relate to the Catholic education movement, and there
has been a virtual explosion of publications on the Irish in
England.

John P. Marmion´s "The Beginnings of the Catholic Poor Schools
in England" is a very brief survey. Its importance for my purposes
derives from the author´s emphasis upon the role of the religious
communities in the education of the Catholic poor. This is a story
not developed in my thesis, and I believe that the Catholic press
should be examined more closely to discern whether there was significant press coverage of the role of religious orders in popular
education. Marmion especially stresses the contribution of the
nuns in establishing two excellent teacher-training colleges that,
he says, were responsible for the "creation of a lay Catholic
teaching profession."[10] Both the general role of religious orders
and their specific part in developing a teacher-training system are

---

[9]John P. Marmion, "The Beginnings of Catholic Poor Schools in
England," Recusant History 17 (1984): 67-83; and J. Matthew
Feheney, "The London Catholic Ragged School: An Experiment in
Education for Irish Destitute Children," Archivium Hibernicum 39
(1984): 32-44.

[10]Marmion, op. cit., p. 80.

significant and require further study.

"The London Catholic Ragged School: An Experiment in Education for Irish Destitute Children," by J. M. Feheney, sketches the history of what was perhaps the only Catholic effort to imitate Lord Shaftesbury's evangelical ragged school movement. Based on archives at the London Oratory and other materials from the 1850s, Feheney's article is a valuable study of an important experiment and gives us a glimpse into the energetic work of William Anthony Hutchison, a member of the Oratory. The ragged schools for boys, girls, and infants were only one of Hutchison's projects. Quite the charitable entrepreneur, Hutchison also organized a model lodging house, a hostel for girls, and a reformatory for girls and established auxiliary organizations for their support. The Association of the Daughters of Compassion was a membership organization for daughters of the aristocracy and upper classes; its purpose was fund raising. The Company of St. Patrick was a group of lay parents of ragged school children; the parents visited neighborhood homes to encourage families to attend church; they also set up reading rooms and a lending library and organized concerts and other neighborhood activities. Feheney demonstrates the extent to which Hutchison imitated Protestant evangelical methods. Once his health broke down, however, directions changed. The new leadership turned away from the less structured style of the ragged school model and adopted more traditional educational methods that placed greater emphasis on academic excellence. The author concludes that "the open structure did not appeal to Catholic leaders. They had more confidence in custodial institutions whether they were orphanages, reformatories, industrial or poor law schools."[11]

Feheney´s article demonstrates that Hutchison and his successor, James Rowe, depended on various types of government grants
available for industrial training. Of greater significance, they
viewed industrial training as the appropriate way to provide education for certain classes of children. One of the questions I raise
in my study is whether the distinction historians have made between
poor schools, industrial schools, reformatories and other types of
schools is appropriate to the realities of the period. Feheney´s
article would suggest that in this case the distinction was not
very important; rather, he shows that Hutchison viewed the various
grant programs as varieties of resources for the one purpose of
education. Feheney´s article is also helpful in portraying educational work as part of a larger effort to meet the needs of poor
children. In Hutchison´s program, schools were one of a whole
array of services essential to poor children. We need to know
whether his approach was characteristic or exceptional.

In the past decade a large number of books and articles has
been published about the Irish in England. Catholic press coverage
of church-state-education issues reveals the extent to which
Catholic poor schools were schools for Irish children. Although
none of the recent publications I reviewed dealt primarily with the
education of Irish children in England, virtually all those concerned with Irish ethnicity, Irish community life, Irish

---

[11]Feheney, op. cit., p. 43.

Catholicism, and the like will help us understand the Irish dimension of the Catholic poor school movement.

Timothy J. O'Keefe has written an informative article, "The
Times and the Roman Catholics: 1857,"[12] on the intense controversy
sparked by Nicholas Cardinal Wiseman's speech delivered at Salford
and printed in the Times in September 1857. Using the circumstances of the recent Sepoy mutiny to complain about the treatment
of Catholics in India, Wiseman voiced two specific concerns: that
it was virtually impossible for the children of Catholic soldiers
to be educated in their own faith because the schools taught
Protestant doctrine; and that Catholic orphans were being raised
Protestant. The furor that ensued in the pages of the Times and
elsewhere is well analyzed by O'Keefe. Its importance here lies in
the fact that the controversy "became confused with broader
questions," including that of the loyalty of Irish Catholics. In
demonstrating how readily the English linked English Catholic complaints to Irish disloyalty, O'Keefe confirms that few topics could
be completely isolated from the Irish question—or from the issue
of education. Concern about Irish disloyalty focused especially on
priests because of their tendency to "interfere" in politics.
Although my study of the Catholic press reveals that Catholic poor
schools were primarily for the Irish, it does not indicate how many
of the clergy involved in the poor school movement were Irish.
This is a question that should be investigated carefully, as the
answer may lead to a fuller understanding of clerical resistance to

---

[12]Timothy J. O'Keefe, "The Times and the Roman Catholics:
1857" A Journal of Church and State 18 (Spring 1976): 253-272.

government grants and a greater appreciation of the tensions surrounding other aspects of church-state negotiations.

Other works that should be mentioned include Sheridan Gilley's "English Attitudes to the Irish in England, 1789-1900" and "The Roman Catholic Church and the Nineteenth-Century Irish Diaspora."[13] Lynn Hollen Lees's _Exiles of Erin: Irish Migrants in Victorian London_[14] is a major work on the realities of Irish ethnicity. Michael Durey's "The Survival of an Irish Culture in Britain, 1800-1845"[15] adds to our understanding of the complexity of Irish life in England before the famine. His argument that there was a segment of Irish well integrated into the English working-class world has important implications for students of the Catholic poor school movement. While my study speaks of "the Irish dimension" of the poor school movement, Durey's work reveals that that "dimension," everywhere, was both complex and multiple. The varieties of the Irish experience now need to be considered in regard to educational politics as well as other areas. On the Irish in specific regions, the following should be noted: W. J. Lowe, "The Lancashire Irish and the Catholic Church, 1846-1871: The Social Dimension";[16] Roger

---

[13]Sheridan Gilley, "English Attitudes to the Irish in England, 1789-1900," in _Immigrants and Minorities in British Society_ (London, 1978), pp. 81-110; also Gilley's "The Roman Catholic Church and the Nineteenth-Century Irish Diaspora," _Journal of Ecclesiastical History_ 35 (April 1984): 188-207.

[14]Lynn Hollen Lees, _Exiles of Erin: Irish Migrants in Victorian London_ (Manchester: University of Manchester Press, 1979).

[15]Michael Durey, "The Survival of an Irish Culture in Britain, 1800-1845," _Historical Studies_ 20 (1982): 14-35.

[16]W. J. Lowe, "The Lancashire Irish and the Catholic Church, 1846-1871: The Social Dimension," _Irish Historical Studies_ 78

Swift, "Anti-Catholicism and Irish Disturbances: Public Order in Mid-Victorian Wolverhampton";[17] and J. M. Feheney's work on delinquent Irish children in London.[18] This rich diversity of scholarship on regional and national history of the Irish in England will help future educational historians better understand the role of schools in the Irish communities in England.

A work which readers will also want to consult is Walter L. Arnstein's Protestant versus Catholic in Mid-Victorian England: Mr. Newdegate and the Nuns.[19] Although the main developments in this case study of Victorian anti-catholicism occurred after 1863, Arnstein's narrative gives texture and reality to the "no-popery" so often referred to by writers in the Catholic press, and his introductory chapters provide a significant addition to the literature.

On the English Catholic press, the most substantial scholarship to be noted is by Josef L. Altholz. His recent contribution is "The Redaction of Catholic Periodicals."[20] Here he unravels the

---

(September 1976): 129-155.

[17]Roger Swift, "Anti-Catholicism and Irish Disturbances: Public Order in Mid-Victorian Wolverhampton," Midland History 9 (1984): 87-108.

[18]J. M. Feheney, "Delinquency Among Irish Catholic Children in Victorian London," Irish Historical Studies 23 (November 1983): 319-329.

[19]Walter L. Arnstein, Protestant versus Catholic in Mid-Victorian England: Mr. Newdegate and the Nuns (Columbia and London: University of Missouri Press, 1982).

[20]Josef L. Altholz, "The Redaction of Catholic Periodicals," in Innovators and Preachers: The Role of the Editor in Victorian England, ed., Joel H. Wiener (Westport, Connecticut: Greenwood

labyrinthine arrangements that constituted editorship in the Victorian period. Editorial committees, theological censors, proprietors, publishers, and printers were all part of this complex arrangement. According to Altholz, Sir John (later Lord) Acton employed the French term "redaction" to describe the totality of the processes involved in editing.[21] Altholz's examination of the Catholic press as a model for redaction points up the need for clarification of the editorial history of several publications treated in the present work. Specifically, he offers useful information on the redaction of the Catholic Standard (subsequently the Weekly Register), Dolman's Magazine, the Dublin Review, the Home and Foreign Review, the Rambler, and the Tablet.

"The Tablet, the True Tablet, and Nothing But the Tablet," also by Altholz, is a delightful account of the episode in 1842 when a conflict between Frederick Lucas and his printer, "one Cox,"[22] resulted in the simultaneous existence of two papers calling themselves the Tablet. Characteristically Lucas called his the True Tablet. The article also describes the origins of the Tablet in relation to the Catholic milieu of the early 1840s and offers a summary of developments after Lucas's death in 1855.

For an excellent review of scholarly writings on the Victorian press, the reader will want to consult Joel Wiener's "Bibliographical Essay" in Innovators and Preachers: The Role of the Editor in

---

Press, 1985), pp. 143-160.

[21]Ibid., p. 144.

[22]Altholz, "The Tablet, the True Tablet, and Nothing But the Tablet," Victorian Periodicals Newsletter 9 (June 1976): 68-72.

Victorian England.[23] In addition, of course, it is necessary to consult the annual bibliographies in the Victorian Periodicals Review and in Victorian Studies to keep up with what Wiener aptly calls this "growth industry" of scholarship on the Victorian press.

Recent work in popular education offers the most striking challenges to my study. Changing approaches and emerging debates are well described in the first few pages of Schooling in Western Europe: A Social History by Mary Jo Maynes.[24] Examining issues from the European rather than a national perspective, Maynes describes the impact of sociology, anthropology and other methodologies on historical questions and outlines the main features of debates between Marxist and more traditional historians of education. The questions recent scholars have asked are many and complex: Was the expansion of popular education progressive, or did educational reform serve to "contain" the "lower" classes"? How did educational reform relate to the rise of democracy? How did working-class parents, families, and children respond to the introduction of education? What was the changing relationship between education and social stratification? What was the relationship between education, literacy, and the Industrial Revolution? The value of Maynes's book to the readers of my dissertation will derive from its breadth of perspective. She touches on many questions I mentioned a decade ago as requiring historical investi-

---

[23]Wiener, "Bibliographical Essay," in Innovators and Preachers, pp. 307-319.

[24]Mary Jo Maynes, Schooling in Western Europe: A Social History (Albany: State University of New York Press, 1985).

gation. Several vigorous historiographical debates now demonstrate how far scholarship has progressed since then.

So many works on English education have appeared, in fact, since my dissertation was completed in 1975 that I am at a loss to know what to say about them in this short space. Perhaps it will suffice to ask what the current debates can tell us about the real connection between religion and education, and on that we can learn a great deal. There are much data on clerical control, secularization, religion as a means of social control, and popular anticlericalism. But there is also the danger of getting lost in competing elitist perspectives--whether radical, Marxist, or clerical--and missing the religion of the people.

I very often have the feeling in reading educational history that we do not know enough about what we might term the religious yearnings of Victorian poor children, whatever their denominational connections--about their desire to be good, about their parents' moral and religious hopes for them, about their questions concerning life and death. To be sure my study, like much recent scholarship, deals with issues of power and control; these are, after all, basic to our understanding of the past. Yet despite the emphasis on these perspectives in studies published since I completed my work, I find that the Catholic press coverage of church-state-education controversies still compels consideration of the religious motivation as a primary element in the extraordinary energy that went into the Catholic poor schools.

This study has been made possible by the kindness and professional assistance of many librarians and historians and by the help of administrators and staff members at many institutions. I wish to express my gratitude in particular to the superintendent and staff of the British Newspaper Library, Colindale, for the expeditious microfilming of materials essential to this research; to the librarians at Farm Street for much generous aid; and to the fathers of the Brompton Street Oratory for making available their valuable collection.

As a student at Catholic University I benefited greatly from the courtesy of administrative personnel who helped make my graduate experience enjoyable and rewarding. Special thanks are due the university for the fellowship that made possible the timely completion of the degree program. Over a three-year period I enjoyed the cheerful support of the professors and staff of the Department of History, and I particularly appreciated the assistance of Rt. Rev. Joseph N. Moody and Professors Thomas West and John K. Zeender. A special debt is owed to those who read and critiqued this dissertation. Professor Catherine A. Cline consistently encouraged my interest and offered helpful direction; Dr. Damian McElrath offered invaluable support and assistance; and as director Rev. Robert Trisco was always ready with insight and assistance. His high standards of scholarship set an important example, and I will remain grateful for his interest and guidance. And for her expeditious preparation of the typescript, I give special thanks to Linda M. Distad.

Above all, I wish to express my deepest appreciation to my husband, James Clarence Holland, whose sanity and unfailing humor have smoothed many rough waters and whose sense of the larger questions of history continues to provide motivation and support.

CHAPTER I

INTRODUCTION

Purpose, Scope and Method of Study

This analysis of the English Catholic press response to the
church-state controversy in education, 1847-1865, attempts to inte-
grate several dimensions of the political and religious developments which contributed to the rise of a national system of education during the Victorian era. Victorians were obsessed with the
idea that elementary education for the poor would solve the ´condi-
tion of England´ problem.[1] Because they believed in religious
education, church-state conflicts were central to all aspects of
the education question. The rise of the popular press was part of
the education mania: because the press had a vested interest in
improving the level of literacy journalists eagerly took sides in
the educational controversies. The religious press existed to
promote sectarian interests and understanding, and its journalists
included some of the most prominent educational lobbyists of the
day; thus familiarity with the development of educational opinion

_____

[1]Richard Johnson, "Educational Policy and Social Control in
Early Victorian England," in The Victorian Revolution: Government
and Society in Victorian Britain, ed. Peter Stansky (New York:
Franklin Watts, New Viewpoints, 1973), pp. 199-201.

1

in the religious press should improve our knowledge of how contemporaries felt, believed and acted. It is hoped this study of the
English Catholic press response to the church-state-education
question will contribute to that understanding.

As there are so many histories of English education another
may seem both unnecessary and irritating, but the literature has
been highly specialized and has failed to answer important
questions concerning the relationship between the rise of modern
education and other major nineteenth-century developments. For
example, it is not altogether clear how the educational revolution
affected the shifting balance in church-state relations or how it
was related to fundamental changes in the structure of local and
central government; nor is the connection between the rise of mass
democracy and the expansion of popular education as clear as many
historians have assumed. This study attempts to deal with the
interplay between certain of these crucial forces which shaped the
church-state-education conflicts in Victorian England.

English Catholics were a minority in possession of little
direct influence in either general or educational politics; however, their position vis-à-vis church-state questions was both
unique and important because of the impact of the Irish question on
English politics and because of the ´popish´ tendencies of the
Oxford movement, which complicated Anglican problems in church and
state. Catholic educational policy was historically important as
part of the opposition to the development of a system dominated by
the civil power and secular or undenominational in character. Thus
an understanding of the Catholic participation in these conflicts
should broaden one´s understanding of other significant aspects of

the problem. This is also a study in English Catholicism, its educational policies and its confessional press. In this context an effort is made to explain how Catholic journalists understood the education question and how they used the press as an instrument for shaping opinion.

The years to be covered, 1847-1865, form appropriate boundaries for the subject. The year 1847 witnessed the formation of the Catholic Poor School Committee, which was the first official organization to have both ecclesiastical backing and the authority to negotiate with the state. The year 1865 saw the death of Cardinal Archbishop Wiseman and thus the end of an era in English Catholicism; the same year saw the death of Lord Palmerston which similarly ended an era in English politics. After 1865 educational policy was much more directly influenced by the parliamentary reform movement and by legislative initiative than it had been during the previous period of executive ascendancy when the Privy Council's Committee on Education and the Royal Commissions dominated the field.

It was originally this author's intention to carry the discussion up to the passing of the Education Act of 1870 because that was such a landmark in English educational history; that plan was abandoned for several reasons which require comment. Following Palmerston's death there was a general shake-up in political affairs which produced the Reform Bill of 1867, the abolition of church rates in 1868, the disestablishment of the Church of Ireland in 1869, the Education Act of 1870, to name only the most outstanding measures of these years. Historical discussion about the connections linking these developments abounds, but it is safe to say that the literature definitely does not emphasize church-state factors even though three of the four measures involved crucial church-state questions. The place of educational reform in this series of developments is not so clear as many historians would like to suggest by their casual reference to Robert Lowe's 'we must now educate our masters' comment of 1867. What is being suggested here is that the 1865-1870 period represents the beginning of a new era, perhaps even the end of the 'Victorian balance,' and that the educational developments of that later period belong to a subsequent era which extended to the passing of the Education Act of 1902.

With specific reference to problems in English Catholic historiography there are equally sound reasons for concluding with 1865. The Catholic concern over the threat to the Temporal Power of the Papacy and over the Vatican Council's definition of Papal Infallibility overshadowed the education question to such an extent that the press coverage of the latter could not be expected to represent Catholic views adequately. Finally, the historical controversy over Cardinal Manning's educational policies up to and during 1870 cannot be resolved without thorough consultation of the Manning papers.[2] Historical questions about the life and contri-

---

[2]See D. E. Selby, "Henry Edward Manning and the Education Bill of 1870," British Journal of Educational Studies 18 (June 1970): 197-212. This treats problems relating specifically to Manning's actions in 1869 and 1870, but there are other problems. For example, what continuity was there between Manning's educational position as an Anglican and the stance he assumed as a Catholic bishop? What impact did the lay anticlericalism prominent within the Anglican body have upon his dealings with Catholic laymen

butions of Cardinal Manning are already so numerous as to demand a
thorough and fully integrated re-evaluation, rather than the numerous piecemeal approaches which have been forthcoming since the
publication of Purcell's unflattering biography;[3] hence the
decision to refrain from contributing still another troublesome
partial solution to a problem which requires a sweeping re-
examination.

The methodology employed in this study has involved the careful analysis of English Catholic newspapers, magazines, journals
and quarterlies. General approaches to social and political problems have received considerable attention, and specific coverage of
church-state-education questions have been studied with great care.
Because of the variety and volume of materials dealt with and the
numerous short-run titles studied, uniformity in analysis has not
been possible; however, certain criteria have governed methodolog-
ical decisions. Attention has been focused on editorial articles
because Victorian journalists were openly editorial and because
'straight news' items tended to be few and of restricted importance; still, an effort has been made to study all pertinent
articles. One qualification should be stated: certain articles
covering local schools or strictly devotional educational literature have received little attention. This is because it was not

---

involved in educational politics? And there are other questions
which suggest the need for a full re-examination of Manning's
career. Particular attention should be given to his pre-1865
educational work.

[3]Edmund Sheridan Purcell, The Life of Cardinal Manning,
Archbishop of Westminster, 2 vols. (New York: Macmillan & Co.,
1896).

possible, helpful or necessary to consult every report about fund-raising dinners, balls and meetings in every town or to read extensively about new prayers or devotional exercises proposed for use in the classroom; this is a study of fundamental church-state questions, not a history of English Catholic schools. An attempt will be made to indicate the extent to which the format, content and editorial policy of each publication have influenced the author's criteria for analysis.

The chronological framework was determined by the progress of state policy because Catholic policy was responsive rather than instigative insofar as church-state relations were concerned. This fact has also governed the content of the following sections of this introduction which are primarily devoted to the broad church-state tensions of the period as they affected and were affected by the education question. The Catholic position is defined in its relationship to that broad current of development.

Educational Background

In 1847 English Catholics formally began negotiations to obtain state funds for their schools. Catholic intrusion into a thoroughly Protestant system aroused 'no-popery' sentiments among Anglicans and Dissenters alike, but this was not the only obstacle; church-state negotiations concerning education had been underway for a decade, and the precedents thus established were not altogether suited to Catholic needs. Educational philanthropy had been in the hands of the two great Protestant societies whose policies had set the pattern for school expansion before government aid was first made available in 1833. In short, Catholics encountered a network of policies and practices which must be described at least briefly if the relative position of Catholics is to be understood.

Since early in the century Anglicans and Dissenters had been well organized for the purpose of spreading education among the poor. They possessed educational societies, national in scope, which derived their operative strength from local component societies. The Dissenters' organization, the British and Foreign School Society dated from 1807 although it was not given that name until 1814. The Anglicans responded to the Nonconformist initiative by founding the National Society for Education of the Poor in the Principles of the Established Church in 1811. These organizations developed two precedents which governed educational policies throughout most of the century: first, education of the poor was to have an unquestionably religious--Christian--basis; and secondly, the establishment of schools was to be the result of local effort supported by national organizations. Since this philanthropic system had been functioning for over two decades when Parliament intervened in 1833, the government followed the path of least resistance by distributing state funds through the existing institutional framework.[4]

This coordination of local and national activity by the religious bodies represented a deep political tradition in English history; in describing this tradition the French historian Elie

---

[4]Discussion concerning the early work of the two societies can be found in almost any general educational history, but the most helpful studies are the following: H. B. Binns, A Century of Education, Being the Centenary History of the British and Foreign School Society, 1808-1908 (London: J. M. Dent & Co., 1908), and R. Gregory, Elementary Education (London: National Society, 1905).

Halévy concluded that "the free organization of the sects was the foundation of social order in England." Halévy credited Methodism with stimulating the rise of such organizational voluntarism which he claimed provided the "antidote to Jacobinism."[5] The Halévy thesis has generated much historical debate which cannot be treated here,[6] but it is appropriate to suggest that voluntarism in education provides another field of battle for Halévy's attackers and defenders. For the purposes of this study it is only necessary to mention that English Catholics were well isolated from such a tradition.

The isolation of Catholics dated from penal times when priests and bishops (vicars apostolic) depended heavily on the provincial Catholic gentry and nobility for patronage and protection. As persecution declined in the eighteenth century the vicars apostolic became more independent of the gentry, but cooperation among the bishops was an off-and-on proposition during much of the nineteenth

---

[5]Elie Halévy, A History of the English People in the Nineteenth Century, vol. 1: England in 1815, trans. E. I. Watkin and D. A. Barker (London: Ernest Benn, 1924; reprint ed., New York: Barnes & Noble, 1961), pp. 590-591.

[6]The debate over the Halévy thesis is discussed by Gertrude Himmelfarb, Victorian Minds (New York: Alfred A. Knopf, 1968), pp. 292-299. Among the prominent critics of this thesis are E. P. Thompson, The Making of the English Working Class (New York: Pantheon Books, 1964); and E. J. Hobsbawm, "Methodism and the Threat of Revolution in Britain," History Today 7 (February 1957): 115-124; and Robert F. Wearmouth, Methodism and the Working Class Movements of England, 1800-1850 (London: Epworth Press, 1937), and Methodism and the Struggle of the Working Classes, 1850-1900 (Leicester: E. Backus, 1955). See also Charles C. Gillispie, "The Work of Elie Halévy," Journal of Modern History 12 (1950): 232-249; and Bernard Semmel's introduction to Halévy, The Birth of Methodism, ed. Bernard Semmel (Chicago: University of Chicago Press, 1971).

century owing to several variables such as quarrelsome bishops, Irish "interference" regarding emancipation, Vatican influences and other factors. Added to this there was confusion of authority between the regular and secular clergy. Finally, the Catholic laity was virtually unorganized in the traditional English sense. The Church has ever been suspicious of too much lay initiative, and the Church in England was not exceptional in this. The Cisalpine influence in emancipation efforts at the time of the French Revolution made the vicars apostolic ever more jealous of their authority; more important was the fact that lay organizations had trouble gaining widespread support even when there was no resistance from the hierarchy.

When Catholics applied for state aid for Catholic schools in 1847, they lacked a well established tradition of local political action to support their newly formed central organization, the Catholic Poor School Committee. This deficiency was exaggerated by internal tensions between Old Catholics and Converts which would soon be complicated by divisions between Liberals and Ultramontanes.

The organizational disadvantages from which the Catholics suffered must be strongly emphasized because the organizational efficiency of the competing societies was a key to the educational politics of the period. It was against this backdrop that patterns of church-state negotiations were worked out between 1833 and 1847.

Among the considerations which shaped church-state negotiations regarding education during this period, seven assume prominence: (1) prevailing attitudes about education were fundamentally Protestant in character, (2) political attacks against the basic underpinnings of the Established church embittered church-state relations during and after the 1830s, (3) the bureaucracy entered the picture in 1839 to assert its own initiative in educational politics, (4) the Voluntarist movement emerged, 1841-1843, to denounce all state interference in education, (5) a substantial percentage of the poor to be educated were Irish Catholic immigrants, (6) the working precedent of the Irish national education system, dating from 1831, was available as a warning and an example to policy makers, and (7) Benthamites, utilitarians and other secularists leavened educational politics with the notion that education should fall under the control of purely civic authorities and should emphasize secular subjects and general morality while excluding religion—especially dogmatic religion. The relative importance of these factors and the interconnections between them are not easily determined. Historical specialization has to some extent obscured that problem, and as this study is itself specialized it cannot provide the solution; but every effort is made to indicate possible connections between the influential factors and to suggest how further research might contribute toward a more fully integrated understanding of the problem.

The fundamentally Protestant character of England is merely mentioned here as one of the underlying assumptions of this discussion, one which would seem to require no modern elaboration.[7]

---

[7]In all fairness to the ecumenical discussions of the present day, as well as to those of the nineteenth century, it must be noted that many High Churchmen deny the fundamental Protestantism of the Anglican settlement. On this point the author accepts the historical arguments underlying Pope Leo XIII's judgment on

Even so, English Protestantism faced new crises during the 1830s which were political, institutional and doctrinal. While the Oxford movement was attempting to re-establish the apostolic and catholic character of the Church of England the institutional establishment came under severe attack from Dissenters and radicals.

The English Reformation settlement represented a sometimes confusing compromise between authority and private judgment, and the weaknesses in that compromise were periodically exploited--by Puritanism in the seventeenth century, Deism in the eighteenth, and by Methodism and Evangelicalism in both the eighteenth and nineteenth centuries. The nineteenth century saw the emergence of a challenge which was at the same time more thorough and more direct, but ironically also more subtle because the claimed reasons for the challenge obscured the underlying realities which made it possible.

That challenge might be called secularism or statism; whatever it is called it represented the gradual increase of the civil power at the expense of the ecclesiastical or spiritual power.[8] In its most forthright form it was severely anticlerical and demanded disestablishment; in its subtlest form it challenged specific rights and privileges of the Established Church. Yet the original

---

Anglican orders; that argument contends that the Anglican settlement was, beyond question, Protestant.

[8]George Anthony Denison, Notes of My Life, 1805-1878 (Oxford: James Parker & Co., 1878), pp. 78-87. He discusses the forces which challenged the authority of the Establishment and stresses particularly the "indifferent power" as a threat. Denison thoroughly discusses the nature of the secularist threat from a strong Churchman's viewpoint.

purpose of the challenge cannot be called secularist, for that
purpose stemmed from Dissenters'--and Catholics'--demands for redress of grievances. In the main Victorians were Christian, and
the type of antireligion which characterizes some modern forms of
statism or secularism were far from dominant. Still, if one
observes England at the death of the Queen and asks what influence
religion exerted on national and local affairs it can be seen that
its influence had narrowed drastically during the long reign. The
attention has been on the rise of the civil power rather than on
the other side of the coin--the constriction.[9] At least two
historians--Owen Chadwick[10] and Olive Brose[11]--have come to terms
with the constitutional changes in church-state relations during
the Victorian era, and their insights remain to be incorporated
into the general historiography. That task falls well beyond the
scope of this study, but aspects of it cannot be avoided because
the question of who would control the nation's schools, church or
civil authorities, was one of the major questions of the nineteenth
century, and the tensions stemming from this question were fundamental and constitutional.

Because the sectarian fragmentation of nineteenth-century
English religious history has obscured some of the characteristics

---

[9]See Sidney Webb and Beatrice Webb, British Local Government,
9 vols. (London: Longmans, Green & Co., 1908). Extensive local
research is needed in this area.

[10]Owen Chadwick, The Victorian Church, 2 vols. (New York:
Oxford University Press, 1966).

[11]Olive J. Brose, The Church and Parliament: the Reshaping of
the Church of England, 1828-1860 (Stanford, Calif.: Stanford
University Press, 1959).

of church-state politics it is necessary to review certain aspects of the Anglican background. The point must be made that the centrality of the Anglican position to the education question was not an isolated fact but one which was intimately related to the whole thrust of reform politics, which was to attack the underpinnings of establishment--church wealth, church patronage and clerical influence in local government. At the same time, utilitarians questioned the general usefulness of the Church of England by ridiculing its apparent incompetence to deal with the problems of a modern industrial society. Olive Brose´s perceptive study, The Church and Parliament (1959), illustrates how Church reform saved Church property from expropriation by Parliament and describes how the Church attempted to answer the utilitarian challenge by demonstrating its usefulness as a national educator.[12]

The question of the Church´s usefulness was linked to the question of whether she was a comprehensive national institution. The constitutional adjustments of 1828 and 1829 gave religious pluralism political legitimacy; the 1835 Municipal Corporations Act incorporated that pluralism into the fabric of local government;[13] the enormous influx of Irish Catholic immigrants, especially during the 1840s, complicated matters further; and the 1851 religious census underlined divisions and emphasized the existence of a growing unchurched population. All these factors undermined the Church´s claim to be comprehensive, which claim cannot, however, be

---

[12]Ibid., pp. 181-206, 35-36, 90-93.

[13]Chadwick, op. cit., 1:108-112.

totally dismissed.

While Anglicans defended the national and comprehensive character of the establishment, Dissenters and Catholics attacked its exclusiveness and challenged its privileges. There was some truth on both sides. The structural base on which the Church of England operated was in fundamental respects both comprehensive and national, but the religious body which benefitted from that structure had been reduced to a privileged and exclusive position. Tensions arising from this situation permeated English life and politics at the local and national level, manifestations of which could be seen in controversies over the church rate, competition between parishes and town councils for local power, divisions caused by the Oxford movement, and struggles over Church property.

Church rate arguments between 1830 and 1868 illustrate the local intensity of church-state controversies. Ancient parish laws made no distinctions among Christians—they predated Dissent. Thus every citizen was a member of the parish and in open vestries could vote on the church rate. After 1830 annual vestry meetings were transformed into local power struggles in which Dissenters challenged the rates; in this struggle Dissenters acted as parish members. From 1832 when Birmingham refused to vote the rate until it was officially abolished in 1868, vestry meetings aggravated sectarian bitterness throughout England. These "tea-cup parochial squabbles" virtually terminated social intercourse between Anglicans and Dissenters and soured many of the real achievements of church reform.[14]

---

[14]Ibid., pp. 146-158.

At the same time politicians in Parliament were attacking Church property. The attack was directed against the Church of Ireland but by implication the question extended to the Church of England as well. Threatened expropriation of Church property stimulated internal reforms involving a drastic redistribution of Church wealth; this was achieved by the Ecclesiastical Commission first organized under Peel in 1835.[15] The Commission's work did not touch directly on the education question, but contemporaries saw a connection. The attack against Church property was coupled with schemes for appropriating excess funds for popular education, which would be controlled by civil authorities. In securing Church control over Church wealth the Ecclesiastical Commission forced proponents of popular education to seek other ways to finance their schemes.

Even more deep-seated changes were taking place in the balance of church-state power. The 1834 Poor Law Act divested the old ecclesiastical parishes of authority over poor rate distribution, and the Municipal Corporations Act of 1835 laid the foundation of town councils which were similarly independent of clerical control. Olive Brose describes the shift of the local power base from the parish to the town council as one of the major facts of the nineteenth century.[16] The 1835 Municipal Corporations Act symbolized the transfer of power from the parochial to the civic unit of government, but it must be kept in mind that the formal structure

---

[15]Brose, op. cit., p. 62. See also G. F. A. Best, Temporal Pillars (Cambridge: Cambridge University Press, 1963).

[16]Brose, op. cit., p. 206.

of the rural parishes and counties was not officially reformed until 1888. Regardless, the transfer of power was a process which continued throughout the nineteenth century; it had the effect of separating secular and religious authority. Although the dismantling of the Anglican-Tory influence in local politics is often mentioned by modern historians, the significance of the detachment of clerical influence from local politics, essential to the development of civic ascendancy in local government, is seldom emphasized. Because clerical influence in the schools was the subject of so much debate, this broad context of anticlerical politics must not be overlooked.

Anglican influence in local politics had traditionally been secured through private patronage controlled largely by the landed families and through patronage controlled by many of the old corporations.[17] In addition, crown patronage and cathedral patronage could be used to strengthen the local power base of the Establishment. As the landed families became increasingly Tory, Church office seekers followed suit. The 1834 Poor Law and the 1835 Municipal Corporations Act undercut the political value of that patronage, though the impact was not felt immediately. The 1835 Municipal Corporations Bill terminated the old corporate patronage by forcing new town councils to sell patronage rights. Chadwick observes that this detachment of the corporation from ecclesiastical patronage isolated the church from the old sense of

---

[17]Ibid., p. 8, and Chadwick, op. cit., 1:109-110.

community interest and responsibility.[18] The separation of clerical and civil power in government was similarly achieved by the Poor Law of 1834 which ended clerical authority over the administration of the poor rates.[19] The 1836 laws transferring responsibility for marriages and registration to civil authorities created under the Poor Law Act further isolated clerics from civil responsibilities.[20] Finally, the deliberate exclusion in 1839 of all clerics--priests, deacons, ministers or bishops--from the Privy Council Committee on Education assured the separation of civil and ecclesiastical authority in education.[21]

In brief, clericalism in local politics was significantly diminished by the Whig reforms of the 1830s, yet this aspect of the reform movement is seldom noted except by church historians.[22] This narrowing of the clerical sphere of influence in local and national politics had an important bearing on the education question in that the one area where clerical influence remained strong was precisely in the area of popular education. Today the importance of the local school to the modern structure of local politics is an assumed fact, as it was in the nineteenth century, and,

---

[18]Chadwick, op. cit., 1:110.

[19]Sir Llewellyn Woodward, The Age of Reform, 1815-1870 (Oxford: Clarendon Press, 1962), pp. 458-459.

[20]Chadwick, op. cit., 1:144.

[21]Ibid., 1:340.

[22]Church historians have not hesitated to note this, but general historical studies by Asa Briggs, Woodward, and even Kitson Clark give very little attention to this fact. This is particularly curious as they all acknowledge the importance of the religious influence on Victorian life.

indeed, a substantial part of the ´national´ education movement aimed at reducing clerical influence in the schools.[23]

Church-state politics during these years was also complicated by the Oxford movement. Irish Church bills of 1833 raised questions about Parliament´s prerogative in basic areas of Church business. We have noted that Church reform was one response to such attacks; another was Keble´s 1833 sermon on national apostacy which occasioned the beginning of the Oxford movement. Catholic historians have emphasized the conversions which emanated from this movement; this is understandable, but here the manner in which the movement affected Church patronage and educational politics must be stressed.[24]

The Oxford movement undermined the Church´s shaky claim to comprehensiveness by defining the apostolic and catholic character-istics of ´Anglo-Catholicism´ in the narrowest sense,[25] as if deliberately to infuriate Evangelicals and Dissenters, not to men-tion doctrinally indifferent anticlericals. Tractarian emphasis on

---

[23]Theodore Zeldin has edited a group of essays dealing with the impact of anticlericalism in local politics in France; this study develops the position that anticlericalism at the local level, especially in rural France, provided the necessary back-ground to the post-1880 laic laws. While the French situation differed greatly from the English, Zeldin´s historical approach might well be applied to the English scene. See his Conflicts in French Society: Anticlericalism, Education and Morals in the Nine-teenth Century (New York: Humanities Press, 1971).

[24]Chadwick, op. cit., 1:167-231. Here Chadwick discusses the patronage problems, especially pp. 226-231. Throughout his study he emphasizes patronage difficulties posed by contemporary theolog-ical trends, both Tractarian and Liberal. The impact of the Oxford movement on educational thought and policies is discussed in later chapters.

[25]The term "narrowest" is used here in the sense of the Evangelical criticism that Tractarian positions were exclusive.

the catholicity of the Establishment necessarily stressed Church authority in institutional as well as doctrinal matters, partly on principle and partly as a means of protecting the Church from interference by a pluralistic Parliament. At the same time the Oxford men pursued paths of doctrinal and devotional renewal which infused new life into the Establishment. Despite this, Tractarians heightened internal divisions at a time when the external challenge was quite pressing. Given the temperament of the day it is improbable that any movement emphasizing ecclesiastical authority would have been popular, but the Tractarians´ Romanizing tendencies ignited anticlerical sensitivities and threatened the basic Protestantism of the nation.

This posed problems for Whig governments during the 1830s and late 1840s. The Government´s exercise of Crown ecclesiastical patronage became a problem because there were so few Whig candidates for bishoprics. Melbourne´s comment, "Damn it, another Bishop dead!" fittingly summarizes his exasperation with Church patronage problems. Lord John Russell later faced even more perplexing problems--and without benefit of Melbourne´s shield of humorous nonchalance.[26] Oxford men complicated this already ticklish problem because their position defied pragmatic compromise and emphasized internal dissension. Both Melbourne and Russell bent over backward to avoid Tractarian bishops and both nearly fell over in the process, because they chose alternates who were so liberal

---

[26]Chadwick, op. cit., 1:122.

in theology that their orthodoxy was in doubt.[27]   But that is
another story; the important fact is that the Oxford movement kept
alive both anticlericalism and ´no-popery,´ which in turn fueled
opposition to clerical control in education.

The third factor relates to the government´s initiative in
education between 1833 and 1847. Only the most important proposals
can be considered here, including those of 1833, 1839-1840, 1843
and 1846. Whig influence, bureaucratic initiative, and a determination to contain Church influence can be seen in all the important
events of these years.

The use of executive power to establish a system of popular
education is especially provocative in that there is so much
emphasis upon the connection between mass education and democracy.
Since aristocratic control in Parliament continued long after 1832
it was obviously impossible to legislate educational reforms in the
direction demanded by those calling for universal education. Thus
it is generally assumed that the application of executive power to
this problem represented a move in the direction of democracy.
Perhaps it did, but in this matter one crucial question has not
been asked--namely, whether the masses wanted education.

Once again the author must plead guilty to raising a question
which is not assessed in this study, but the legitimacy of the
question would seem self-evident. Contemporary sources leave no
doubt that the ruling elite wanted the masses to have some kind of

---

[27]Both Melbourne and Russell encountered difficulties over
appointments involving R. D. Hampden; see Chadwick, op. cit.,
1:112-121, 237-249.

education that would render them less troublesome, but those same sources also indicate that school inspectors encountered considerable parental resistance to elementary education. This was especially so in rural areas where half the population resided.[28] The nagging problem of low and irregular attendance could also be construed as an expression of popular disinterest. So the historian might well ask whether there was in fact genuine popular support for mass education. Doubtless the Chartists were interested in education, but were they ´representative´? If interest in education was democratic in the sense that interest in wages or workhouse conditions could be said to have been democratic, then historians are justified in depicting the struggle for control as a democratic phenomenon.

Regardless, the struggle has been so portrayed, and this poses a considerable problem for church-state historians. The assumption that Church control over education was incompatible with democratic trends or with the development of a genuinely national system of education permeates the vast majority of studies on nineteenth-century English education.[29] Thus it is imperative to ask whether

---

[28]Charles Kenneth Francis Brown, The Church´s Part in Education, 1833-1941 (London: National Society, 1942), p. 11. Brown describes the opposition of farmers to the education efforts of the clergy; quoting from Richard Dawes, Schools and Other Similar Institutions for the Industrial Classes (n.p., 1853), he elaborates upon this theme. Brown also quotes from a school inspector´s report: "Strange as the truth may be, I believe that one of the greatest, if not the greatest, hindrance to education comes from those who ought to be the most forward to support it--from the parents of the children," p. 5.

[29]To confirm this one need only consult, more or less at random, a half dozen histories of nineteenth-century education, to find the Church named as the greatest obstruction to the advance of national education. This was the view of the proponents of nation-

the movement for popular, national and civic-controlled education did in fact have a democratic base. The importance of the question to church-state historians can be expressed in the following proposition: if there was not a popular demand for education in general then the struggle for control of the schools was a struggle between elites, the one defending ecclesiastical or spiritual authority in the name of religion, the other defending civil supremacy in the name of the people. Because the proponents of civil supremacy also claimed to represent the best interests of religion the battle lines were anything but clear, and the historian must determine whether concern for religion or for civil supremacy ranked higher. All of which is to suggest areas requiring further study while at the same time to indicate that the educationalists' use of executive power raises critical questions regarding conventional historiography.

The events of 1833, 1839-1840, 1843 and 1846 established precedents which governed church-state-education affairs until the passing of the 1870 Education Act. State aid to education began in 1833 with a ₤20,000 grant voted by Parliament and distributed by the Treasury to the two educational societies. Funds were distributed according to the amount of subscriptions raised locally, which system greatly favored Anglican parishes.[30] Over the first

---

al education, who regarded the religious difficulty as the chief obstacle to be overcome. Because they viewed undenominational or non-doctrinal education as the only solution to the problem, they saw the Church's insistence on doctrinal teaching as obstructionist.

[30]Raymond G. Cowherd, The Politics of English Dissent (New York: New York University Press, 1956), p. 118. He notes that

five years the National Society received Ⴆ70,000 of the total
Ⴆ100,000 awarded.[31]

The Whigs were too busy with other problems to attend to
education questions again until 1839 when the government created,
by executive order, a central agency to manage the distribution of
state funds and otherwise further the advancement of education. At
the same time the Privy Council Committee on Education was formed
wherein the government proposed, (1) to found teacher-training
colleges, or normal schools, to which ´model schools´ were to be
attached, and (2) to institute a system of school inspection upon
which state grants would be conditional. Powerful Church opposition forced the Whigs to abandon the normal school plan, but con-
cession on this point failed to quiet opposition to the formation
of the Privy Council Committee on Education or the institution of
an inspection system. This opposition reflected distrust of any
vaguely defined central powers, and the Church´s resistance to
anything resembling state supremacy in education.

The Whig leadership attempted to claim a posture of religious
neutrality for the state. Russell boasted that the government
proposed to entrust management of its plan to a committee made up
not of representatives of any religious body or sect or of members

---

during the first year the British and Foreign Schools Society
schools received funds nearly equal in amount to that received by
the National Society but that the distribution soon became unequal.
Chadwick, op. cit., 1:338, implies that the system of distribution
remained the same throughout the early period but suggests that the
National Society received more government money because it was able
to maintain a higher level of private subscriptions.

[31]Chadwick, op. cit., 1:338.

of the various sects, but of "official servants of the crown" as though their religious commitments could be neutralized by affiliation with the bureaucracy.[32] This supposed neutrality of "official servants of the crown" requires comment.

The men most responsible for the make-up of the Privy Council Committee on Education and for its early policies were Lord Russell and Dr. James Philip Kay (later Kay-Shuttleworth).[33] Russell was Home Secretary for Melbourne when he proposed increasing the education grant and establishing undenominational state-controlled normal schools. At that time he was also vice-president of the British and Foreign Schools Society and his attitude toward the Church (of which he was a member) was decidedly anticlerical, which fact was no mystery to his contemporaries. Russell believed in the supremacy of the laity over the clergy, he opposed Tractarians and Catholicizers, and he encouraged liberal theologians--so far as he

---

[32]G. F. A. Best, "The Religious Difficulties of National Education in England, 1800-1870," Cambridge Historical Journal 12 (1956): 155, 173, 169. Best quotes, on p. 169, Russell's remark from Hansard; see Great Britain, Parliament: Hansard's Parliamentary Debates (Commons), 3rd series, vol. 45 (1839): 273 ff. In this footnote Best remarks, "this was a good Whig position, rather like Macaulay's when contesting Leeds in 1833, he refused to tell a Methodist questioner more about his religion than that he was a Christian."

[33]Sir James Philips Kay-Shuttleworth was born at Rochdale, Lancashire, 1804, the son of Robert Kay. He studied medicine at Edinburgh University and settled in Manchester during the late 1820s. There he developed a great interest in the factory poor, in public health and popular education. He was appointed Poor Law Commissioner in 1835, and in 1839 became the first secretary to the Privy Council's newly established Committee on Education. See Encyclopaedia Britannica, 11th ed., 15:703, and Frank Smith, The Life and Work of Sir James Kay-Shuttleworth (London: n.p., 1923). Certain important aspects of his views remain obscure, especially his religious views; John Hurt, Education in Evolution: Church, State, Society and Popular Education, 1800-1870 (London: Rupert Hart-Davis, 1971), p. 23n.

encouraged theology at all.[34] Dr. Kay was about as neutral as Lord Russell. He described the normal school proposal as "the most direct mode of asserting the emancipation of the common school from the surviving claims of a priestly class," and he claimed that the plan "asserted the supremacy of the Civil Power in education in order that it might invoke the aid of the laity in securing to parents and scholars the rights of conscience."[35] He was responsible for excluding priests, bishops and ministers from the newly formed Privy Council Committee on Education, which was scarcely viewed as an expression of neutrality by Churchmen.[36] Finally, he called the Churchmen who opposed his scheme the "medieval party" and thereby invoked ´no-popery´ sentiments.[37]

Consequently, the very idea that Russell and Kay-Shuttleworth would formulate neutral policies was preposterous. In 1839 the Whigs had assured Kay-Shuttleworth that "their object was to frustrate the claims of the Church to the national system of education and to assist the claims of the civil power to control the education of the country—to prevent the growth of inordinate ecclesiastical pretensions . . . to vindicate the rights of conscience and to lay the foundation for a system of combined education."[38]

---

[34]Chadwick, op. cit., 1:234, 232-237.

[35]Sir James Philip Kay-Shuttleworth, Public Education as Affected by the Minutes of the Privy Council from 1846-1852 (London: Longman, Brown, Green and Longmans, 1853), p. 4.

[36]Chadwick, op. cit., 1:340.

[37]Kay-Shuttleworth, op. cit., pp. 7-11.

[38]Chadwick, op. cit., 1:340.

Neutrality was not among the assumptions of the participants in this struggle; it was a propaganda weapon skillfully used by those who favored a ´combined´ system of education, which group included most supporters of the British Society. In the language of the day the term ´combined system´ meant one in which the scholars received secular instruction from the schoolmaster and separate religious teaching from priests or ministers of the respective denominations represented by the student body.[39] Such a system necessarily involved the separation of religious and secular instruction, which was precisely what the Anglicans and Roman Catholics opposed. Anglicans--especially the Tractarians--insisted on denominational instruction in which perspectives informed by dogmatic Christian beliefs were infused into all instruction secular and religious. Moreover, they denied the very possibility of dividing the learning process into religious and secular components, insisting that all so-called secular subjects were related to questions ultimately religious.[40] In large measure this view underlying the Anglican position has been dismissed as a dishonest pretense intended to disguise the supposedly "real" reason for

---

[39]Francis Adams, History of the Elementary School Contest in England: The Struggle for National Education, by John Morley, ed. Asa Briggs (Brighton, Engl.: Harvester Press, 1972), pp. 98-99.

[40]This discussion was carried on in terms of "instruction" vs. "education." Instruction meant the training of the intellect only while education meant the combination of spiritual formation with intellectual training. This language was used by Protestants and Catholics alike. The denunciation of "mere instruction" was intended as an attack against the assumptions of rationalism as the adequate basis for education. This distinction hardly makes its way into modern studies, which results in much historical confusion. This is difficult to explain since this distinction was clearly made by Members of Parliament in their debates, which constitute the chief source for many educational histories.

Anglican obstructionism--defense of Church powers, property and privileges.[41]

Historians have emphasized the economic and political vested interests of the opponents of a national ´combined system.´ These interests were impressive and loudly defended,[42] but there was also an area of argument related not only to the political, economic and social interests of the Church of England but to the very survival of religion as the basis for civilized society. This argument dealt in its political dimensions with the problem of separating religious and secular instruction.

G. F. A. Best came close to acknowledging this problem when he noted that "we have inherited the system and overcome the Victorians´ peculiar problems, but the ship has been saved by overthrowing half the cargo--their preoccupation, especially through the formative period up to Forster´s great act, that the education of the children of England should have a really religious as well as what is called (somewhat misleadingly) its secular side."[43] Yet even Best, who recognizes that state education in

---

[41]Mary Sturt, The Education of the People: a History of Primary Education in England and Wales in the Nineteenth Century (London: Routledge and Kegan Paul, 1967), p. 82. In discussing the bishops´ objection to the 1839 proposals, which were based on opposition to the separation of secular and religious comment, Sturt comments: "When the main debate opened the dishonesty of the whole opposition became apparent," citing the fact that there was not "a vestige of religious teaching proposed in any part of the scheme" as proof that there was no basis for honest opposition. The whole point of the opposition was that secular and religious instruction could not be separated. This is only one example of many--but it is typical of the historiography.

[42]Denison, op. cit., p. 80.

[43]Best, op. cit., p. 156.

fact overthrew "half the cargo"--namely its religious basis, does not give serious consideration to the arguments of those who predicted this would happen if religious and secular instruction were permitted to be separated under the control of the civil power.

During the nineteenth century the belief that religion and civilization, church and state, are inseparable was inverted into the belief that religion is a purely private concern. Neither that transformation nor the role played in it by popular education can be appreciated unless the opposing positions are given full and objective study, which is beyond the scope of the present work. Even so, reference to related questions must be made continually if the political and doctrinal realities of the Anglican and Catholic positions are to be made clear.

To return to the 1839 proposals it should be clearly stated that opposition was not limited to the normal school scheme. There was substantial opposition to the very existence of a central agency and even more powerful opposition to the inspection scheme.[44] The House of Lords passed a resolution expressing dis-

---

[44]Opposition to the centralization of power was not restricted to government action in education. In a recent study by Nicholas Edsall, The Anti-Poor Law Movement, 1834-1844 (Manchester: Manchester University Press, 1971), opposition to the new Poor Law system is discussed. One of the themes stressed is that there was powerful opposition to the creation of centralized bureaucratic machinery. Historians have been so interested in the development of new social agencies of government they have tended to place little emphasis on how drastically this revised the local power structure as the basis of English government. The Parliamentary debates of this period contain frequent references to fears expressed by Commoners and Lords alike that increased centralization represented a movement in the direction of the French--toward ´state despotism´ as it was often called. The tone of such discussions indicates deep commitments to the traditions of local government. This has been the conservative position, but it has

approbation of the Order in Council creating the Privy Council Committee on Education though a similar resolution was defeated in the House of Commons.[45] The bishops and the National Society carried their opposition to the inspection plan much further by virtually refusing to deal with the state. Of ₤19,895 offered the National Society schools in 1839-1840, only ₤5,369 was accepted.[46]

This was not what the Privy Council Committee wanted. Plans for educational expansion were useless without cooperation from the Church which operated the vast majority of the existing schools.[47] The Church held the trump card, which fact escaped no one's notice at the time. The compromise which was worked out was in reality a Church victory. Initially the government tried to placate the Church by offering an inspection system which would exclude religion, but that violated the principle that religion could not be separated totally from other subjects.[48] A year later the state conceded to the bishops, giving them power over the appointment and dismissal of inspectors, the right to formulate instructions for inspectors to use in examining religious matters, plus the right to see the general instructions, religious and secular, before their promulgation; this virtually amounted to the right of approving all instructions issued to the inspectors. The bishops also won the

---

not received even-handed historical treatment.

[45]Graham Balfour, The Educational Systems of Great Britain and Ireland, 2d ed. (Oxford: Clarendon Press, 1903), pp. 5-6.

[46]Sturt, op. cit., p. 96.

[47]Denison, op. cit., pp. 96-100, 113.

[48]Sturt, op. cit., pp. 96-97.

right to receive (and by implication to approve) official copies of all inspectors´ reports to the Privy Council Committee on Education.

The Committee on Education Minutes implementing this agreement guaranteed the integration of religious and secular instruction by insuring that inspectors would inquire "with special care" into the teaching of Church doctrine. Instructions to inspectors called for careful attention to all religious aspects of the parish schools: attendance at church, prayer, catechetics and Bible studies. In addition, the general moral formation of the children was to be looked into and inspectors were to determine how the school contributed to the various aspects of spiritual and moral growth of the scholars.[49] In short, the Church of England received nothing less than state support for teaching religion--and all other subjects--according to the doctrines and perspectives of the Establishment. Dissenters were outraged because this meant the extension of the very influence which they hoped to curtail and because at this point there were no provisions for appointing separate inspectors for Nonconformist schools. It was feared that Anglican inspectors--who were usually clerics--would impose Anglican doctrine on all schools. The British and Foreign Schools Society soon negotiated with the Committee on Education which then agreed to appoint separate inspectors for the British Society schools. This partially alleviated the tension, but there has been confusion regarding the similarity between these agreements. They

---

[49]J. Stuart Maclure, Educational Documents; England and Wales, 1816-1963 (London: Chapman and Hall, 1965), p. 51.

are usually described as similar, which misses the point.[50] The
point may seem trivial, but this inaccuracy goes to the heart of
the problem and illustrates how historians have failed to appre-
ciate the Church's opposition to the separation of religious and
secular instruction.

There is no evidence that the Committee on Education initially
intended its inspection system to be sectarian; in fact, the thrust
of the 1839 proposals was against denominationalism. The bishops'
demands changed the whole scheme, a fact which is seldom noted.
The Dissenters favored the original proposal precisely because it
was not denominational and contained provisions which were expected
to weaken denominationalism, which they equated with the
Established parish school system. When the bishops forced the
Committee on Education to relinquish its undenominational stance on
inspection they transformed the system into a thoroughly denominational one by forcing inspectors to examine both religious and
secular instruction. Such a turn of events proved intolerable to
Dissenters. That they were able to obtain limited concessions
protecting them from Anglican inspectors was almost beside the
point; there was little appeal in winning the skirmish while losing
the war.

In order to understand the context of the Nonconformist mentality a brief reference to the Church rates battles might be

---

[50]Binns, op. cit., p. 130, mentions a similarity between the
agreements having to do with approval of the appointment of inspectors; but this was only part of the agreement made with the
Anglicans. The other part--and the most important part--guaranteed
sectarian instruction, which was against the fundamental principles
of the British Society.

helpful. Chadwick's discussion of this subject shows how deeply Dissenters were committed to the fight against the rate. The Church rate was but a small tax levied to cover the cost of church repairs, yet one man went to jail because he refused to pay 5s.6d. The circumstances of his incarceration were so complicated and he was so stubbornly committed to principle that it required an act of Parliament to get him out of jail. Dissenters were able to turn vestry meetings into affairs nearly as boisterous as English elections--no laughing matter.[51] Now, Dissenters willing to face jail over a pittance could not have been expected to welcome any policy guaranteeing the tax-supported extension of Church influence in education.

On the contrary, the Concordat of 1840 must be seen as the initial cause for Voluntarism as it provided the background to the Nonconformist response to Sir James Graham's factory bill of 1843. Therefore, the resentment Dissenters harbored over the 1840 agreement exploded into outrage when the Conservative Government's Home Secretary proposed a scheme involving compulsory education for factory children in schools to be built with state funds and maintained out of the local rate.[52] Teachers and school managers were to be Anglican, largely clerics, and the curriculum was to conform to the Church of England's standards, though children could be withdrawn from formal catechism by Dissenting parents. Peel had tried to dissuade Graham from introducing such a measure, but the

---

[51]Chadwick, op. cit., 1:146-158.

[52]Charles Birchenough, History of Elementary Education in England and Wales from 1800 to the Present Day (Baltimore: Warwick and York, 1914), pp. 82-83.

latter persisted; the outcome surprised nearly everyone.[53]   A record number of petitions denounced the scheme, and the protests were so vehement that all efforts at compromise failed; hence, the affair proved beyond doubt that Church extension through education could not be funded by local rates and would probably not be tolerated so long as it required public monies.[54]

An important offshoot of the factory bill controversy was the rise of Voluntarism. The Congregationalist Union officially proclaimed the policy in 1843 and formed a Central Board of Education that December. The Baptist Union followed suit. Although the British Society officially resisted this position, most of its local committees refused to deal with the state after 1840.[55] During 1841 only £1,337 went to British Society schools, while over the following two years only one of eighty-six schools established by that organization applied for state aid.[56]

The extent to which Voluntarism permeated Nonconformist schools is not altogether clear. Some British Society schools availed themselves of state aid after 1847, and there was overlapping leadership in the British Society and the Congregational and Baptist Unions.[57] The key to Voluntarism would seem to be found at the local level, since the three central organizations

---

[53]Brose, op. cit., pp. 195-198.

[54]Ibid.

[55]Binns, op. cit., pp. 132-133.

[56]Cowherd, op. cit., p. 124.

[57]Binns, op. cit., pp. 132-133, 141-145.

possessed only persuasive, not coercive power. Before 1843 local committees had begun to balk at the state system because it implied state interference; that trend was solidified in 1843 and continued to dominate Dissenters´ educational efforts well into the 1860s. The decline of Voluntarism during the 1860s similarly appears to have been linked with local developments. In the interim Dissenters consolidated their influence in local politics, and as their confidence in the new machinery of municipal government increased they became convinced that locally elected civic bodies could manage an educational system acceptable to Nonconformists.[58] But that is to leap too far ahead in the story. What must be remembered is that voluntarism established itself as a powerful force in educational politics during the 1840s and remained strong throughout our period. Ironically, this fact contributed to the general denominationalism of English schools because the Voluntarists, free of state interference, introduced a more denominational curriculum into their schools. The extent to which this was done is not clear, but it is generally acknowledged that the Congregationalists pursued such a policy.[59]

---

[58]Two studies are particularly helpful in defining the connection between local politics and the rise of national education: Samuel Edwin Maltby, Manchester and the Movement for National Elementary Education, 1800-1870 (Manchester: Manchester University Press, 1918); and Sylvia A. Welch, "The Role of the Birmingham Reformers in the Movement for Change in the Educational System of England, 1840-1877" (Ph.D. dissertation, New York University, 1970).

[59]Binns, op. cit., p. 152. He notes that the Central Committee of the Congregational Education Board was denominational but that many schools were undenominational. R. K. Wilson, The First and Last Fight for the Voluntary Principle in Education, 1846-1858 (London: Eastern Press, 1916), pp. 28-29, contended that Edward Baines Jr., who was leader of the movement, favored denomi-

Not until after Peel's spectacular defeat over the corn law crisis were educational questions again prominent. After the formation of Lord John Russell's Government in 1846 there were several efforts to extend bureaucratic influence in education. In July Lord Russell announced his intention to give special attention to education. By the end of the year the Privy Council Committee on Education's new policies and regulations had been announced.[60] The purpose of the 1846 Minutes was to upgrade the quality of elementary teaching by, (1) augmenting teacher salaries, (2) creating a class of assistant teachers or student apprentices called "pupil-teachers," (3) establishing a Queen's Scholarship program whereby pupil-teachers could compete for scholarships to normal schools, and (4) implementing a teacher-certification program. By offering financial aid to training colleges, teachers, and pupil-teachers the state hoped to devise means of drawing prospective teachers from the poorer classes. By making the schoolmasters financially dependent on the state the Privy Council Committee's control over the schools would be extended. The state's 1839 plan for gaining control over teachers had been rejected; this was a substitute plan for achieving the same end, perhaps more gradually.

The Privy Council Committee Minutes were discussed in Parliament in 1847 when Russell's recommendation for increasing the education grant to ₤100,000 came up for a vote. This debate will

---

nationalism and opposed the separation of religious and secular instruction. Important questions remain regarding the impact of Voluntarism in education.

[60]Kay-Shuttleworth, op. cit., pp. 45-64.

be discussed in greater detail in the next chapter, but it should be noted here that Dissenters denounced the government plan as one which would strengthen parish schools. By giving parish school-masters additional financial advantages, by enticing students into parish schools with pupil-teacher stipends, which in turn offered scholarship possibilities, the measure was deemed monstrously dis-advantageous to Dissenters. Nonconformist anger was further aroused by rumors about a Government offer to negotiate Roman Catholic participation in the plan. On the other hand churchmen welcomed these measures as enlightened and fair, which did nothing to placate opponents.

This is where Roman Catholics officially entered the picture. In general terms government aid to education had been greatly extended since 1833. Money was being distributed to schools for buildings, books, maps, and teacher housing, and to normal schools for buildings and training. Stipends were being offered to teach-ers and pupil-teachers.[61] And the school inspectors were on the government payroll. The most important condition upon which such grants were based was school inspection.

In practical terms, given the Voluntarists' withdrawal from state programs, the system amounted to a subsidy for Church of England schools, which fact served to inflame sectarian bitterness.

Three additional general factors which influenced church-state-education negotiations remain to be discussed: (1) the large

---

[61]Minutes of August 25, 1846, and December 21, 1846, dealt with teacher and pupil-teacher stipends and scholarships. That of July 23, 1847, funded books and maps.

and growing numbers of Irish Catholic children among the poor to be educated, (2) the example of the Irish national education system, and (3) the influence of the secularists.

Though statistics pertaining to the Irish Catholic poor during this period are rather inadequate, both contemporaries and historians have agreed that a significant percentage of the lower class poor, especially in new industrial centers, were Irish.

Philip Hughes estimates the Catholic population at nearly 680,000 in 1851, including about a quarter of a million English-born and 430,000 Irish-born Catholics.[62] As the English population totalled nearly eighteen million, the Irish-born comprised close to three percent, which seems hardly significant at first glance; however, the Irish population was concentrated in the new industrial cities where 'little Irelands' became prominent in terms of population and in terms of the social, economic and religious difficulties which their presence crystallized. As early as 1835 it was estimated that one-fifth of the Manchester population was Irish-born.[63] The massive immigration which came with the famine swelled the Irish population in all major industrial centers. The following listing of cities reporting over 5,000 Irish-born suggests the scope of the situation:

---

[62] Philip Hughes, "The English Catholics in 1850," in The English Catholics, 1850-1950, ed. George A. Beck (London: Burns, Oates, 1950), pp. 42-45.

[63] Asa Briggs, The Age of Improvement (London: Longmans, 1959), p. 302.

Table 1

IRISH POPULATION, 1851

Town	Irish-born Population	Total Population
London	107,548	2,363,236
Liverpool	83,813	376,000
Manchester-Salford	52,304	400,000
Birmingham	9,341	233,000
Leeds	8,466	172,000
Ashton-under-Lyme	8,090	31,000
Newcastle-on-Tyne	7,124	88,000
Stockport	5,701	54,000
Preston	5,122	70,000
Wigan	5,506	32,000

SOURCE: Philip Hughes, "The English Catholics in 1850," in The English Catholics, 1850-1950, ed. George A. Beck (London: Burns, Oates, 1950), pp. 80-81. Hughes´ table is based on the census of 1851, Religious Worship in England and Wales (London, 1853).

Available statistics apply only to Irish-born, not to their English-born relatives who also crowded into the ethnic communities and were just as much a part of the ´Irish sector´ as the Irish-born. Statistics thus tell us little about the communities themselves which were the concern of those who wished to minister to them. Regardless, these figures do reveal a great deal about the concentration of the Irish in various regions; in this context the following table giving the breakdown of Irish-born in certain Catholic dioceses may be helpful. Of the thirteen dioceses formed by the restoration of the hierarchy the following eight had over 25,000 Irish-born in 1851:

Table 2

IRISH-BORN POPULATION IN CERTAIN DIOCESES, 1851

Diocese	Irish-born Population	Total Population of Diocese
Liverpool	112,875	886,567
Westminster	86,508	2,414,299
Salford	79,635	1,180,834
Beverly	43,682	1,789,047
Hexham	41,640	969,126
Southwark	38,394	2,245,021
Birmingham	30,304	1,539,645
Shrewsbury	28,422	1,072,752

SOURCE: Philip Hughes, "The English Catholics in 1850," in The English Catholics, 1850-1950, ed. George A. Beck (London: Burns, Oates, 1950), pp. 48-50.

Statistics tell us little about the school-age children, but if the estimate that one-fourth of the total population was made up of children between the ages of five and fifteen is accepted, it can be assumed that there were well over 100,000 Irish children requiring education.[64] Notwithstanding the lack of accurate data, it is known that 'street children' were a problem in London and the industrial towns and that a vast percentage of them were Irish.[65] As Charles Buller, M. P., noted during the education debates of 1839, the Irish Catholics constituted a large proportion of the Manchester population. He remarked on their being "entirely under

[64]Maltby, op. cit., p. 47. He assumes that one quarter of the population consisted of children; whether this estimate applied to Irish families is not indicated.

[65]Richard Cobden, Cobden's Speeches on Questions of Public Policy, ed. Bright and Rogers, vol. 2, p. 583, quoted by Maltby, op. cit., p. 81. Cobden said, "I do not want to have my Bible read in schools because if so the children of 60,000 people must go uneducated." There were nearly 60,000 Catholics in Manchester at this time.

the influence of their priests," and asked, "whose interest is it that these people should be educated?" He answered that question by saying that "their ignorance makes them more dependent upon their priests," and suggesting that English self-interest demanded that they be educated.[66]

It would seem that historians have failed to ask the obvious question: to what extent was the attempted education of the poor a means of proselytizing the Irish Catholic poor? Any thorough assessment of that question would involve an enormous undertaking in local history, which is not the purpose of this study; what this study does attempt to do, however, is to indicate how English Catholics viewed the question.

The impact of the Irish national educational system is considered by Mary Sturt who notes that

> the two great influences in the beginning of state educa-
> tion in England came from Ireland and the new Poor
> Law. . . The example of Ireland supplied the political
> techniques and the forms of organization; the experience
> of the new Poor Law supplied the men, a consciousness of
> the need and the methods.[67]

It is unfortunate that she does not develop this theme with greater thoroughness by providing supportive comparative analysis of administrative and political details; but she does list points of similarity, observing that the Irish had dealt with the principal problems--central and local control, distribution of funds, school accommodations adjusted to local needs, teacher training, teacher salaries and professional status, and inspection. Sturt's grasp of

---

[66]Hansard, 3rd series, vol. 48 (1839): 558-559.

[67]Sturt, op. cit., p. 64.

the religious problem, however, is singularly weak: "the thorny
question of religion had already been settled by mutual toler-
ance,"[68] she observes, which description of affairs in nineteenth-
century Ireland could not be farther from the truth. Donald H.
Akenson's recent study of the Irish system generally supports
Sturt's contentions, but the best source on this subject remains
Hansard. The educational debates are filled with references to the
Irish system, which was so much a part of the thinking of the day
that those who sat in Commons and Lords generally called the new
Privy Council Committee on Education the "Board," which was the
name used to refer to the central agency of the Irish system.[69]

The importance of the Irish precedent was especially significant to the religious question. The Irish Commission, or National
Board, included Catholic, Anglican and Nonconformist (Presbyterian)
representatives. Through the influence of the Protestant and
Catholic clergy the system which was designed to be undenominational became thoroughly denominational, and schools throughout
Ireland were controlled by Protestant and Catholic clerics.[70] This
process was well underway by the late 1830s, which fact undoubtedly
influenced the decision to exclude clerics from the Privy Council
Committee, an influence which became all the more understandable
when it is remembered that the English greatly feared priestly
power in Catholic Ireland. Just how far the English educational-

---

[68]Ibid., p. 76.

[69]Hansard, 3rd series, vol. 48 (1839): 530-567, 227-299.

[70]Donald H. Akenson, The Irish Education Experiment (London:
Routledge and Kegan Paul, 1971), p. 224.

ists were influenced by what they knew of the Irish system cannot be determined with exactness, but it is clear that the two systems cannot be viewed in total isolation.

Finally, no introduction concerning the church-state-education problem would be complete without some reference to the influence of the secularists. Most historians contend that their direct influence was minimal during the nineteenth century, that the education problem was religious to such an extent as to exclude unbelievers from prominence. This would seem the obvious conclusion to draw from what is known about Victorian religion, but if the secularist influence is ignored altogether it is difficult to explain how "half the cargo" of education was thrown overboard. It is a delicate problem touching on the difficulty of differentiating between the secular humanist and the liberal Christian perspective in church-state questions. In Christian theology there is presumably all the difference in the world--that between human self-sufficiency cut off from eternity and human dependence on the Son of God for eternal life. In educational politics the distinction is less clear. Again, G. F. A. Best provides a helpful summary of the problem in which he insists that the problems of education were "mainly religious." He concluded that the context was not between religious and secular educationalists but "between two irreconcilable ideas of what was really religious education--the doctrinal idea and the undenominational idea, which could and in fact always did coexist within the bosoms of both established and dissenting churches."[71] Here Best treads on troublesome ground, as there is good reason to argue that much of what was put forward as "undenominationalism" was in fact secularism and that this was understood at the time by both the proponents and the opponents of undenominationalism.

Victorians not only wanted religious education, they wanted a practical system which would serve the needs of the whole nation immediately. The desire to reconcile demands of Christians with the needs of the state was intrinsically related to the problem of defining a national faith. Given the proliferation of doctrinal differences among Protestants, only a diffused multidenominational notion of Christianity could be called national. Best notes that such a generalized concept of Christianity was "new only in its wide acceptance and its political significance." He describes it as the "religious dimension of that ´Liberal´ movement in thought and politics which High Churchmen and Conservatives and the more dogmatic Evangelicals were fighting . . ." Precisely how the historian is to distinguish between secularism and "generalized Christianity" Best does not say, but he includes Edward Miall among the proponents of it, citing Miall´s claim that "all the ends of Christian education could now be achieved without ever a mention of Christ." According to Best this was justified by "the popular sentimental paraphernalia of the Christian fireside, the innocent childhood and the prayers lisped at the mother´s knee." The problem was that "there was significantly little analytical inquiry

---

[71]Best, "Religious Difficulties of National Education," p. 161.

into where mother got her religion from, or how much religious backbone her children might be expected to retain in adult life."[72]

The problem with this analysis is that Best ignores the secularist leaven and the warnings made by the doctrinalists at the time. He acknowledges that the proponents of "scarcely religious" education shared their position with the enemies of organized religion but attributes their complacency over the future of Christian morality to the fact that they lived in such a religious age.[73] That explanation ignores the fact that denominationalists provided a significantly large volume of analytical inquiry into "where mother got her religion from" and concluded that Christian morality depended upon the teaching of Christian doctrine. In short, the undenominationalists were not "complacent" because such indifference was not part of the religious temperament of the time and because their opponents made such indifference impossible. If it is not good history to suggest that Victorians were complacent on this point, then it is necessary to look elsewhere for an explanation of the willingness of Victorians to overthrow half the cargo.

Religion was important to Victorians. Was something else more important? It is necessary to examine their priorities to discover what it was that permitted them to make common cause with the secularists who wanted to eliminate doctrine from education for non-religious or even antireligious reasons. The truth is that Dissenters who favored undenominational but more-or-less Christian

---

[72]
  Ibid., pp. 168-171.

[73]Ibid., pp. 170-171.

education shared with the secularists a desire to contain--if not eliminate--clericalism in education. By 1869 the struggle over Church control of education had consolidated into a national movement headed by the National Education League which favored unsectarian or undenominational education. It was clear from the debate within the National Education League that the distinction between ´secular´ and ´undenominational´ was not at all well-defined. The following excerpt from Francis Adams´ description of the debate clarifies this point:

> Then, as ever, it was the religious difficulty which raised its head to confront progress. The chairman was challenged by the Rev. Mr. Dowson of Hyde, to say whether the League supported secular education or the British school system. Mr. Dixon replied, "We do not use the word ´secular´ but we exclude all theological parts of religion, and I am sure that what is left is what even Mr. Dowson himself would call secular." In answer to further questions on the same subject, Mr. Dixon stated that the word "unsectarian" excluded all dogmatic and theological teaching, and all creeds, and catechisms, and also that if the Bible were read it must be without note or comment.74

This is but one of the more conspicuous examples of the extent to which secularism invaded undenominationalism, but it is an example sufficient to dismiss the general claim that the secularist influence was nominal. Historians have taken on good faith the Dissenters´ assurance that secularism was not their goal, which may or may not be open to question; but such a claim has to do with intentions and not with results. The undenominationalists risked that outcome--which was predicted on all sides--because they were more concerned with achieving the ascendancy of the civil power as

---

74Adams, op. cit., p. 202.

a means of reducing the Church's influence.

The above discussion has been intended to suggest the need for broad comparative studies which would relate these various influences to one another. Many of these problems will be discussed again in terms of perspectives expressed in the Catholic press, but before turning to that task it is necessary to describe certain specific aspects of the Catholic position vis-à-vis education prior to the establishment of the Catholic Poor School Committee.

The Catholic Position

What advantages and disadvantages did the Catholics bring to their negotiations with the state? Beyond question the disadvantages outweighed the advantages. First, the English Catholics were poor; their aristocracy was in decline at the same time that hundreds of thousands of penniless Irish immigrants were flooding England; and there was no substantial middle class population to offset the imbalance. As the provision of minimal pastoral care was a burden in itself, there was certainly no surplus for schools. Secondly, there was a shortage of personnel--teachers, priests and religious--necessary to manage a large-scale school system. Thirdly, Catholics possessed no teacher-training system or facilities. Fourthly, they lacked precisely those traditions which accounted for the success of Protestant educational efforts: well organized educational societies which could coordinate local and national efforts; working relations with the state; and well-established traditions of local voluntary political activities which could support specific educational efforts. Finally, Catholics were burdened with the Irish problem: the religious hysteria which could be triggered by ´no-popery´ could be perpetuated and exaggerated only by the influx of immigrants whom the English regarded as little better than barbarian heathens. It was not only English Protestants who viewed the Irish with distaste; many old stock English Catholics shared this prejudice, which served to multiply Catholic burdens by generating division.

It is more difficult to characterize Catholic advantages. A certain unity was enjoyed on important questions: they believed in doctrinal education and were united on what the doctrinal content should be, and they generally agreed that the best teachers were religious. In addition there were potential advantages to be derived from the Irish problem, which could be used as a lever to pry concessions from the state, assuming matters were adroitly handled. Beyond these conditions it is essential to consider general tensions within the Catholic body which had an indirect bearing on the development of a Catholic position on the state´s role in education.

There has been much discussion about the tensions which disrupted English Catholic unity during these years, most of which has focused on divisions between Old Catholics and Converts or on divisions between Liberal Catholics and Ultramontanists.[75] Many of the most prominent controversies of the day can be seen in this

---

[75]For discussions on Ultramontanism and Liberal Catholicism see the following: Wilfred Ward, William George Ward and the Catholic Revival (London: Longmans, Green, 1912), pp. 84-153; Damian McElrath, "An Essay on Acton´s Critical Decade," in Lord Acton, the Decisive Decade, 1864-1874; Essays and Documents, Damian McElrath and James Holland, eds. (Louvain: Bibliothèque de l´Université, 1970), pp. 3-49; and Josef Altholz, The Liberal Catholic Movement in England (London: Burns and Oates, 1962), pp. 1-6, 130-151.

context. For example, the restoration of the hierarchy and some of the disputes which it generated reflected the different hopes and expectations of Old Catholics in England and Ultramontanists at the Vatican. The Old Catholics saw the restoration as a means of achieving greater independence while Vatican officials hoped thereby to increase their control over the English bishops. Converts had only an indirect influence upon these differences, but it must be noted that Wiseman hoped that the restoration of the hierarchy would help overcome Old Catholic resistance to his work with the Converts.

Another example of disunity can be seen in liturgical, architectural and devotional styles. Because such differences penetrated all levels of public worship they had a great capacity to sow discord. Proponents of the Gothic revival in architecture tended to be Old Catholics who saw the Gothic as the true embodiment of the Catholic spirit, while Converts associated it with the Anglican cathedrals. As they fled the Church of England they also fled its Gothic cathedrals, turning toward Italian styles in both architecture and devotion. In terms of devotional style Old Catholics preferred the restraint of ´Garden of the Soul´ piety and were offended by the flourish and sentimentality which characterized both Italianate architecture and continental devotional styles.[76]

Perhaps more to the point were the conflicts over political and intellectual authority in the Church. In the area of church

---

[76]Bernard Ward, The Sequel to Catholic Emancipation, 2 vols. (London: Longmans, Green, 1915), 2:261-278.

politics the Ultramontanist position was the more radical because it demanded an increase in papal power out of keeping with the traditional English understanding of the relative influence enjoyed by laity, clergy, episcopacy and papacy. In this sphere Liberal Catholicism tended to favor the maintenance of the older decentralization of power with less emphasis upon the prerogatives of the papacy, though their emphasis upon the role of the laity was considered radical at the time. In its intellectual aspect--which was its raison d'être--Liberal Catholicism championed freedom of inquiry in a way which was believed to constitute a radical departure from the traditional understanding of Catholic authority.

Certainly differences over church authority and intellectual freedom penetrated all levels of Catholic life, but it remains to provide the complementary historiography focusing on tensions arising out of major pastoral challenges. The most prominent pastoral problem which English Catholics faced had to do with the influx of increasing numbers of destitute Irish who crowded into city slums and greatly outnumbered English Catholics.

This pastoral problem may seem unrelated to the troubles between Liberal Catholics and Ultramontanists or between Old Catholics and Converts, as pastoral care of the poor was never a major issue between these factions. As it happened, however, the regional, social and economic orientation of the majority of Old Catholics removed them from problems affecting the urban poor, and circumstantially those who were most involved in social, pastoral and philanthropic efforts in the London slums also happened to be prominent Ultramontanists. The Old Catholic gentry came largely from the land, from rural England where they and their "satellites of tenants" formed a world in itself.[77] There were whole areas of life which they did not penetrate, particularly the clerical and academic world of the universities, the industrial cities, the expanded bureaucracy, and the world of the rising middle classes whence came so many of the post-1829 Converts.[78]

The most prominent Converts had been prominent as Anglicans; this meant they understood dimensions of English life from which the Old Catholics had been removed. For example, the National Society was a very prominent Anglican organization at the national and local levels; this enabled many Converts to bring to English Catholicism a sophisticated understanding of the innuendoes of educational politics. They enjoyed a similar awareness of political realities in other areas of social and pastoral concern-- particularly those having to do with the Poor Law. In short, they had a working knowledge of the fine line between politics and philanthropy in areas of social importance; in this they were set apart from Old Catholics. Consequently there was a mutual lack of comprehension between Old Catholics and Converts which facilitated the accumulation of differences. Undoubtedly these regional, social and economic factors separating Old Catholics and Converts contributed to differences in their perspectives concerning the Church's pastoral priorities, but such differences are not altogether accounted for by Old Catholic vs. Convert tensions. There

---

[77]David Mathews, "Old Catholics and Converts," in Beck, op. cit., pp. 223-228.

[78]Ibid. Mathews' entire essay, pp. 223-242, is helpful with regard to the social orientation of Old Catholics.

were tensions between rural and urban Catholics, particularly between London and Provincial Catholics long before converts constituted an identifiable element. Similarly, tensions between metropolitan and provincial bishops are not easily categorized, though Philip Hughes´ description of the problems arising from London´s central place in English Catholicism is helpful here:

> London, as always, is <u>sui generis</u> and so--let the question be put . . . does London as such ever understand, has it ever known, how England lives, what England thinks, and why England thinks as it does? Few questions are more important for whoever would arrive at the meaning of Catholic history in England . . . One problem that leaps immediately to mind, in illustration of the need to ask the question, is the different policy and point of view that has guided the building of parish schools in, say, London and Lancashire during the last fifty years.79

Hughes stresses the fact that London remained a traditional "home of small businesses" where industrial habits underwent few of the changes which revolutionized the Midlands and the North. In this context he emphasizes the importance of Ullathorne´s leadership in Victorian Catholic affairs, which remains to be treated adequately by historians.80 It might be said that Ullathorne was a typical representative of Old Catholic interests, and there is much truth in the assertion; but Ullathorne was also Bishop of Birmingham and therefore a representative of a world hardly known to many landed Catholic families.

79Hughes, <u>op.cit.</u>, pp. 67-68.

80<u>Ibid.</u>, pp. 74-75. Hughes notes that the projected title for the biography of Ullathorne which Bernard Ward hoped to write was <u>Bishop Ullathorne and His Times</u>. Hughes thus implies that Ward shared his views that Ullathorne was the most prominent prelate of the period.

Since little attention has been given to conflicts over pastoral priorities[81] too little is known about the composition of circles concerned with the care of the Irish poor. But it is clear that those most prominent in this work in London--which was, after all, the place where most Catholic newspapers and periodicals were published--were converts who also happened to be Ultramontanists.[82] Particularly noticeable in such circles by the mid-fifties was Manning. Now it is necessary to know more about the Catholics who took an active interest in these problems in other areas; we know Old Catholics were as prominent if not more prominent than Converts in Liverpool's educational and social philanthropy,[83] but intensive diocesan studies are required before any adequate statements can be made about the men who supported these pastoral efforts. Regardless, the work of the Converts in London earned them widespread publicity. There is little reason to assume that there was any necessary connection between their Ultramontanism and their concern for the poor, but there is every reason to assume that their care of the poor won a popular base for Ultramontanism. This is a theme which may only be suggested in these pages, but this research effort definitely confirms the need to examine with greater care

---

[81]See John Bennett, "The Care of the Poor," in Beck, op.cit., pp. 559-584. See also the articles by Sheridan Gilley cited in the Bibliography.

[82]From the names which appear repeatedly in the Tablet and the Weekly Register reports of meetings for the promotion of schools or redress of social grievances it is clear that Manning, Oakeley, Faber, John Morris (Wiseman's Secretary) and even William George Ward were prominent in such efforts.

[83]Thomas Burke, Catholic History of Liverpool (Liverpool: Tinling & Co., 1910), pp. 93-97, 105, 115-125.

the social basis for the strength of Ultramontanism in England.

A great quantity of energy and talent was consumed by Catholics in these conflicts, many of which were of secondary importance. This divisiveness undermined what potential may have existed for a strong educational movement. How these tensions affected Catholic educational policies is not always clear, but the general atmosphere of disunity certainly infected later educational developments.

The French example had a more direct impact on Catholic educational politics. The thousands of French Catholic refugees who poured into England during the Revolutionary era provided English Catholics with a permanent awareness of the anticlericalism and fierce antireligion of the Revolution and its radical component in England. State education in France was viewed as a product of the Revolution itself and English Catholics believed the French Ministry of Public Instruction to be fundamentally anti-Catholic and anti-religious. Thus, anything which could be construed as tending toward the creation of a Ministry of Public Instruction became anathema to them.

The background to the formation of the Catholic Poor School Committee must be understood in the broad context of Catholic educational activities dating from penal times when the teaching of Catholic doctrine had been defined as treason. Despite evidence of clandestine Catholic education in England, no real achievements in popular education can be substantiated before the eighteenth century relief acts were passed. Beales attributed the beginning of Catholic work in popular education to the efforts of several societies which provided schools, clothing and foster homes for Catholic poor children. In 1811 the Charitable Association for the Relief of Poor Children,[84] the Benevolent Society for Apprenticing Out Poor Catholics,[85] and the Laudable Society for Maintaining and Clothing Catholic Destitute Children[86] merged to form the Associated Charities. Beales described this organization and its components as the "lineal ancestor" of the Catholic Poor School Committee.[87]

Much historical work remains to be done with respect to the connections between the local societies and these organizations, but Marie Gertrude Diamond's thesis brings together many of the influences at work in the area of popular education. The Associated Charities' constitution provided for the integrity of its constituent societies and for the formation of subcommittees to coordinate the different but related efforts to clothe, feed, apprentice and educate poor children and orphans. It should be noted that this unified approach to child care must have suffered somewhat as attention came to focus primarily on schools. Diamond notes that the functions of Associated Catholic Charities were identical with those of the Catholic Poor School Committee--namely the sponsoring, through financial aid, of the opening of schools,

---

[84]Marie Gertrude Diamond, "The Work of the Catholic Poor-School Committee, 1847-1905" (M. A. thesis, University of Liverpool, 1963), p. 14. The Charitable Association was founded in 1765.

[85]Ibid. The Benevolent Society was founded in 1784.

[86]Ibid. The Laudable Society was founded in 1796.

[87]A. C. F. Beales, "Beginnings of Catholic Elementary Education in the Second Spring," Dublin Review 205 (October 1939): 307.

the increase of efficiency of such schools, and the training of Catholic teachers.[88]

Beyond London schools were most concentrated in Liverpool where the Irish population was very prominent.[89] The beginning of Catholic schools in Liverpool was related to a town council attempt to create locally funded corporation schools permitting denominational instruction according to parental desires. This consisted of Bible reading plus some doctrinal instruction; Catholic children read the Douay version of the Bible and were taught some catechism by Catholic monitors.[90] Since the monitors were little more than slightly literate older children the instruction could hardly have been considered doctrinal; nevertheless, even this amount of 'popish' instruction aroused public indignation. The program begun in 1835 came to an end with the election of a Conservative council in 1842; at this time a new policy was introduced permitting only the authorized version of the Bible and demanding that all children join in daily prayers. At this point the Liverpool Catholic clergy denounced the system and persuaded the parents of over 900 children to withdraw them from the school.[91] Subsequently Catholics opened their own schools, and between 1831 and 1845 five such poor schools were established accommodating over 3,000 pupils. Catholic schools were also opened in other areas. The Northern District reports

---

[88]Diamond, op.cit., pp. 17-18.

[89]Ibid., pp. 19-32.

[90]Ibid., pp. 21-22. Her discussion is based primarily on the work of Thomas Burke, op.cit.

[91]Ibid.

indicate places for over 6,000 students in addition to whatever was provided in Manchester, Salford, and Lancaster.[92] Despite evidence of real progress, local financial support was inadequate and a national effort was needed.

That national effort came with the formation of the Catholic Institute, which grew out of the Metropolitan Catholic Tract Society, organized during the 1820s to circulate cheap literature among the poor as a means of counteracting Protestant calumnies. The Catholic Tract Society had been in decline for some time when its founder, William Eusebius Andrews, died in 1837. The Catholic Institute was then formally established in the summer of 1838, not only to publish Catholic literature but also to defend the legal rights of Catholics and to assist in the support of Catholic schools. The bishops supported the movement and, with the clergy, became ipso facto members. Provincial branches were founded in Liverpool, Manchester, York, Darlington, North and South Shields, Leicester, Norwich, Bury St. Edmonds, Bath, Lyme Regis and other towns. The chairman of the general committee was the Hon. Charles Langdale, a member of an old Yorkshire Catholic family and sometime Member of Parliament.[93] The Catholic Institute moved from great promise to decline rather quickly and by 1845 Langdale resolved to confine his energies to the education of the poor. An indication of the Institute's success in education is its collection: in 1843 Langdale compared the Catholic contribution of ₤1,100 with the

---

[92]Ibid., pp. 30-31.

[93]B. Ward, op.cit., 1:195-197.

₤568,000 raised by Dissenters, and in 1846, out of 520 Catholic congregations in England and Wales only 74 contributed a total of ₤483.[94]

It cannot be said that ₤483 represented the total Catholic contribution to education because the charity schools still continued to function at the local level. But the failure of the national effort underscores the Catholics' inability to coordinate national and local activities.

The Catholic Institute was soon dissolved and its educational functions assumed by the Catholic Poor School Committee. The story of that development will be treated when the details of Catholic negotiations with the state are discussed in the next chapter. At this point it is necessary to turn to the other aspect of our subject--the press--and provide a general background sketch of the rise of the popular press. It is also necessary to attempt to assess the relative place of the English Catholic press in this national spectrum.

The Press

The power of the modern press is a subject which has fascinated historians for generations, yet precise characterization of that power remains illusive because it is never quite possible to show that the press was responsible for particular historical events. Quarrels over the use of and access to the printed word date from the invention of modern printing and have had religious importance since reformers challenged the Catholic hierarchy's

---

[94]Diamond, op.cit., p. 35.

right to control access to Holy Scriptures. Origins of the secular and political dimensions of the modern press clearly predate the French Revolution, but that historical event polarized attitudes which shaped the struggle for and against censorship in the nineteenth century.

Today we use the term "press" to denote organs which stress political, economic and social news often to the exclusion of clearly defined religious issues, and the separation of religious and secular subject matter has become characteristic of much present-day journalism. So it is not inappropriate to remind readers that this is a recent development which would undoubtedly have dismayed Victorian publishers, editors and readers alike, for at least half of the periodicals published at mid-century were frankly religious in their orientation.[95] As for the remainder, attitudes about religion permeated all Victorian journalism from the avowedly doctrinaire to the antireligious publications.

Many of the transitional forces at work in mid-Victorian society were reflected in the movement to expand popular education, so the Victorian press assessment of that movement provides first-rate evidence for the educational historian. Similarly, the growth of the modern press itself reflects major transitional forces at work. The application of steam printing to newspaper publication in 1814 greatly increased the speed of printing; the radical press of the post-Napoleonic years aroused conservative fears and appealed to the class hostilities which came to dominate so much

---

[95]P. G. Scott, "Richard Cope Morgan, Religious Periodicals and the Pontifex Factor," Victorian Periodicals Newsletter, no. 16 (June 1972), p. 1.

nineteenth-century thinking. Thus the combined influence of the machine and class antagonism came together to politicize journalism in a new fashion.

Politicians had responded to radical or openly seditious journalism with the taxes on knowledge--or stamp taxes. The earliest such tax was imposed in 1712; it was increased in 1756, 1765, 1773, 1789, 1798, 1804 and 1815. In addition the government imposed severe regulations against blasphemous and seditious publishing, especially after the crises of 1819. During the 1820s opposition to restrictive taxes and censorship was reasonably limited, presumably because times were good, but the ʹwar of the unstamped pressʹ revived in 1830 and continued until the tax was substantially reduced in 1836. During those years hundreds of periodicals were published illegally in defiance of the archaic libel laws, and some seven hundred vendors, publishers and printers went to jail because of that defiance; thus they helped to "define a new political and journalistic awareness." Joel Wiener describes the 1815-1840 period as one of transition from traditional, restrictive rural-oriented journalism to the modern popular urban-oriented journalism with its emphasis on social, political and economic protest.[96]

The problem of the press during the early nineteenth century is easily related to that of education. The number of prosecutions reflected the increase of radical--even seriously revolutionary--publications. While the political radicals encouraged popular

---

[96]Joel H. Wiener, "The Press and the Working Class, 1815-1840," Victorian Periodicals Newsletter, no. 11 (February 1971), p. 1.

political protest, a sense of alienation and class hostility, the blasphemous press, which included a substantial number of penny and half-penny journals, encouraged vice and crime. The whole field of lurid publishing, which offered to the poor the most indulgent narratives of vice and crime, was a major concern of religious publishers, Bible societies, educationalists and other philanthropists who feared for the souls of the poor as well as for the moral stability of the nation. They saw cheap literature making dangerous inroads against Christian morality. Presumably one does not need a history of Victorian vice literature to satisfy curiosity about the character of the blasphemous press, but it is not without interest that the legitimate press of the day always referred with typical Victorian horror to the abundance of wicked materials being distributed among the poor. It is no overstatement to suggest that educationalists of all persuasions were anxious to protect the poor from the worst of the cheap literature. As for the attitudes toward the spectrum of political and religious opinion offered through the press, no such consensus existed. Some educationalists wanted education to gain the masses for radical causes espoused by radical rags, while others wanted to provide the ´right kind´ of education as a means of countering the influence of the revolutionary press.

These sketchy remarks cannot adequately characterize the Victorian press, but as one historian has noted, it is a mistake to say that Victorian journalism was all of a piece.[97] The only

---

[97]L. W. Brady, "Penny-a-Liners and Politics: the Growth of Journalistic Influence," Victorian Periodicals Newsletter, no. 11 (February 1971), p. 17.

generalization that can be made here is that Victorian journalists were concerned about education, and educationalists were concerned about the impact of the press on the masses. Beyond that the problem of whether press coverage "ought to be considered the mirror of all or some segment of public opinion, or simply its creator"[98] cannot be decided with accuracy. This study assumes that the press both mirrored and created opinion.

The importance of the Roman Catholic press at mid-century cannot be said to have been very great. That changed somewhat after the Ecclesiastical Titles Bill debates aroused interest, however unfavorable, in Catholicism, and after the flow of converts from Canterbury to Rome placed a number of prominent intellectuals and journalists within the Roman camp. Even so, the Catholic press never really rivaled the organs of Church and Dissent, not to mention the Times. General awareness of the Catholic press was no doubt quite limited. Reasonably well informed Englishmen might have been familiar with three or four Catholic titles such as the Tablet, the Dublin Review, the Rambler, and perhaps the Weekly Register. Beyond that it must be assumed that the English Catholic publications were important only to Catholics themselves. For that matter the familiarity of the general public with even those few titles must be attributed in part to the intellectual status of individual contributors and editors, such as Lord Acton, Richard Simpson, William George Ward, Cardinal Wiseman, and certainly John

---

[98]McElrath, The Syllabus of Pius IX, Some Reactions in England (Louvain: Bibliothèque de l'Université, 1964), p. 39.

Henry Newman.

All save Acton and Wiseman were converts, which raises the question of the general intellectual and social status of English Catholics. W. G. Ward expressed a typical attitude toward Catholics when he reportedly said, "when a Protestant meets a Catholic in controversy, it is like a civilized man meeting a barbarian."[99] Newman stated his qualms about English Catholics when he wrote to Keble, "I am setting my face absolutely towards the wilderness."[100]

As for the reputation of Catholics in general, little need be said for little can be said. Roman Catholics were simply not in the mainstream of English life until long after their emancipation. Of course everyone knew the Irish were Catholic--but to Victorian society they did not count. If some Catholic intellectuals achieved prominence it was seldom on the basis of their Catholicism alone. In short, the intellectual and social isolation of Catholics had the effect of isolating the Catholic press.

This has a particular significance in that one thing that can be said with safety is that Victorian journalists were anything but isolated professionals. Today journalism is thought of as clearly defined as a profession. That state of affairs did not exist a century ago. Included among the ranks of journalists and editors were all the great political, religious, economic and social leaders and thinkers of the day; similarly, almost anyone who

---

[99]B. Ward, op.cit., 2:236.

[100]Charles Stephen Dessain, John Henry Newman (London: Adam and Charles Black, 1966), p. 79.

functioned in the public realm had some contact with newspapers and periodicals, as proprietors, editors or writers. In this sense Victorian journalism was more representative than its twentieth-century counterpart. When this is kept in mind, the isolation of Catholics and their press assumes even greater proportions, and it is one of the chief aims of this study to discern the way that fact affected the capacity of the Catholic press to address problems in church and state which could not be reduced to such isolated perspectives.

Too little is known about the Catholic press during this period. The publication of the Acton-Simpson correspondence provides a wealth of information, as does the Newman correspondence. The Wellesley Index has contributed immensely to knowledge about the contributors to the Dublin Review and the Rambler; beyond this there are a number of general articles providing cursory outlines.[101]

Despite the meager historical analyses of the English Catholic press it can be said that certain difficulties which had to be faced by Catholics troubled their Protestant counterparts much less. The prominence of the laity in modern journalism posed the problem of authority for the Catholic press. Tensions between Catholic journalists and their bishops were bound to erupt on occasion, and as confessional newspapers having extremely wide circulation presented a new phenomenon, the Church had not worked out means to deal with such tensions. Hence, Catholic editors and

---

[101]The best single article is that by J. J. Dwyer, "The Catholic Press, 1850-1950," in Beck, op.cit., pp. 475-514.

writers operated in an uncertain world where the distinction between what was uncertain and what was purely arbitrary was not
always clear.   In the world of church-state-education negotiations
Catholics faced even greater uncertainties.   Not surprisingly,
then, the press treatment of the education question posed serious
questions for editors, contributors and bishops alike.

In the following chapters an attempt is made to examine how
Catholic journalists understood the education question on the basis
of what they published.   Keeping in mind the generally accepted
notion that the modern press and secular education have served the
cause of popular democracy effectively, it will be helpful to
ascertain whether Catholics learned to use the press with comparable effectiveness in the furtherance of their own educational
interests in church and state.

CHAPTER II

THE BEGINNINGS OF CATHOLIC RELATIONS WITH THE STATE

Formation of the Catholic Poor School Committee: Press Response

Between the reorganization of the Catholic Institute in 1845 and its formal dissolution in the fall of 1847, Charles Langdale, acting for the Institute, began negotiations for Catholic participation in the government education grant. Langdale's exchanges with the government were unproductive until 1847. Of the four Catholic publications in existence at the time[1] only Dolman's Magazine and the Tablet treated the question at all, and only the Tablet provided extensive coverage. For the year 1847 attention is focused almost entirely on the Tablet's coverage of this matter.

The Tablet

The Tablet was responsive to the education question because its editor was intimately involved in events leading to the formation of the Catholic Poor School Committee. Frederick Lucas has been described as the perfect model for John Bull; both his countenance and build fitted the description, and his tenacity of pur-

---

[1]The Dublin Review, Dolman's Magazine, the Catholic Weekly Magazine, and the Tablet.

65

pose and fierceness in controversy complemented that appearance.[2]
Lucas belongs to that line of militant Catholics who, while making
enemies inside and outside the Church, have left an important mark.
Among such figures in English Catholicism one thinks immediately of
Bishop John Milner, William George Ward and Hilaire Belloc. Such a
man was Veuillot, the talented editor of L´Univers which excited
much religious controversy and served as a powerful force in mold-
ing French Ultramontanism.

Lucas was born in 1812, the son of Samuel Hughes Lucas, a
London corn merchant. He grew up in the family´s religious tradition which was Quaker. Following studies at the newly established
University of London, he read law and was called to the bar in
1835. Meanwhile his religious views changed drastically; from the
strict Quaker practices of youth he moved toward skepticism and
doubt, flirting with Benthamite perspectives. Seeking a resolution
of the conflict between faith and reason he turned to the writings
of Bishops Berkeley and Butler; despite the aid he received from
their works, nineteenth-century Anglicanism was not to be his
stopping place. An avid follower of the Oxford Movement, Lucas saw
that its logical terminus was Rome, and in 1839 he converted.
According to his friend and biographer, Christopher Reithmüller, he
"stood absolutely alone" in making this choice--that is, he was not
assisted by contemporary Catholics nor had he read the writings of
English Catholics, with the significant exception of Milner´s End

---

[2]Dwyer, op. cit., p. 482.

of <u>Religious</u> <u>Controversy</u>.[3]

Lucas´ Catholic life was almost synonymous with the history of the <u>Tablet</u> until his death in 1855, though he wrote for the <u>Dublin</u> <u>Review</u> for a short time.[4] The <u>Tablet</u> first appeared on Saturday, May 16, 1840; soon Lucas encountered trouble with his partner, and for a time there were two <u>Tablet</u>s. Characteristically, Lucas called his the <u>True</u> <u>Tablet</u>. With the weight of Daniel O´Connell´s support the rival paper was driven out of business, and Lucas remained in control of the one <u>Tablet</u> which then resumed its initial title.[5]

Lucas was a man of unhesitating vehemence and soon stirred up controversy. It is not possible to describe in detail the con- flicts of the <u>Tablet</u>´s early years, but the editor´s disregard for conciliatory approaches to Catholic difficulties should be char- acterized. Lucas had a special fondness for abusing the Catholic aristocracy, which the following excerpt illustrates:

> We know that a great deal of our language has given offence to what is called "good society." We heartily rejoice at it. "Good Society" owes us no gratitude and we owe it no allegiance. On the contrary, we regard it as a corrupt heap of religious indifference, of half faith, of cowardice, of selfishness, of unmanly impotence.6

Reithmüller applied what was said of Burke to Lucas, namely

---

[3]Christopher James Reithmüller, <u>Frederick</u> <u>Lucas,</u> <u>a</u> <u>Biography</u> (London: Bill and Daldy, 1862), pp. 13, 19, 23-24, 61.

[4]<u>Ibid</u>., p. 73. It is of some interest that Reithmüller indi- cated that many earlier writers for the <u>Dublin</u> <u>Review</u> were Protestants.

[5]B. Ward, <u>op</u>. <u>cit</u>., 2:31-46.

[6]Edward Lucas, <u>The</u> <u>Life</u> <u>of</u> <u>Frederick</u> <u>Lucas</u>, 2 vols. (London: Burns and Oates, 1886), 1:120, citing the <u>Tablet</u>, n.d.

that "he formed his opinions like a fanatic and then defended them like a philosopher."[7] Any form of timidity he viewed with abhorrence. When the 1844 Queens Colleges scheme was proposed the _Tablet_ asked, "are the bishops awake?"[8] Similar questions were put to friend and foe alike. Lucas was a Whig when the paper commenced, but the party was never his highest priority. An Irish friend said that he could not have been bought with all the gold in the Bank of England or frightened by a charge of the Life Guards.[9] His only permanent and chief commitment was to Catholicism, and he seldom missed an opportunity to denounce its assailants. Whig treachery was a favorite target for Lucas, and it qualified for serious attention on the education question time and again.

It is somewhat ironic that an ex-Nonconformist and sometime Whig should have taken up the Whigs´, not to mention England´s, greatest vulnerability, the Irish question, as a journalistic crusade. Lucas´ stand on the Irish question probably generated more opposition than any other single position he ever maintained. His coverage of that matter provides fascinating reading and a wealth of historical evidence, but that is another subject. The important point is that by 1847 the _Tablet_ had already aroused the anger of many Catholics by its uncompromising coverage of controversial questions. Despite this it enjoyed unrivaled prominence as the only Catholic weekly.

---

[7]Reithmüller, _op. cit._, p. 13.

[8]Dwyer, _loc. cit._, citing the _Tablet_, n.d.

[9]Reithmüller, _op. cit._, p. 90.

The _Tablet_ had taken the lead in educational controversy in 1843 when Graham's factory bill aroused such widespread hostility among Dissenters. Without going into the particulars it must be noted that the Earl of Arundel and Surrey (a son of the Duke of Norfolk) had spoken favorably on the measure in Parliament. He suggested that so long as the Established Church existed "it must predominate and must also of necessity be administrative in any system of national education."[10] The statement was in keeping with a long tradition by which English Catholics emphasized their allegiance to the Crown, and the Catholic aristocracy applauded. At the Catholic Institute meeting the Earl was given a special vote of thanks.[11] When Langdale carried his praise of the Earl of Arundel and Surrey's position into the columns of the _Tablet_ by a letter to the editor, Lucas published a hearty rejoinder:

> Mr. Langdale asks us who can doubt that it is right and just for the English legislature to provide a national religious education according to the principles of that Establishment. Who can doubt it? We can, and deny it too . . .12

Lucas attacked Graham's bill with powerful logic, and the bishops and clergy rallied to his position. Catholic meetings were held throughout the country protesting the measure, and even a few Catholic aristocrats joined the protest. In the main Lucas argued that it was one thing for the Church of England to educate its own children and quite another for it to educate non-Anglicans, espe-

---

[10]B. Ward, _op. cit._, 2:51.

[11]_Ibid._

[12]_Ibid._

cially with the help of tax money. The important fact that the Tablet, rather than Langdale, the aristocracy or the Catholic Institute, was first to champion Catholic educational rights in the context of an official church-state struggle was not forgotten by Lucas, who in turn did not let his opponents forget.

When the education question became prominent again in 1847 Lucas reminded Langdale that the Tablet, not the Catholic Institute, had upheld Catholic principles in 1843.[13] Lucas' purpose was not to quarrel with Langdale but to obtain justice for Catholics because they paid taxes and therefore had a right to share in the tax-based education grant.

Lucas' efforts to generate support for the Catholic demand for state educational funds played no small part in shaping Catholic negotiations with the government in 1847. He believed that Catholic political power in the constituencies should be groomed to support Catholic demands. A former Nonconformist, Lucas understood the kind of pressure Dissenters had used effectively for decades; he also understood that the government's resistance to Catholic emancipation had been overcome only by fear. Thus he concluded that the appropriate function of the Institute was to develop its constituency as a power base to be respected and feared by the English government.

It was over the question of whether the Institute should engage in politics that Lucas and Langdale disagreed; that disagreement arose over the specific problem of education and con-

---

[13]The Tablet, May 29, 1847, p. 345.

tributed to, if it was not the main cause of, the dissolution of
the Institute. Because the quarrel was carried on in the columns
of the _Tablet_, as well as in the committee meetings of the
Institute, the press response to the church-state-education
question was especially significant.

The necessity of such a strategy had been stressed by Daniel
O'Connell for years before 1847, and there was a general understanding that redress of Catholic grievances necessitated political
action. In fact that understanding partly motivated the founding
of the Catholic Institute in 1839. One need only consult speeches
at the annual meetings to find English Catholics enthusiastically
applauding O'Connell's highly political appeals urging English
Catholics on toward organized political action according to the
Methodist example, and asking the laity to form themselves into a
body of collectors for Catholic causes. The enemies were combined,
he argued, so why should Catholics not imitate that example?[14] The
Catholic Institute always honored O'Connell but never followed his
advice. When he asked, "Why not have your public meetings as your
opponents do?" there was applause but no follow-up.[15] Even Charles
Langdale supported these pleas for political action. The following
paraphrased report of Langdale's speech in 1839 illustrates this
point:

> He remembered very well when it was much the fashion for
> our enemies to speak of British Catholics as "respect-
> able" persons who had no relish for agitation; and great

---

[14]B. Ward, _op. cit._, 1:197.

[15]_Catholic Magazine_ (1839), pp. 452-453, cited by Herbert
Lucas, "The Catholic Institute and Frederick Lucas," pt. 1, _Month_
51 (May 1884): 219.

praise we got for this "respectability." But those who
praised us, nevertheless, did not cease to oppose and
persecute us; and if we had never stirred we might have
never obtained relief from those who complimented us
about it.16

But the Catholic Institute never developed organizational or polit-

ical momentum. It circulated Catholic tracts in answer to the type

of 'Maria Monk' literature everywhere distributed, and it raised

school funds, but by 1841 O'Connell commented about the English

Catholics' failure to develop a wide base of support. The _Tablet_

picked up O'Connell's theme:

It is positively sickening--we beg the pardon of the
speakers at this meeting--to hear such eulogums on our-
selves, such boasting, such triumphant exultation--at
what? . . . One would imagine from the speeches of yes-
terday and our self-congratulations . . . that the character of the English Catholics was energy, enterprise,
perseverance, undaunted courage. But is it so? God
knows it makes us laugh and half cry merely to write
the words. To express the English Catholic character in
three words we should describe them thus: "Apathy,
apathy, apathy."17

The unstated assumption underlying O'Connell's appeal was that

a wide base of support meant the Irish Catholic masses in England.

O'Connell constantly urged the English to follow his lead by en-

listing the membership of the poor at low rates, predicting enor-

mous sums would be raised. This aspect of the political failure of

the Institute is glossed over by English Catholic historians[18] as

it was avoided by English Catholics in the 1840s. In 1841 the

---

[16]_Catholic Magazine_ (1839), p. 455, cited by H. Lucas, _ibid._,
p. 220.

[17]_Tablet_, May 15, 1841, cited by H. Lucas, _ibid._, p. 228.

[18]H. Lucas, _ibid._, pp. 218-225, and B. Ward, _op. cit._, 2:53-
54. Neither Ward nor Lucas explain that the Institute's lack of
popular support was a problem involving the Irish.

question of the Irish in England was less politically sensitive than in later years; even so, upper class English Catholics were not ready to take up an active political alliance with the Irish poor--certainly not an alliance which pursued the ´Monster Meetings´ strategy of what was viewed as mob politics in Ireland. The important point is that Lucas, in advocating an organized laity for the promotion of Catholic interests, was imitating O´Connell´s example, and was not opposed by Langdale, the bishops or other prominent Catholics until later. The above quoted denunciation of Catholic apathy won the approval rather than the rebuke of bishops and others. Bishop Briggs voiced his thanks and the Catholic Magazine, which was edited by the secretary of the Catholic Institute, James Smith, reprinted the article in full.[19]

Differences between Langdale and Lucas came into the open in 1847. It is possible that so long as O´Connell lived and enjoyed considerable respect among the English Catholics, lip-service was paid to his cause. But by 1847 many things had changed. The famine was bringing Irish immigrants into England in droves, and the prominent Catholic laity began speaking out against mixing religion and politics. At this point Lucas launched his offensive.

On January 2, 1847, the Tablet asked, "What is the Catholic Institute doing?" about the education question. Holding that the Catholics could not expect justice from the government he urged them to "agitate and make known their discontents." He then wrote that the committee of the Institute which had taken up the job of collecting and distributing money for schools was doing useful work

---

[19]H. Lucas, op. cit., p. 227.

but insisted that this was only a small part of the larger task of protecting Catholic interests. The protection of those interests required political action. Thus it was argued that Catholic voters should learn to use the vote to uphold their religious interests.[20] The following week the Tablet published Charles Langdale's reply. He was furious that his educational work had been characterized as "small" and described that work in touching terms, saying that he trembled for his very soul should he neglect it.[21] In the next issue Lucas re-stated his initial position about the need to organize Catholics for all causes related to Catholic needs and to fit the education question into that larger scheme. Langdale's letter, published the previous week, had said that what the Catholics needed was a leader of Montalambert's stature. Lucas denied this and maintained that it was not valiant leadership that was required so much as a wide base of support:

> It is not the great genius of one man that is needed, but earnestness and magnanimity on the part of the multitude of small men that make up our community . . . [Of this] we have a right to complain, because these qualities are virtues which more or less are within the reach of every man . . .22

Lucas went on to urge that Catholics press their demands vigorously and immediately upon the government. These demands, he insisted, should be backed up by the "power of annoyance" which constituent politics should provide.[23] That "power of annoyance" should be

---

[20]Tablet, January 2, 1847, p. 2.

[21]Ibid., January 9, 1847, pp. 18-19.

[22]Ibid., January 16, 1847, p. 34.

[23]Ibid.

used by Catholics as it had been used by the Dissenters; moreover, he argued, the Catholic Institute was the proper agency for bringing that power into play:

> If the possession of this influence is necessary to give weight to the remonstrances and representations of the Institute, then it is the natural business of the Institute to take care that in this weight its remonstrances and representations are not deficient.24

Lucas predicted that many would say that "the course to which you would invite the Institute is a political course, and the Institute cannot meddle with politics." So he asked, "What are politics we should like to know?" He answered as follows:

> Depend upon it, that what terrifies us in the matter is not politics but religion. What those men whom Mr. Langdale complains of fear, is, we shrewdly suspect, the being thought guilty of such heinous bad manners as to avow themselves Catholics before everything. To come before the world as Conservatives, or Whigs, or Liberals, has nothing displeasing to their sensitive natures; but to proclaim with a loud voice that to them Whiggism and Toryism are comparatively nothing and religion everything--this it is which they cannot stomach--this it is of which they are afraid.

Concerning the problem of party allegiance he went on to note:

> What is asked is, not that man shall leave his party, or vote against his party, but that he shall make the condition of his supporting his party what we may call justice to God; that he shall use his vote, whether in Parliament or at the hustings, to coerce either his candidate, his fellow-member, or his peer, into paying attention to Catholic interests which justice and the law of God imperatively demand. What sort of Catholic--what sort of Christian--what sort of man--must he be who is too great a coward or too great a traitor to find the performance of this simple duty above his miserable capacity? We shall leave the answer to those who are more skillful than we are in the epithets of reproach.25

24Ibid.

25Ibid.

Such statements hardly require interpretation, but it is important to place them in the long-term historical context. A segment of the English Catholic aristocracy had displayed uncommon readiness to give way in important questions in order to win state recognition.[26] Lucas was clearly interpreting the political timidity of "respectable" Catholics in 1847 in this context and insisting that the right order of priorities be spelled out and adhered to.

On January 23, Langdale's answer was published. Acquiescing in the Tablet's judgment about the apathy of Catholics, he expressed embarrassment over the inadequacy of Catholic voluntary contributions to education, which contributions would provide the basis for computation of a government grant:

> I have trembled lest my demand should be complied with, and that in the presence of a Protestant minister I should have had to point to the paltry collection of a few hundred pounds to meet the education of three times as many thousands of our children. . . . I was spared that degradation.27

Langdale also denied that the Institute should be responsible for politically arousing Catholics, which responsibility he said lay with the press.[28] This effort to shift responsibility for political action to the Tablet was repeated later; Lucas always answered that the press could--and should--help, but that it could not do more because political action required organized effort. That was

---

[26]This was exemplified by the behavior of the "Protesting Catholic Dissenters" during the 1780s.

[27]Tablet, January 23, 1847, p. 51.

[28]Ibid.

why the Catholic Institute had been established.[29]

Lucas was not willing to let the matter rest, and he again replied to Langdale. In the February 6 _Tablet_ he denied ever having said the committee's educational work was small and repeated the statement about its being only part of a much broader work. Langdale, it was said, had confused the _Tablet_'s position. Lucas went on to list six conclusions about the state of Catholic affairs, the most important of which were: that Catholics had failed to put their claims before the government prior to the formation of official policy; that they had failed to stimulate Catholic constituencies; that they had made no progress toward the establishment of a normal school; and that "the committee of English Catholics sitting in London--representatives of the whole body--thinks it has performed an almost superhuman task (and believes itself capable of nothing more or greater) when it has collected a few hundred pounds and passed a dozen votes dividing the gross sum into a dozen unequal portions." He added:

> A sixth conclusion we venture to draw for our own private instruction: it is that we English Catholics are in a very bad way, and that we need the blast of a trumpet to waken us from this sleep of death.[30]

These exchanges between Lucas and Langdale continued well into June with the same themes being reiterated on both sides. Langdale insisted that the business of the Institute was not political while Lucas claimed it was. Both lamented the inadequacy of general support from the Catholic population. Despite these confrontations

---

[29]_Ibid._, February 13, 1847, p. 98.

[30]_Ibid._, February 6, 1847, p. 82.

Lucas and Langdale were not really working at cross purposes. Lucas saw nothing incompatible between hostility in controversy and amiability in personal relations. His friends knew him as a gentle man, a generous host and a devoted friend. Honest disagreement he believed to be part of friendship.[31] Those who knew Lucas well enough to fight with him in the columns of the Tablet probably had some appreciation for such qualities.

We know too little about the relationship between Lucas and Langdale. One of their contemporaries who knew Langdale well said he "must have very keenly felt the harsh tones of the articles," but went on to quote Langdale's daughter on the same subject:

> We used to be present when Papa opened the paper, and he used to read these attacks on himself, at which we used to be very indignant; but we never could get him to express the least soreness or annoyance. On the contrary, he generally turned it into a joke, and said the editor had a perfect right to say what he pleased about him.[32]

At one point Lucas went out of his way to make it known that Langdale was not his main object of attack; rather, his arrows were aimed at those who failed to sustain the Institute's efforts.[33]

These confrontations in the Tablet's columns presaged trouble for the Catholic Institute. Its annual meeting was held just a few days after a government decision against aid to Roman Catholic

---

[31]John Moore Capes, "Frederick Lucas," Rambler, 2nd ser., 4 (December 1855): 450-460. This provides some contrast with Reithmüller's appreciation of Lucas, which stressed Lucas' capacity for friendly disagreement. Capes much regretted the tone in which Lucas carried on public disputes.

[32]William J. Amherst, S. J., "The Hon. Charles Langdale," pt. 3, Dublin Review 113 (October 1893): 861-862.

[33]Ibid.

schools was announced. The Government´s handling of this situation lent force to Lucas´ warnings that Russell and the Whigs could not be trusted and to his argument that since all they understood was fear Catholics must frighten them into supporting their demands. There remains some uncertainty about the actual course of events between April 1847, when the Government conveyed its refusal to support Catholic demands, and December 1847, when the first Minutes prescribing conditions for aid to Catholic schools were published, but the broad outlines of these developments can be sketched.

Langdale´s 1846 correspondence with government officials had yielded nothing; he resumed his efforts with a letter to Lord Lansdowne, President of the Council, in January 1847. Exchanges dating from January 23 to April 15 between Langdale and the Committee on Education convinced Langdale and his colleagues that Russell´s Government would approve their requests for aid. Then on April 16 Kay-Shuttleworth wrote to Langdale advising that the Committee´s Minutes prohibited such aid because the 1839 Minutes required the use of the authorized version of the Bible.[34] Kay-Shuttleworth indicated that preparation of separate Minutes for Catholics would be deliberated soon; however, the next day Lord Russell sent word to Bishop Thomas Griffith contradicting Kay-Shuttleworth´s suggestions. Bishop Griffith had requested an interview with Russell, who replied he would be glad to receive a

---

[34]Tablet, April 24, 1847, pp. 260-263. Here the official correspondence was published in full. The same correspondence was abstracted by H. Lucas, "The Last Days of the Catholic Institute," Month 51 (August 1884): 509-511. In a footnote, p. 511, Lucas showed that the 1839 Minutes did not call for the authorized version. Similarly, the Tablet, May 22, 1847, p. 322, indicated that this claim was false.

deputation of Roman Catholic bishops before introducing measures regarding aid to Catholic poor schools, but he added, "Her Majesty's Ministers . . . have no immediate intention of promulgating Minutes of the Privy Council on that subject."[35]   Two days later, on April 19, the debate in Parliament touched on this question, and both Russell and Lansdowne made it clear that aid would not be forthcoming soon.   Several Members spoke in favor of the Catholics, including Sir James Graham, Sir Robert Peel, Sir William Molesworth, and John Arthur Roebuck, but their efforts were fruitless.[36]

The reasons for the Government's about face are not altogether clear, but the Tablet often complained that Methodists had exerted strong pressure against aid to Catholics.   When the Catholic Institute met for its annual gathering on April 21 the official correspondence was disclosed and speakers liberally denounced the treachery of the Russell Government.   At this meeting a resolution was passed calling for a public meeting of all Catholics for the purpose of protesting the Government's position.   At the same meeting Bishop Ullathorne moved for alterations in the constitution of the Catholic Institute which were designed to improve its efficiency with respect to dealings with the government; Ullathorne's motion was also intended to empower the Institute to call public meetings concerning the difficulties of the moment.[37]   The

---

[35]Lord John Russell to Bishop Griffiths, April 17, 1847, cited by H. Lucas, op. cit.,   p. 512.

[36]Diamond, op. cit., pp. 40-42.

[37]Tablet, April 24, 1847, pp. 260-263.   "The Government and

Institute subsequently sent out circulars to all congregations in the country requesting support for such a meeting; numerous favorable responses were returned.[38] At some point in the interim, however, Langdale determined against this course of action.[39] His change of opinion occasioned another confrontation with Lucas who was also a member of the Institute's education committee. Accounts of this confrontation are inadequate, but the outline can be pieced together. At the Institute's education committee meetings Lucas, Dr. Ferguson, Mr. W. J. Amherst and others pressed for the public meeting, but Langdale said he had pledged himself against such a course of action. Lucas said he had never heard of such a pledge, that it was little more than a cowardly invention and that it was invalid because it was--if it existed at all--unofficial. The confrontation between Lucas and Langdale was carried on partly in committee meetings and partly in the Tablet.[40]

Lucas insisted that political action was necessary to overcome the Government's obstinacy, and he believed the mass meeting appropriate. Langdale backed away from that course because of pressure from the Catholic gentry and nobility.[41] In this context it is

---

the Scheme of Education and the Catholic Institute," Dolman's Magazine (May 1847), pp. 417-418, also blames Methodists for influencing Government policy.

[38]Tablet, May 22, 1847, pp. 321-322.

[39]H. Lucas, "Last Days of the Institute," pp. 519-520.

[40]Amherst, "The Hon. Charles Langdale," pt. 2, Dublin Review 113 (July 1893): 527-529.

[41]H. Lucas, "Last Days of the Institute," pp. 519-520; and Amherst, "Langdale," pt. 2, pp. 526-528.

necessary to understand Langdale's relationship with that select body. Langdale was born Charles Stourton, fourth son of the seventeenth Baron Stourton; his Godfather was Bernard Edward, Duke of Norfolk; his maternal grandfather was the last Lord Langdale of Holme Hall, Yorkshire, and Draycott, Staffordshire. He assumed the name Langdale when he was willed Houghton Hall in Yorkshire by Phillip Langdale, his mother's cousin. Though not the possessor of munificent estates, Langdale was prominent among the most illustrious families of England, and it is clear that by virtue of his extraordinary efforts in Catholic philanthropy he was an unquestioned leader of the upper class Catholic laity.[42] Clearly his position concerning the public meeting was not merely personal but was representative of the attitude of the most prominent gentry and nobility. What Langdale's personal views were remains unknown; he told Lucas and his associates, 'call a meeting and I will attend it'--but that was quite beside the point. As Amherst observed, under such circumstances,

> Mr. Langdale might have been there as he said he would be; but he would not have been expected to issue circulars and use his influence to induce the Catholic nobility and gentry to follow him.43

Lucas then determined to issue his own appeal in favor of the "aggregate meeting"; this appeared in the May 8 Tablet. "Is the generous warmth which the Ministerial fraud and insult have

---

[42]Amherst, "Charles Langdale," pt. 1, Dublin Review 111 (October 1892): 395-425. This article sketches Langdale's early career; ibid., pt. 2, pp. 527-529, reiterates the importance of his leadership of the Catholic laity in the context of the Catholic Institute controversy.

[43]Ibid., pt. 2, p. 530.

occasioned to be allowed to cool into the usual frigid indifference?" he asked. He reminded Catholics how well the Methodists
used political pressure to overcome Government resistance and obtain for themselves the education grant, and he bemoaned the extent
to which Catholics "have been such fools as to vote for these
miserable Whigs throughout the whole of our Prostitute career." He
called for mass meetings in London to be coordinated with others
throughout England so that Catholics might call to account those
"who have kept and who have broken their promises."[44]

The question of the mass meeting was apparently settled once
and for all at a meeting of the education committee of the
Institute. Lucas had moved that the chairman should call a public
meeting, and a date was set for discussion of the question. Both
sides gathered forces for the fight. When the meeting took place
the defeat of Lucas' motion was assured by the presence of "a great
many members who had not often shown themselves on the committee."
According to Amherst, who was present, "every one of this class of
men voted with Mr. Langdale." Amherst noted that this action "gave
the coup de grâce to the Institute" by demonstrating beyond
question its inability to function.[45] Though the date of this
meeting is not known, the May 29 issue of the _Tablet_ spoke of the
issue as having been settled.[46]

On May 29 an article entitled "The Miserable Pusillanimity of
the Committee of the Catholic Institute" appeared in the _Tablet_; it

---

[44]_Tablet_, May 8, 1847, p. 289.

[45]Amherst, "Langdale," pt. 2, p. 529.

[46]_Tablet_, May 29, 1847, p. 345.

vehemently denounced the committee's refusal to call a public meeting. "If the Committee had possessed half the courage of mice," it said, an "Aggregate Meeting" would have succeeded. Catholics were reminded again of the Institute's 1843 betrayal of Catholic educational causes and a variety of other accusations were hurled at it. Reference was made to a proposal for making the Catholic Institute the standing agency for dealing with the state. Of this the following was said:

> We deprecate with all our might any such arrangements. To consent to it is to sell the Catholic interests to the enemy without hope of redemption. We would as soon place our interests in the hands of the Whigs themselves as in the hands of their Whig deputies. God save us from all Whigs, but especially from all Whig Catholics.47

On June 5 the Tablet published Langdale's "Defense of the Committee of the Institute" but prefaced it by saying, "to us he seems to have surrendered the whole case." The preface also attacked Langdale personally, describing him as "timid, cautious to excess . . . deficient in nerve." On the matter of political action Lucas said, "Mr. Langdale is pledged to their damnation rather than to allow the Institute to remind a Catholic elector of the religious obligations under which he exercises his vote . . ." And again Lucas called to mind Langdale's failure to stand up for Catholic principle in 1843.[48]

In his heated response to Lucas, Langdale defended his own honor as a gentleman, while at the same time attacking "those inspired in the retirement of the study, and proved by the heroism

---

[47]Ibid.

[48]Ibid., June 5, 1847, p. 354.

of the pen" and such like Victoriana. Langdale denied that his actions had ever been guided by party feeling--Whig or Tory--and insisted that Catholicism had been his chief priority. The crux of the answer, however, was that the Institute had never been directly responsible for political action as such and that he was thus acting in keeping with its tradition. Rather than give an explanation concerning his pledge against political action, which Lucas had questioned, Langdale merely turned the question:

> Most assuredly, nobody ever heard of, or as far as I know even thought of, the proceedings into which you, Mr. Editor, would choose as you say to plunge the Institute headlong, "to take our chances in the black and bottomless pit of politics" until within these last six months.49

While the reply lists other instances when the Institute refrained from actually calling public meetings--which were entirely managed by independent committees--it fails altogether to define or defend the pledge which Lucas had challenged. It will be remembered that Langdale originally agreed that a public meeting should be called; when he changed his mind he said he was bound by a personal pledge to oppose the calling of such a meeting. Neither his change of policy nor his supposed pledge were adequately explained by this reply, though the letter does reveal that Langdale believed the Catholic aristocracy had been always and legitimately reluctant to become involved in disreputable political activities.

On June 12 the Tablet published Bishop Briggs´ letter condemning the manner in which Langdale had been attacked; Lucas hastened to publish an apology in which he regretted that his manner had

---

49Ibid.

offended a bishop, but the apology defended the crux of his position. He said he had simply intended "to convince our readers how grossly our affairs have been mismanaged recently." Of the Bishop's expression of confidence in Mr. Langdale, he said:

> If by unbounded confidence [of the] Bishops Dr. Briggs means to imply that all believe Mr. Langdale to be endowed with a force of mind, energy, activity, courage and discernment, which make a man a safe guide in times of difficulty and qualify him to rescue a disunited and sluggish people from the thraldom beneath which their own apathy bows down--if this be his Lordship's meaning, so signal and so honourable a testimony must make Mr. Langdale indifferent to, and the world at large careless about every meaner opinion; and we know therefore that we do no injury to Mr. Langdale, but merely throw discredit on our own judgment when from this opinion we venture our very humble, most respectful, but most unqualified dissent.50

It is indeed worth noting that the bishop's letter restricted itself to condemning the Tablet's manner; issue was not taken with any particular position.

This was the last issue in which Lucas focused chiefly on the Catholic Institute and its failures. In the meantime the Catholic negotiations with the state had been revived. One writer notes that at the end of April the Russell Government had pledged itself to support aid to Roman Catholic schools.[51] By May 25, 1847 correspondence between the Privy Council Committee's George Keppel and the Rev. Thomas Tierney Fergusson, secretary of the Catholic Institute, indicated that the Privy Council Committee had been formulating plans to offer aid to Catholics.[52] Lucas sat on the

---

[50]Ibid., June 12, 1847, p. 370.

[51]Diamond, op. cit., p. 46.

[52]Ibid.

education committee of the Institute and must have been aware of these developments, but the Tablet published little information relative to them. The May 29 article mentioned above, which suggested the possibility of the Institute becoming a permanent agency for dealing with the government,[53] probably related to the May 25 letter just cited which did propose that the Institute be made the official agency for negotiating with the government. The other terms proposed, which were not publicized in the Tablet, included inspection of secular instruction only, with provisions for ecclesiastical certification of religious instruction, the appointment of a Catholic inspector to be approved by the Catholic hierarchy; in addition Catholic schools were to permit parents of non-Catholic children to withdraw them from doctrinal instruction, and anyone in Holy Orders was to be excluded from the post of schoolmaster.

Lucas soon shifted the Tablet´s focus of attention to the local meetings in the borough of Marylebone where the Association of St. Thomas of Canterbury originated. The first report of such meetings appeared in the June 19 Tablet. The education question was prominent among the topics discussed, but the main purpose of the meeting thus reported was to set an example for local political organizations which could defend Catholic interests in the constituencies. In his speech as chairman Lucas asserted that the existing machinery for redressing grievances had failed because it began "at the wrong end" by forming a general organization before local committees existed to support its work. This, he said, was like

---

[53]Tablet, May 29, 1847, p. 345.

building a house without first making the bricks. The theme
stressed was the religious responsibilities of Catholic voters,
especially where the education problem was involved. A petition
was signed protesting the exclusion of Catholics from the education
grant; it stated that Catholics had been "robbed of wealth conse-
crated by their Catholic forefathers to purposes of education."[54]
Such references to the confiscation of monastic property clearly
represented an attack on the Establishment's property settlement
and must have horrified some of the good Whig Catholics whose
readiness to uphold the Establishment so angered Lucas. The petition also protested laws preventing religious from becoming teachers. The latter referred to sections of the Emancipation Act
prohibiting the existence of male religious orders in England.[55]

On July 3 the Tablet reported a later meeting in the same
borough. At this time Amherst summarized the Catholic grievances
to be dealt with. The first was the exclusion of Catholics from
the education grant, the second involved the 1829 penal law concerning male religious orders. This, Amherst noted, was especially
devastating because the male religious orders traditionally fur-
nished the teachers of the Church.[56] Concern about this matter was
quite timely because there were discussions in Parliament about
whether the Privy Council Committee on Education would permit any
clerics to teach in state-funded schools. In a June 7 debate in
the House of Lords, Lord Stanley questioned Lord Lansdowne about

---

[54]Ibid., June 19, 1847, p. 389.

[55]B. Ward, op. cit., 2:73-74.

[56]Tablet, July 3, 1847, p. 417.

the character of the government's discussion with Dissenters, particularly Methodists, concerning the 1846 Minutes on education. Stanley wanted to know if schoolmasters could hold minor Anglican orders and if Nonconformist agitation focused on this issue. After some hedging Lansdowne told Stanley that the Methodists had been interested in this very question and admitted that the Committee on Education would consider a deacon disqualified for the office of schoolmaster.[57] The Bishop of Exeter brought the matter up again on June 11, moving that persons in Holy Orders but not exercising ecclesiastical functions not be considered ineligible for the office of schoolmaster in schools receiving Parliamentary funds. Lansdowne responded by accusing the Bishop of having concealed motives and wanting "to create a separate profession of schoolmaster" in which Anglican clerics would have a guaranteed place. After lengthy discussions the Bishop withdrew his motion.[58]

These discussions underline the Privy Council Committee's intention, as expressed by Lord Lansdowne, to exclude any and all clerics from the teaching profession. Put another way they reveal the firm determination of the Committee on Education to create a purely secular teaching profession. This is an aspect of the church-state education question which has received almost no attention but constitutes one of the basic themes of the period.

On many occasions the Tablet took note of debates over Anglican problems which touched on Catholic interests. Since the

---

[57]Hansard, 3rd series, vol. 93 (1847): 176-178, 370-380.

[58]Ibid., p. 380.

question of Holy Orders went to the heart of the Catholic belief that religious should take up the responsibilities for the schools, it is surprising that the Tablet did not call readers´ attention to these debates. The question of Holy Orders was doubly problematic for Catholics because of the strictures against male religious orders dating from 1829, but the Tablet did not take up this problem at the time.

For the remainder of 1847 there was a general decline in the number of articles about education. The Lucas-Langdale confrontations stopped, and after the bishops took the matter under their wing Lucas turned to other problems, principally the work of the Association of St. Thomas of Canterbury for the Vindication of Catholic Rights. This body was intended to be primarily political, modeled after the politics of Dissent. The Tablet always reported the Association´s meetings where the education grant was a prominent topic; but from July to December almost nothing is to be found in the pages of the Tablet about Catholic negotiations with the state.

The dissolution of the Institute and the formation of the Catholic Poor School Committee were reported on November 20. This report emphasized the fact that the creation of the Catholic Poor School Committee was the work of the bishops, who had assumed full responsibility for Catholic educational policy; the article also published the circular distributed among clergy and Institute members announcing these plans; and within the circular was printed the September 27, 1847 letter under the bishops´ signatures con-

cerning their scheme.[59] Thus were these new developments
announced. On December 4 the Tablet reported the Catholic
Institute meeting at which that body was officially dissolved.
This meeting made it clear that the fate of the Institute had been
directly influenced by the formation of the Association of
St. Thomas of Canterbury, which received what was left of the
general fund of the Institute, while the Institute's education
committee funds were formally passed over to the Poor School
Committee.[60] Ironically these events meant the separation of political efforts from the negotiations, but the Tablet did not take
notice of that fact. By the end of 1847 the paper and its editor
appeared to be content with the way things had been resolved.

During 1847 the Tablet published over forty articles about
aspects of the church-state-education problem; some were nothing
more than letters or documents; some were well-developed editorial
policy statements. In addition, the Tablet had the practice of
publishing excerpts from the Parliamentary debates which supplemented regular coverage of the matter.[61]

In these columns of the Tablet are found the editor's views as
well as those of his opponents who submitted correspondence for
publication. Not only did the Tablet provide full coverage of
events during the first half of the year, its columns also reveal
better than any other source the extent to which the education

---

[59]Tablet, November 20, 1847, p. 743.

[60]Ibid., December 4, 1847, p. 772.

[61]This practice was also followed by the Catholic Standard.

question went to the center of Catholic relations with the government. While we have only made references in these pages to the
most representative articles, an effort has been made to sketch the
major characteristics of the paper's position and to suggest how it
related to the evolution of Catholic policy.

During the first half of 1847 the paper focused primarily on
the Langdale-Lucas dispute over whether Catholics should organize
politically to obtain state funds. From the first the _Tablet_
insisted that because the state was inherently hostile to
Catholicism and had manifested that hostility at every opportunity,
Catholic demands for redress of any and all grievances--including
educational ones--should be backed by political pressure. In particular, the _Tablet_ argued that the Catholic Institute's education
committee had the responsibility of coordinating politics and negotiations and seeing to it that Catholic electors learned to exercise their vote in behalf of Catholic interests. This assumption
that the political and educational questions were inseparable penetrated nearly everything said in the _Tablet_. Just as the _Tablet_
asserted that politics and religion were not and could not be
totally separate, it also insisted that secular and religious
instruction could not be separate. The relationship between these
inseparable factors, it was said, must be determined by the priorities of religion; when politics touched on religious values or
questions in any way, the interests of religion had to take prece-
dence; when instruction touched on religion--as all instruction
did--the interests of religion must take priority. This was the
broad position of the paper in 1847, and so long as Lucas lived it
did not change.

With regard to more specific questions, the Tablet urged the Catholic Institute to pursue certain policies which involved the use of political pressure. Langdale preferred a wait-and-see policy. In April 1847 the Institute got stung. Lucas and the Tablet called for protest meetings to demonstrate the force of their demands, but Langdale balked. Langdale's policy prevailed, but the government made another about-face and offered aid to Catholics in December 1847. Precisely why and when Russell made his second policy shift is not clear, so it cannot be determined whether Lucas' publicity in the Tablet had any impact on the government's decision to offer aid to Catholics. What does seem certain is that the dissolution of the Catholic Institute and the formation of the Catholic Poor School Committee were partly the result of Lucas' attack on the Institute--in the columns of the Tablet, in the meetings of the Institute's education committee, and through the formation of the Association of St. Thomas of Canterbury.

Another theme developed during 1847 was the unreliability of the Catholic-Whig alliance. Lucas was an astute observer of Lord Russell's opportunism. He described the "Parliamentary conscience of the present day" as one of the "curiosities of casuistry." Russell, he said, was a "two-fold" man whose priorities were not predictable. Elaborating on this theme of Russell's "two-foldedness" he pondered over "which of the two brains" he used to say his prayers.[62] Lucas was never convinced by Russell's pose as

---

[62]Tablet, May 1, 1847, p. 274.

the friend to Catholics. Ironically, in the short run Lucas was proved wrong when Russell favored aid to Catholics later in 1847. In the long run, however, Russell proved the correctness of Lucas´ opinion with his Ecclesiastical Titles Bill in 1851.

When the Privy Council Committee on Education resumed negotiations with the Catholics in earnest and the bishops took the matter officially into their hands, Lucas suspended public criticism for a time and let matters proceed under proper authority. But before these developments for the remainder of the 1847-1852 period are studied the treatment accorded by Dolman´s Magazine to the 1847 problem should be reviewed.

Dolman´s Magazine

Little has been written about Dolman´s Magazine, a rather short-lived monthly published from March 1847 through August 1849 under that title and then through 1850 under different titles. The publisher, Charles Dolman, had also published the Catholic Magazine, 1838-1844,[63] and later published the Lamp.[64] Dolman was the nephew of a Bond Street publisher, Thomas Booker, whose business he took over.[65] F. C. Husenbeth noted that the magazine was a continuation of the Catholic Magazine which had been edited by the secretary of the Institute, but there is no indication of any

---

[63]Dwyer, op. cit., p. 503.

[64]According to Dwyer, ibid., the Lamp was being published by Dolman in 1855. This contradicts statements by other authorities that Dolman went out of the periodical publishing business in 1850.

[65]F. C. Husenbeth, "History of Catholic Periodicals," Catholic Opinion, January 30, 1867, p. 1. This was based on an unspecified article in Notes and Queries.

official connection between Dolman´s Magazine and the Institute.
About the only information available concerning Dolman is that his
printing firm was responsible for much of the progress made in the
area of Victorian Catholic publishing.[66] When Dolman´s Magazine
ceased publication under that title in August 1849, it merged for a
brief time with the Weekly and Monthly Orthodox Journal and was
published as the Weekly Register, August 1849 through January 1850;
following that, from March through December 1850, it appeared as
the Catholic Magazine and Register. Subsequently the publication
ceased to exist.

Dolman then turned from periodicals to more sophisticated,
higher quality and more costly publications, but Catholic buyers
were not sufficiently numerous to sustain such a business. He went
bankrupt and retired to Paris, where he died in 1863.[67]

Insofar as Dolman´s involvement in Catholic life was concerned
there is little evidence that his influence extended much beyond
the world of his business and his publications. The Catholic
Directories for 1846 and 1848 respectively show him to have been
secretary to the London Catholic Charitable Fund and Vice President
of St. Edward´s Catholic Literary Institution.[68] This would merely
represent minor affiliations with the usual Catholic social and
philanthropic organizations which one would expect from a middle-
class businessman. There is no evidence that he wielded influence

---

[66]John R. Fletcher, "Early Catholic Periodicals in England,"
Dublin Review 198 (April 1936): 295.

[67]Fletcher, op. cit., p. 296.

[68]The Catholic Directory: 1846 (London: C. Dolman, 1846),
p. 165; Catholic Directory: 1848, p. 166.

beyond this sphere.

Editorship of the magazine, 1845-1846, has not been identified prior to April 1846, when Miles Gerald Keon was editor. He was succeeded in November 1846 by the Rev. Edward Price.[69] Both men remained somewhat obscure but appear several times in the Newman correspondence. Keon, a member of an old Irish family, was educated at Stonyhurst. Apparently his only prominence in English Catholic affairs derived from his work on Dolman's Magazine for a few months during 1846. Newman mentioned both Keon and the Magazine in a letter to John Moore Capes in July 1846. Capes and Newman were discussing the possibility of establishing a new Catholic periodical, and Newman told Capes that Keon had been pressing him to write for Dolman's Magazine, but that he had refused on the ground that he had never written for a "mainly literary publication." Explaining his refusal further, Newman said, "certainly the tone and style is not such as I should like to take part in." At the same time Newman made it clear to Capes that he would consider contributing to "a religious magazine--if it really were professedly religious; or at least critical, philosophical, etc., I mean grave."[70] In a subsequent letter Newman remarked that he respected Keon's zeal and implied that his relations with him had been friendly, but he added:

> . . . yet I do not think he can conduct a periodical--he is too young, (in Aristotle's sense)--I wish you could

---

[69]Fletcher, op. cit., p. 302.

[70]John Henry Newman to John Moore Capes, July 13, 1846, in The Letters and Diaries of John Henry Newman, ed. Charles Stephen Dessain (London: Thomas Nelson and Sons, 1961), 11:205.

make some arrangement with him, yet do not see how; for
when you cast off Editor and Publisher, a very poor
identity would remain between his Magazine and yours,
supposing a coalition were possible, yet I think this is
a difficulty; and (without meaning to say that Catholics
should take up Mr. Keon's publication) yet it will be one
of your collisions with the Old Catholics.[71]

This very brief reference suggests that Dolman's Magazine had
the loyalty of the Old Catholics and lacked Newman's support. In
this respect matters were not improved by the change of editors.
In 1846 Price took over, but he soon got into a major controversy
with Newman over Faber's Lives of the Saints.[72] Though the details
of that controversy do not concern us, the magazine's incapacity to
get along with Newman may have been significant. Newman's intellectual weight and the shortage of competent Catholic writers must
certainly have combined to weaken the magazine's chances for success in days when Catholic publishing was marginal at best. As for
Price, little seems to be known about him except that he was a
convert from Presbyterianism, a graduate of St. Edmund's College
(1829), was ordained in 1832 and served from 1844 at the Sardianian
Chapel at Lincoln Inn Fields.[73]

Despite Newman's view that the magazine was not serious as an
intellectual publication, it contains much informative material on
English Catholicism, 1845-1850, and deserves more study than it has
received or can be given here. In politics it was clearly Whig,
and its political articles mildly favored Catholic political action

---

[71]Newman to Capes, July 14, 1846, ibid., 11:207.

[72]Price is identified by Dessain, ibid., 12:437. Here Dessain
indexes the correspondence relative to this matter.

[73]Joseph Gillow, Biographical Dictionary of English Catholics,
5 vols. (London: Burns and Oates, 1887), 5:366.

at times. For example, an article published in March 1845 said that because English politics were in fact sectarian Catholics must learn how to play sectarian politics effectively.[74] How this was to be done was not elaborated; moreover, Keon´s stated editorial policy would have hampered the development of a strictly Catholic political line. That policy included first the conciliation of Protestants and secondly the reconciliation of Catholic factions.[75] On church-state issues the magazine tended to favor the separation of church and state and to oppose the endowment of religions.[76] Perhaps one of the most valuable articles published in the early years was one by Charles Edward Jerningham, a prominent Old Catholic. Entitled "The Catholics of England," the article provides a defense of the Catholic-Whig alliance that acknowledges that the Tories had been the "natural allies" of Catholics following the seventeenth-century Whig settlement. In the nineteenth century, however, the ´no-popery´ cry was taken up by the Tories, especially during the Melbourne administration. Thus were the Catholics forced to look for support from those who had been their most bitter enemies. This new alliance Jerningham termed a "forced affinity" over which he exhibited not a little uneasiness.[77] If

---

[74]"The Policy of Catholics," Dolman´s Magazine (March 1845), p. 32.

[75]Miles Gerald Keon, "To the Catholics of Great Britain and Ireland," Dolman´s Magazine (April 1846), p. 318.

[76]"A Peep at All Things and a Few Others," Dolman´s Magazine (May 1845), pp. 297-301. This was a general news column; the particular section cited here had to do with the Maynooth grant debate.

[77]Charles Edward Jerningham, "The Catholics of England,"

that uneasiness was typical of other Old Catholics, then they would have felt especially uneasy about Catholic-Whig dealings concerning education. Langdale's defensive posture supports such a hypothesis and suggests the need for further inquiry into the strength of the Old Catholic-Whig alliance.

In May 1847 Dolman's Magazine published a fourteen-page article on the education question entitled "The Government Scheme of Education and the Catholic Institute." This article summarized the events leading up to the Privy Council's rejection of Catholic requests for educational funds, and presented excerpts from the correspondence between Langdale and the bishops on the one hand, and the various government officials on the other. Clearly the article was occasioned by the April 21 meeting of the Institute, and much of the material presented is repetitious of that presented in the Tablet. The author identified himself as "Fiat Justitia," a priest, and cannot be further identified. His concern for political action was surprisingly in line with that developed by Lucas. Pressure from Methodists and the problem of the forthcoming election were given as reasons for the Government's duplicity toward Catholics. Here Catholics were urged to follow the example of the Dissenters, who were frequently praised in these pages for their fight against ignorance and for their capacity to bend the government to their will:

> Their strength is in union, and they have made Lord John feel it. They are strong in the registry--they are strong in combination--they are strong in long-winded

Dolman's Magazine (May 1846), p. 527.

orators--they are strong in the well-paid advocates of the press, and the Whig government bends beneath this well-combined and simultaneous attack.[78]

Catholics were urged to form committees in every congregation in England and to monitor and encourage Catholic voter registration. Organization at both the local and national level was called for on the model of the anti-Corn Law League.[79] Catholics were reminded of their numerical strength which, if they were but united, could not be despised. The writer said that the "mean, and insulting, and treacherous conduct" of the Government, and particularly of Lords Russell and Lansdowne "should be exposed to the just and merited censure of every just and honourable mind." The author admitted that this was his first political article, but he insisted that the government's treachery left him without a choice.[80]

The two most noteworthy aspects of this article are its expression of surprise at Russell's duplicity and the insistence on political action as the remedy to it. If Dolman's Magazine was an Old Catholic organ as Newman suggested, its call for political action is especially important. It would suggest that Lucas was by no means alone in advocating such a policy and that Langdale's resistance to that policy developed some time after the Catholic Institute meeting. That, in fact, is what the Tablet implied.

A third factor to be noted about this article has to do with its emphasis on the role taken by the bishops in negotiations with

---

[78]"The Government Scheme of Education and the Catholic Institute," Dolman's Magazine (May 1847), p. 411.

[79]Ibid., p. 422.

[80]Ibid.

the government. Lucas´ onslaught against Langdale and the gentry overshadowed the Tablet´s coverage of the active role of the bishops in these matters. Jerningham´s article lays greater stress on episcopal efforts. Though the Tablet provided details about bishops´ activities, their significance is better highlighted in the Jerningham article. Bishop Walsh´s work was especially important, but Bishop Briggs, along with Bishops Brown, Sharpless and Ullathorne, clearly took an active interest in the church-state-education questions at this time.

It is difficult to compare a single article in one publication with over forty in another, but accuracy requires the attempt. That Dolman´s Magazine only turned its attention to this matter after the Government´s refusal to aid Catholics had generated a general cry of indignation, and that it published no follow-up articles after that outcry subsided, indicate the extent of the editor´s concern. This may also suggest the extent of concern felt by Old Catholics, though that conclusion cannot be substantiated. In contrast, the Tablet indicated a sustained and detailed concern with all elements of the church-state-education question by its thorough if controversial coverage.

CHAPTER III

THE CATHOLIC PRESS AND THE PROGRESS OF CATHOLIC
RELATIONS WITH THE STATE, 1848-1852

In 1848 the Tablet ceased to be the only Catholic organ concerned with educational questions, so it is necessary to introduce
the additional periodicals under discussion. At the same time it
should be helpful to say a word or two about the way the power of
the modern press was understood by Catholic journalists--rather by
the Rambler editor, whose commentary on the meaning of this new
phenomenon will serve to introduce the English Catholic understanding of contemporary journalism during these years.

These bibliographic and background remarks will set the stage
for the main questions under discussion here: the Catholic press
assessment of the progress of Catholic relations with the state,
1848-1852. It is necessary to discuss general questions having to
do with the way Catholic publications treated problems such as the
definition of education, authority in education, and the general
importance of Protestant educational efforts. Attention is also
devoted to specific church-state questions in which Catholics became involved--those having to do with the conditions established
for school trust deeds (especially the so-called "management

102

clauses"), inspection, and curriculum. Finally, an attempt is made to summarize characteristics of the general press assessment of the work of the Catholic Poor School Committee. As this period was crucial in the development of opinion on church-state-education questions, it is necessary to indicate the full spectrum of interests and opinions expressed in the Catholic press, insofar as this is possible.

Catholic Newspapers and Periodicals, 1847-1852

In addition to the two publications discussed in the preceding chapter (the Tablet and Dolman's Magazine), there were seven others published during this period which have been analyzed for the purposes of this study. In the following paragraphs an attempt is made to provide background information about them—to give fundamental bibliographic data and to characterize the significance of each.

The Rambler

The Rambler has received more attention from historians than any other Catholic periodical of the Victorian era, and it is unnecessary to provide a repetitious account of its significance and history. The prominence and competence of its editors and of the controversies they generated accounts for the extent to which historians have been fascinated by this publication.

At first viewed as an organ of the Converts, the Rambler gradually became the organ of a select body of English Liberal Catholics, among whom the most prominent spokesmen were Lord Acton, Richard Simpson, John Moore Capes, J. S. Northcote, and others. As a Convert publication begun by Capes[1] in January 1848, the Rambler soon became the focus of controversy because of its boldness in proclaiming, by example, the need for Catholics to exercise freedom of thought in areas open to discussion by the laity or not pronounced on authoritatively by the Church. The tension within Catholicism between free inquiry and authority has troubled the Church throughout the ages, and the eloquent way in which the Rambler's contributors focused on these tensions was bound to cause trouble, which it did. The editors' confrontations with the English bishops were wide ranging and involved not only theological questions but also politics, the role of the laity and the press, and education. In the present study it will be necessary to restrict discussion to those conflicts which arose in connection with the educational controversies of the day.

Capes' interest in social problems was reflected in the Rambler's pages from the start; these volumes contain many valuable articles on the problems of poverty, emigration, Catholic duties to the poor and education. The Rambler's first controversy having to do with education came in 1848 when an article on the deplorable state of clerical education prompted a fierce rebuttal from Ullathorne. At the time Newman observed that what most angered authorities was the accuracy of the accusations, but Newman himself was critical of the Rambler's tone.[2] This was to become character-

---

[1]For a detailed study of Capes' association with the Rambler, see Frances Dowling, "The Liberalism of John Moore Capes (1812-1889)" (Ph.D. dissertation, Catholic University of America, 1974), pp. vi-viii, 80-165.

[2]Walter E. Houghton, ed., The Wellesley Index to Victorian Periodicals, 1824-1900, 2 vols. (Toronto: University of Toronto

istic of its history--competent argument clothed in terms bordering on irreverence and defiance. The _Rambler_ hit authorities where they were most vulnerable and thus invariably inflamed tempers. Though this initial educational controversy involved no church-state issues, it will be seen that later articles occasioned controversies which did focus on church-state questions. In subsequent chapters the _Rambler_'s conflicts with the hierarchy over church-state-education questions are discussed more fully; for the moment it is sufficient to point out that _Rambler_ articles on education had important repercussions.

Generally speaking this issue has not received much attention except as an example of the conflict between Liberal Catholics and their bishops.[3] But it is this author's position that it was not coincidental that the church-state-education question occasioned such serious confrontations. The church-state-education question everywhere plagued the Catholic Church in the nineteenth century-- and it was a problem in which the role of the laity as well as the press was especially important. This was particularly true in England where the bishops could not totally control education: they lacked both the personnel and the resources to do so. The Church was exceptionally vulnerable on this question, and that vulnerability goes a long way toward explaining why the bishops retaliated so powerfully against the _Rambler_. Historically, the _Rambler_ generated controversy over the most sensitive problems of

---

Press, 1972), 2:733.

[3]See pp. 282-307 below for a discussion of this matter.

Catholicism during this period--the temporal power, papal infallibility, and the role of free inquiry in the pursuit of truth--
within and without the Church--and the church-state-education
question. The one question which has been treated least by historians has been the last.

The Dublin Review

Like the Rambler, the Dublin Review has received considerable
attention from historians, and so only the briefest sketch of its
early history which dates back to 1836 is needed here. During
Wiseman's visit to England in 1835 and 1836, he was approached by
Michael Quinn, an Irish lawyer in London, about founding a Catholic
review. Wiseman viewed this proposal favorably, hoping to serve
the English Catholics while wooing the Tractarians. Quinn obtained
the support of O'Connell, and the three launched their venture.
Proprietorship was in the hands of Wiseman and O'Connell. Speculation on the selection of the name has not settled the question of
whether the Dublin Review was so named in deference to O'Connell,
in an effort to counter the influence of the Edinburgh Review, or
for other reasons.[4] Financial troubles, irregularity of publication and other problems plagued this periodical for many years.[5]
According to J. J. Dwyer, Wiseman was the "presiding genius" in the
early years, and it was his stipulation that no political extremes
be presented in the Review.[6] The Dublin played an important part

---

[4]Wellesley Index, 2:11-12.

[5]Ibid.

[6]Dwyer, op. cit., p. 575.

in developing Wiseman's liaison with the Oxford men, and a number
of important theological articles were instrumental in attracting
men Romeward. The most startling example was Wiseman's article on
the Donatist controversy, which gave Newman a stomachache and was
not a little influential in undermining his defense of the
apostolic character of Anglicanism.[7]

Editorial control of the Dublin Review was somewhat confused
because of the mutual efforts of Wiseman and two others--H. R.
Bagshawe and C. W. Russell.[8] When Wiseman returned from Rome in
1840 he virtually assumed direction of the publication; Russell
shared heavily in editorial work. According to the summary description of the Dublin provided in the Wellesley Index, Bagshawe
served primarily as executive editor, which would have enhanced the
degree of control held by the bishop.[9]

Until the restoration of the hierarchy the Dublin Review's
pre-eminence remained largely unquestioned, but when the Oxford
Movement reached its peak the Catholic body was left with many
internal tensions and the problem of assimilating Converts and Old
Catholics. The Review became part of these tensions.

Wiseman's hope that it would become the instrument of unity
was sadly disappointed. With the establishment of the Rambler as a
Convert organ ably edited and attracting talented contributors, it
was not long before the two came into conflict. As already noted

---

[7]W. Ward, The Life and Times of Cardinal Wiseman, 2 vols.
(London: Longmans, Green, 1912), 1:320-344.

[8]Wellesley Index, 2:12-13.

[9]Ibid., p. 13.

the conflict came into the open over the education question and the bishops´ authority with regard to it.

During the 1850s the Dublin moved from crisis to crisis. Finally, in 1863 William George Ward assumed editorial responsibilities and commenced a new series.[10] Though Ward proclaimed a conciliatory policy, he was hardly the man to carry out such a policy: it was another of his policies to fight liberalism with all his abilities, which were considerable.

These struggles were central to the Dublin Review´s editorial line during the early 1860s, but however fascinating they are it is sufficient to refer readers to other accounts and to look at the Dublin´s position as it touched on the theme of this study.[11]

As a review in the strict sense the Dublin Review did not publish editorial commentary on current events apart from reviews of contemporary literature. Occasionally the publication of proposed or enacted legislation served as a pretext for political commentary, but during the 1847-1852 period no major article devoted to the subject of popular education or to the church-state-education confrontation appeared in this journal. Even so, there will be occasion in the following chapter to refer to peripheral articles; thus it seemed appropriate to include this introductory sketch here.

The Catholic Weekly Instructor

Not much is known about the Catholic Weekly Instructor which

---

[10]Ibid., p. 14.

[11]Dwyer, op. cit., pp. 474-482; Wellesley Index, 2:11-22.

ran for over three years, was said to have had one of the largest circulations enjoyed by any Catholic periodical of its day, and was edited by a member of the original Catholic Poor School Committee. Published as a weekly under that title through July 11, 1846, it then became a monthly and appeared as the Catholic Instructor from August 1846 through December 1847; at that time it ceased publication. At its commencement in June 1844 the editor explained that the magazine was intended to be an answer to the trashy papers, "the large pernicious penny sheets" of the day.[12]

Never pretending to be a serious intellectual publication, its contents included natural history, practical, common-sense philosophy, articles on antiquities, travel, history, biography and poetry. The Catholic Weekly Instructor was addressed to the poor and "simple of heart."[13] The prevalence of articles about temperance suggests an Irish readership. The social tone of this paper was short of being radical, but it certainly displayed no great fondness for the rich. Articles tended to focus on practical problems of the poorer classes--such as the dangers of poisoning children with narcotic syrups, lead poisoning and the like--but a certain element of condescension may have marred the effect.

This periodical arose out of the Derby Reprints, a series of cheap publications which could be reprinted at minimal cost, for distribution among the poor, because of copyright expirations.[14]

---

[12]Catholic Weekly Instructor, June 15, 1849, pp. 1-2.

[13]Ibid., p. 2.

[14]Thomas Sing, "A Few Words to Our Readers," Catholic Weekly Instructor, January 1847, p. 1.

Rev. Thomas Sing of St. Mary's in Derby was responsible for the series and was also editor of the Instructor. One source estimated that the circulation reached 20,000 at one point, but this was contradicted in the paper's columns where the problem of low circulation was discussed, and a comment was made indicating that no Catholic periodicals circulated over 7,000.[15] It failed for want of support, and the following from the final issue suggests the editor's appraisal of the venture; after noting how much Catholics needed a weekly such as the Catholic Weekly Instructor the editor said:

> But in truth we despair of such a result; we remember the old adage, that what is "everybody's business is no one's," we have little organization and little disposition to go out of our private paths to walk together on the highways in masses, and continuously the each one feeling himself secure in the infallibility of his faith, does not estimate highly those ordinary usages which are found very effective by sectaries.16

The only remaining bit of information of great significance to be gleaned from the sources is that Sing was actively involved in the formation of the Catholic Poor School Committee; in fact, he is said to have authored its declaration of principles concerning the need to extend religious education throughout England and Wales.[17] Certainly this publication deserves attention as a representative Catholic paper directed at the Irish poor. Unfortunately for the purpose of this thesis it contained almost nothing on the topic of

---

[15] Husenbeth, op. cit., p. 1, estimated its circulation at 20,000, but Sing, loc. cit., mentioned the 7,000 figure.

[16] The Catholic Instructor, December 1847, p. 529.

[17] Gillow, op. cit., 5:509-510.

education having to do with church-state problems during its last year of publication, 1847.

The Catholic School

This was the official publication of the Catholic Poor School Committee, edited by its secretary, Scott Nasmyth Stokes. It was circulated free of charge to the English Catholic clergy and to all subscribers of the committee.[18] There is no evidence that it was independently circulated as a regular periodical, but it was reviewed regularly in many contemporary publications.

Given the very official and specialized character of this publication the criteria used in analyzing it should be spelled out. The issues of this magazine provide an extensive but very partial history of the work of the committee during its early years. Any thorough assessment of the periodical as a whole would necessarily have to be supplemented by full analysis of the Catholic Poor School Committee reports, not to mention Parliamentary debates, Minutes of the Privy Council Committee on Education, and correspondence of its editors--especially correspondence with members of the hierarchy and other committee members. The nature of the publication gives it the character of an official document, not just a periodical; this was especially true insofar as the Catholic School served as a major source for much of the regular press coverage of school problems.

Because the necessary background study materials are not available and would in any event constitute an enormous project for

---

[18]"Catholic Poor School Committee," Catholic School 1 (June-July 1849): 110.

research beyond the scope of this study, Catholic School reports have been analyzed here only insofar as they specifically treated church-state questions.

The Catholic Vindicator and Irish Magazine

This penny weekly was launched on February 22, 1851 in answer to the so-called Papal Aggression upheaval. Patrick Burke Ryan, Esq., was the founder; his control lasted into 1852 when burdens derived from a large inheritance on the western shore of Ireland called him away from London.[19] This editorial change was announced in January 1852 and brought into full effect in April, when John Eugene O'Cavanaugh became owner and editor.[20] One source identified George Vickers as one-time publisher, but it is not certain if or when this was the case.[21] Originally published as the Catholic Vindicator, the title was changed by O'Cavanaugh to Catholic Vindicator and Irish Magazine, appropriately descriptive of its purpose and readership.

Though short-lived, the Catholic Vindicator provides valuable evidence about the interests and concerns of the Irish in London. The general tone of the magazine was exceedingly hostile to the "base spirit of heretical Saxon hostility to Ireland" and attentive to the social and economic problems of Irish immigrants. One finds

---

[19]Husenbeth, op. cit., p. 1; he identifies Ryan as the founding proprietor of this publication. Reasons given for his resignation were stated in the Catholic Vindicator and Irish Magazine, April 17, 1852, p. 65.

[20]Catholic Vindicator and Irish Magazine, April 17, 1852, p. 65.

[21]Fletcher, op. cit., pp. 306-307.

here particularly good coverage of such institutions as that for
Catholic Servants, which helped place immigrant employees, and of
the various life assurance associations which attempted to provide
a degree of financial security for the near-destitute. But the
scope of the topics covered in this periodical was wide-ranging and
included ecclesiology, history, art, science, biography and literature. Though not intended in any way as an intellectual publication of scholarly merit, its popularizing had the merit of lacking
the condescending tone so often complained of with regard to
similar cheap literature for the poor.

Little can be said about the contributors except that they
were described in one issue as "gentlemen who number amongst them
names distinguished in their universities, of highest literary
rank, of great practical experience, and devotion to
Catholicity."[22] Except for one report that the Vindicator's circulation reached nearly 12,000, little else is known about this
publication. Professing to be an organ of Irish nationalism and
reflecting social, spiritual, economic and political concerns of
the Irish masses, it has been too much ignored.

The Weekly and Monthly Orthodox Journal

Husenbeth described this as a "very respectable, learned and
ably-conducted periodical" published by Mary Andrews and edited by
the Rev. Richard Boyle.[23] Its short duration, from January 6, 1849

---

[22]Catholic Vindicator and Irish Magazine, April 17, 1852,
p. 65.

[23]Fletcher, op. cit., p. 303; and Husenbeth, op. cit., p. 1.

through July 8, 1849, probably accounts for the difficulty of obtaining information about it, though it seems certain that this publication was a continuation of the old Orthodox Journal which gained great notoriety in the days of Bishop Milner. A cheap (3d) illustrated sixteen-page weekly, this publication included the usual columns--correspondence, Catholic news, reviews, a weekly calendar and occasionally serious essays. As noted above, it merged with Dolman's Magazine in 1849.

The Catholic Standard subsequently
the Weekly Register

Given the duration of this periodical it is surprising that little historical information can be obtained concerning its early history. It first appeared on October 14, 1849 as the Catholic Standard and continued to be published under that title until May 19, 1855, when it became the Weekly Register and Catholic Standard. Continuing under that title until March 14, 1902, it was changed to the Monthly Register but appeared under that name for only a few issues prior to its discontinuance in 1902.[24] The standard sources say that it was originally published by Anthony Williams of 3 Bridges Street, Covent Garden, but this now appears to be incorrect.[25] Williams' name appeared on the masthead after the beginning of 1850; before that John Ringrose was listed as

----

[24]Fletcher, op. cit., p. 304, claims it ceased publication in 1890, but the British Museum Newspaper Library catalog lists the Weekly Register and Catholic Standard as continuing from May 19, 1855-March 14, 1902, and followed by the Monthly Register, April-November 1902.

[25]Fletcher, loc. cit.

publisher.[26] It would seem that Ringrose and Williams successively functioned as printers, but the identity of publishers and proprietors remains obscure or at least unverifiable. In the December 8, 1849 issue there is an editorial reference to a group of proprietors and editors.[27] Then in 1852 reference is made to the resignation of proprietor E. Robillard. Robillard published a letter in the paper claiming full responsibility for the founding and carrying on of this periodical; his letter was occasioned by the financial ruin into which the paper had thrust him. Robillard was a French Catholic, not a native Englishman, and it appears that he had considerable dealings with Cardinal Wiseman who lent his support to the effort made to raise funds to rescue Robillard from his financial embarrassment.[28] Whether Robillard acted as sole editor has not been determined, nor has it been learned how the publication was carried on subsequent to his resignation. The very considerable attention given to Anglicanism in its columns suggests that there must have been a few Oxford converts involved in the venture--but anything more than what has just been said would be pure speculation at this point.

Henry Wilberforce purchased the paper in 1854; from whom he bought it or to whom it was sold in 1863 remains unknown. Dwyer notes that Manning acquired the Weekly in 1881, but the intervening eighteen years remain a mystery.[29]

---

[26]Catholic Standard, December 15, 1849, p. 8.

[27]Ibid., December 8, 1849, p. 1.

[28]Ibid., December 11, 1852, pp. 5, 8.

[29]Dwyer, op. cit., p. 505.

The Catholic Press on the Power of the Press

Before turning to the way the above mentioned publications treated the specific problems of church-state-education, 1847-1852, it seems appropriate to review the way the power of the press was understood by Catholic journalists. This is tantamount to reviewing what was said in the Rambler about the power of the press, for only the Rambler treated this problem with great seriousness or in depth.[30]

Practically all the other periodicals paid frequent tribute to the power of the press by stressing the need for a Catholic press to answer the anti-Catholic forces at work in the English newspapers, magazines and journals. Thus it can be assumed that editors of all the organs analyzed here were quite sensitive to the power of the press, but during this early period only the Rambler published serious articles on the subject. The caliber and significance of the articles published in the Rambler demand attention.

In its early years the Rambler published at least five substantial articles about the power of the press. Leading articles in the third and fifth issues treated this subject, raising questions about the impact of the press on the English mind and on the fundamental religious values and beliefs of men. Presumably written by editor John Moore Capes,[31] these two articles satirized

---

[30]See also [John E. E. D. Acton], "The Catholic Press," Rambler, 2nd ser., 11 (February 1859): 73-90. This is a major statement on the press; it was stimulated by the fear of episcopal censorship.

[31]These first issues were not indexed in the Wellesley Index

the superficiality of the daily paper, captioned by the phrase, "have you seen today's paper?" which question expressed the absurd notion that truth could be captured by a quick morning glance. The writer complained that the speed and pressure under which the daily paper was produced degraded content and style, thought and word; even so, the fact that so great a proportion of the nation's talents and energies were devoted to this vast engine made it a power to be reckoned with by all who loved truth.[32]

The leading article of January 29, 1848 pondered whether the daily paper was a curse or a blessing. On balance, the writer concluded that it was a curse. Though it served progress in trade, commerce, politics and law, and constituted a significant obstacle to "individual enormities, and to the tyranny and corruption of the state,"[33] nevertheless, it tended to the destruction of principle, the worship of mere intellect, violence, dogmatism and personality, and to the substitution of humbug and superficial talk for real, honest thought and knowledge. The pressure of deadlines prevented writers from taking a "calm half-hour, to allow reason and charity to suggest an idea," or to reconsider sentences which destroyed men's reputations. "What will be the value of a man's thoughts?" Capes asked, and "What will become of the thought of a nation?" when its opinions are formed through the influence of the daily

---

but this article seems so similar to later articles attributed therein to Capes that it is reasonable to assume that he was the writer.

[32][Capes], "Periodical Literature," Rambler, January 15, 1848, p. 33.

[33]Idem, "The Daily Paper," Rambler, January 29, 1848, p. 73.

paper. Capes repeatedly denounced the superficiality of the press, particularly its tendency to encourage the "adoration of mere talent" or "mere intellect." He described the daily paper as an "engine of warfare" having an overwhelmingly negative influence. Because its very existence depended upon popular support it became the victim of that public which it assumed to govern and a slave to the popular appetite for "what is rapid, showy, and effective." Thus it threatened to destroy both genuine thought and the sense of tradition.[34]

In March 1849 Capes spoke of the "sovereign power" of the press, suggesting that the great power of the era lay not in scientific mastery over nature or in the rise of constitutional democracy but in the power of the fourth estate. This power, unknown to former ages, claimed undivided sovereignty by virtue of its ever-growing control over men's thoughts and actions, by its absorption of an enormous proportion of the civilization's talent, genius and knowledge, and by its capacity to persuade, convince, cajole, and terrify. Its power was shrouded in the mystery of its corporate "we" and its anonymous constitution. The press, he said, was becoming an idol god. It had the potential to become a force for either good or evil, but "to treat it with contempt is the part of a fool."[35]

Since it was a problem which the Church could not ignore, the Church faced the task of finding a way to reconcile the press with

---

[34]Ibid., pp. 74-76.

[35]Idem, "The Fourth Estate," Rambler 3 (March 1849): 471-475.

Church authority. Such a task involved great peril:

> Great is the peril of authority when it undertakes to
> direct a power, the condition of whose existence it is to
> labour without claim to any authority whatsoever.36

Bishops, parliaments and judges could not manage the press without

either plunging themselves into such a "vortex of agitation and

conflict as to diminish their honour" or so severely restricting

content as to render the results dull and useless. Capes defined

the chief task of the church and the state alike in terms of the

problem of ruling "an independent world by means of its independ-

ence." If the utmost skill was called for, the Church possessed

both talent and unique advantages stemming from the Catholic jour-

nalists´ submission to Church authority on all essential matters of

faith. Capes argued that no one outside the Church could claim

such an advantage, but he cautioned that the press could only be

turned to the service of mankind and of God by being "taken as it

is." It was, he concluded, a "gigantic power which no indignant

contest could ever wrest from its herculean grasp."[37]

Though none of the above referenced articles discussed the

specific impact of the press on the education question, all were

concerned with the educative function of the press, its manner of

shaping opinion and intellect. Clearly the _Rambler_ editor feared

that influence with its attending superficiality--not to mention

its capacity for destruction. Capes was above all concerned about

the impact on the educated classes, but there is an implied under-

standing that the press´ control over the thoughts of the masses

---

[36]_Ibid._, p. 476.

[37]_Ibid._, pp. 476-477.

posed grave problems. But the main theme related to the fundamental character of the press, particularly its independence; Capes
was pleading for a profound understanding of the freedom of the
press as it related to Catholicity. He claimed that those outside
the Church could not understand that Catholics may differ on
matters outside the boundary of the teaching authority while remaining unified on the essential matters of faith and morals; the
proper use of the press, he insisted, would show the world that
Catholics were "as wonderful in our unanimity, as we are vigorous
in making use of our liberty, where liberty is our due."[38]

In February 1852 the Rambler published a translation of excerpts from Monsignor Pierre-Louis Parisis' work on the problem of
Catholic journalism. Parisis was described here as "one of the
most able, most fair, and most respected of the French episcopate."
Many of the matters covered in the article applied primarily to
conditions in France, but the article as a whole offered a very
strong apology for and defense of the work of lay journalists in
defending the faith, even when that work involved discussion of
doctrinal matters. Parisis argued that the shortage of priests and
bishops precluded bishops and clerics from conducting journals;
thus it was the duty of lay journalists to defend Catholicism from
the hostile press. Ignorance in religious matters and indifference, its inevitable result, he said, were the two great plagues of
the day; the laity was obligated to combat them. Parisis was
careful to state that lay journalists must always defer to author-

---

[38]Idem, "The Duties of Journalists--Catholic and Protestant
Education," Rambler 3 (January 1849): 328.

ity where the teaching authority was involved, but that condition did not preclude all lay discussion of theological questions. Developing the theme that the cooperation of the laity had always been necessary and important, he insisted that it was all the more essential in modern times when so many matters controlling the lives of the faithful were being decided by laymen outside the Church.[39] The work of lay journalists was not only permissible but urgently necessary, Parisis said, because his silence might well lend tacit encouragement to the progress of evil. He concluded:

> . . . and when the ruin of religion in a great kingdom is the matter at stake, such connivance is a tremendous sin, even in the sight of men, much more before God.40

General Educational Questions

Modern bureaucracies--secular and spiritual alike--have a seemingly infinite capacity to confound outsiders by the mere device of piling detail upon detail. Even in its embryonic stages the educational bureaucracy displayed this capacity well. As anyone familiar with the successive Minutes of Education dating from 1833 can testify, unscrambling the details of state policy is no mean task. The church-state-education question is also a church-state-bureaucracy question, which means that a certain amount of bureaucratic red tape must be untangled.

An examination of the contemporary press, even a segment of it, can help identify those details of bureaucratic policy which

---

[39][Pierre Louis Parisis], "Monsignor Parisis on Catholic Journalism," Rambler 9 (February 1852): 67.

[40]Ibid., p. 100.

attracted the most attention and generated the most debate and can indicate whether historians have emphasized in correct proportion those issues most vexing to contemporaries. The press was not solely concerned with bureaucratic details, however, so it must be analyzed for its response to broad general questions as well. Given the enormous number of details, the substantial number of general questions and the fairly large number of periodical titles under examination for the 1847-1865 period some schematization is imperative.

In an effort to achieve a semblance of balance and order the broad questions are considered under two general headings. The first is called the Protestant competition. The phrase is used here to describe Protestant proselytizing efforts ranging from the distribution of Bibles and sectarian literature to formal school-room persuasion. Evidence from the press and other sources indicates that the Irish poor were often the focus of such Protestant efforts, so the matter of Protestant competition is bound up with the larger problem of the Irish poor in England. The competitors included Anglicans, Dissenters and the proponents of secular education whom the Catholics regarded as unusually misguided Protestants. Discussion here focuses on the Catholic response to this competition, which was most often described as apathetic. Another form of proselytizing was the ´no-popery´ which influenced what Catholics could and could not hope to obtain from the state, but it is difficult to show how ´no-popery´ affected educational policy except in isolated instances.

The second and even broader category is called the nature of education. This refers to the very basic problems of philosophical definition and to questions of authority, and curriculum as they touched on church-state relations. Because fundamental philosophical precepts cannot be considered as completely separate from their implementation it is essential to compare the press treatment of theoretical questions with its treatment of actual difficulties which arose. There were numerous technical problems which could be construed as questions of church and state, but only the most important and most representative practical difficulties are touched on here.

The Protestant Competition

Coming to terms with the Catholic press assessment of the Protestant competition in education involves determining whether the concern expressed over proselytizing was serious or whether it was a rhetorical device intended to arouse apathetic Catholics to their social and charitable duties. It also involves identifying the proselytizers and their intended victims.

It cannot be forgotten that Catholics were inclined to blame all the failures of contemporary English society on the Protestant Reformation. This was a convenient rug under which could be swept all the political, moral, spiritual, social, economic and educational woes of the day. The education problem was thus easily disposed of with the following explanation: the confiscation of monasteries destroyed the old Catholic educational system which was both charitable and democratic in that it served rich and poor alike; ignorance and poverty were the fault of Henry VIII and Elizabeth. An infinite variety of elaborations on this theme was possible, and one or two may be helpful. An 1850 issue of the

Dublin Review contained an article treating the Poor Law problem and provided the following explanation for England's plight:

> Lutheran and Calvinistic doctrines, which deny the merit of suffering and of works of charity, have sapped the foundations at once of patience in the poor and of charity in the rich; poverty and suffering, in their system, is again a purposeless evil, or at best, an unredeeming punishment.41

An earlier *Rambler* article blamed English Puritanism for driving the poor to gin and worse. By forbidding innocent amusements for the poor, such as those associated with traditional Catholic feast days and holy days, and by providing no equally wholesome and harmless substitutes, the poor became easy prey for the "profligate and designing" peddlers of debasement. This *Rambler* article asserted that innocent amusements were as essential to education as religion.42

Another element ever present in the Catholic appraisal of Protestantism was a deep awareness of the fundamental causes of Protestant disunity--to wit, the abandonment of the principle of Church authority. Protestant disunity was one of the few advantages Catholics enjoyed in educational work, and it was often stressed by journalists.

The Catholic appraisal of Victorian Protestantism offers a tempting subject for further study because Catholics, aloof from sectarian strife, enjoyed a unique perspective on Protestant troubles. Insofar as the English press was an institution

---

41Myles O'Reilly, "Poor Administration at Home and Abroad," *Dublin Review* 29 (December 1850): 326.

42"The Amusements of the Poor," *Rambler*, April 1, 1848, p. 274.

Protestant in itself, Protestantism could be said to have been the driving force behind the growth of a Catholic press. Despite impressive internal motives for establishing Catholic periodicals, the desire to answer calumny and to keep Catholic readers from the clutches of the infidel press appears to have been stronger; references to the power of the press generally identified that power in England with the power of Protestantism.[43]

Catholic press coverage of the Protestant educational movement focused heavily on the political power of the sects, giving minimal attention to the specific impact of Protestant schools as such. The Protestants´ facility for obtaining state aid for their schools concerned Catholics, as did their ´no-popery´ politics which could prevent Catholics from getting similar aid. In the various Catholic publications there were many articles about Bible societies, relief work among the poor, lodging houses, baths, soup kitchens and other forms of ´Protestant bribery.´ Articles focusing specifically on Protestant Sunday schools, night schools, ragged schools and day schools were fewer in number. In short, the Catholic press as a whole evidenced considerable concern over Protestant activities among the Catholic poor, while coverage of their actual educational activities was highly uneven.

Proselytizing among the poor was a worry to Catholics because of the inadequacy of Catholic missions. The rise of the Irish population in the cities long predated the Irish famine of the mid-

---

[43]T. W. Marshall, the first government inspector of Catholic schools, wrote a very interesting book on this subject: <u>Protestant Journalism</u> (London: Burns and Oates, 1874).

forties when the influx of destitute Irish only served to emphasize an existing Catholic failure. Sheridan Gilley has raised important questions about the Irish immigrants, suggesting that the Catholics may have been more charitable toward the Irish poor than some historians have supposed,[44] and that Protestant proselytizing was not solely aimed at the Catholic poor;[45] even so, the Catholic poor remained a peculiarly Irish problem, one which was viewed as an educational problem by Catholics and Protestants alike. The background to this problem has only been dealt with in bits and pieces. Unfortunately the present essay contributes more of the same, but the Catholic press treatment of the problem provides a helpful guide to further work in that it identifies many of the questions which must be investigated if this dimension of English Catholic social history is to be understood.

Discussion of Protestant educational work focused prominently on workhouse schools and ragged schools while devoting little attention to the work of British and Foreign Society or even National Society schools. References to the attendance of Catholic children at Protestant schools are seldom specific--that is, all Protestant schools seemed to be viewed as equally bad for Catholic children. One cannot find in the contemporary Catholic press many distinguishing comments about Baptists, Methodists or Quakers or Congregationalists insofar as their schools were concerned. In fact, this author found no articles which singled out any of the

---

[44]Sheridan Gilley, "Protestant London, No-Popery and the Irish Poor, 1830-1860," pt. 1, Recusant History 10 (October 1969): 216.

[45]Ibid., pp. 210-213.

Protestant sects in such a way. Protestant schools were a threat because they were Protestant--not because they were Baptist, Congregational or Anglican. Catholic journalists took a more discriminating view of the political power possessed by the sects. They were especially wary of Methodist ´no-popery,´ which, as we have seen, was responsible for the government´s refusal to grant aid to Catholics in the spring of 1847; in connection with this they displayed considerable respect for Methodist organizational capacities and often cited them as models for imitation. Anglican efforts also came in for special treatment because of their connection with the state.

The Protestant influence exerted through Ragged Schools and workhouse schools was almost exclusively Anglican. Workhouse proselytizing was especially vexatious because it was protected by law and by the power of the local Boards of Guardians who were notoriously anxious to preserve the workhouse as an Anglican sphere of influence.[46]

The _Dublin Review_ article on the poor law system mentioned above acquiesced in the theory that workhouse children were fully the responsibility of the state, the "common parent of all."[47] As the _Dublin_ was very much under Wiseman´s thumb it seems surprising to find in its pages such support for state prerogatives in education, especially workhouse education. Close to the top of the English Catholics´ list of grievances was the treatment of

---

[46]Chadwick, _op. cit._, 1:96-97.

[47][O´Reilly], _op. cit._, p. 334.

Catholics in workhouses, yet this article suggested that the state follow the Belgian example by establishing state work forms for children. The aim was to separate them from the influence of hopelessly pauperized adults. In itself this was not inconsistent with Catholic principles, perhaps, but the article hardly mentioned the spiritual aspect of the problem. Another Dublin Review article did mention the religious question but only vaguely by suggesting that religious education would have a purifying impact and thus reduce crime.[48]

In Dolman's Magazine workhouse schools were mentioned in only one article about the Manchester Board of Guardians and its treatment of a Catholic pupil-teacher. This article was not unusual but illustrates the type of difficulties Catholics encountered. The Catholic chaplain had complained to the Catholic Poor School Committee about a Catholic boy losing a pupil-teacher appointment because of his religion. The priest was distraught because the boy had been deprived of the job and because the priest had been deprived of needed assistance in his work of providing religious instruction for Catholic children--outside school hours. The Catholic Poor School Committee had then complained to the Poor Law Commission which turned the matter over to the local Board of Guardians. Its meeting occasioned the Dolman's Magazine report. Probably hundreds of such cases were reported in the Tablet and elsewhere over the years following the enactment of the 1854 Poor Law. The way the local Board treated this case, however, is appro-

---

[48][James Morris], "The Government Criminal Returns," Dublin Review 28 (June 1850): 353.

priately mentioned here. The local board decided that the conduct of the chaplain had been "highly culpable in that he had communicated with the Poor Law Commission without having proper authority to do so; it was resolved that he should be called before the board to account for his behavior.[49] _Dolman's_ _Magazine_ failed to print a follow-up story relating the outcome, which suggests that there was not extraordinary interest in the subject and that no form of justice was expected from the Board of Guardians.

The _Catholic_ _School_ hardly touched on the workhouse school problem at all. This is understandable because the Catholic Poor School Committee dealt mainly with the Privy Council Committee on Education which had only indirect influence over workhouse schools.[50] One article, however, did raise questions about workhouse education.[51] The author, Scott Nasmyth Stokes, described Catholic negotiations with the Marylebone Workhouse where an experiment had been proposed whereby children would be sent to schools outside the workhouse. The Poor School Committee wanted Catholic children withdrawn to Catholic schools. Describing the workhouse as the Protestant substitute for monasteries and condemning their unique facility for turning out infidels and hopeless paupers, the writer urged that Catholics had certain rights in workhouses and demanded that they be respected. In this particular case he re-

---

[49]"Catholic Intelligence: Manchester Board of Guardians," _Weekly_ _Register_ continuation of _Dolman's_ _Magazine_ January 19, 1850, pp. 395-396.

[50]The relationship between the Privy Council Committee and the workhouse schools requires further study.

[51]Scott Nasmyth Stokes, "Children in Union Houses," _Catholic_ _School_ 2 (May 1851): 139-142.

ported that the Catholic effort to remove 60 to 200 children from the workhouse during school hours, when they should attend Catholic schools, had met great resistance. Authorities found that some difficulty had been discovered in an act of Parliament--which they refused to specify. The matter was submitted to the Poor Law Board and the Privy Council Committee on Education; officials from both bodies expressed sympathy for the Catholic cause but were powerless in the face of the Guardians.[52] Stokes´ report indicates that Cardinal Wiseman took an active part in these negotiations. Though his efforts were fruitless, the fact is significant in that historians have hardly mentioned such efforts on the part of the Cardinal.[53]

On the same subject the Tablet´s coverage was more extensive. Few editions of the Tablet were entirely without reference to some aspect of Poor Law abuses, a favorite concern of the editor who, in founding the Association of St. Thomas of Canterbury in 1847, listed this as one of the major Catholic grievances. Lucas´ contributions toward the founding of the Brotherhood of St. Vincent de Paul in England also testified to his concern for workhouse inmates and other destitute poor.[54] Specific references from the Tablet

---

[52]See also "Destitute Catholic Children," Catholic School 1 (February 1850): 212-213.

[53]It may be significant that Ward´s Wiseman includes no index reference to the Cardinal´s efforts with regard to workhouses; similarly it contains no references to the Poor School Committee schools, or education. There is, however, a very brief discussion of such matters, pp. 450-453 of the second volume.

[54]Tablet, July 17, 1847, p. 848; and Jack Kitching, "Roman Catholic Education from 1700-1870" (Ph.D. dissertation, University of Leeds, 1966), p. 87. Kitching indicates that Lucas, William Amherst and C. J. Pagliano were active in this effort.

hardly seem necessary here, for it would mean repetition of discussions about cases of abuse such as those just mentioned. Still, it must be stressed that the Tablet provides a wealth of evidence on this question which must be consulted if Catholic relations with the state are to be assessed adequately. In general, the evidence suggests that Catholics greatly feared the power of local boards which safeguarded anti-Catholic policies and that staunch 'no-popery' at the local level inclined Catholics to look to the central bureaucracy for greater leniency.

The total Catholic population in workhouses cannot be ascertained because religious registers were not faithfully kept, if they were kept at all. This makes it difficult to judge the importance of workhouse education. As late as 1861 the Newcastle Commission report revealed that local Boards of Guardians displayed little zeal in providing education for workhouse children.[55] Yet England had literally hundreds of workhouses sheltering thousands upon thousands of children, which suggests that the connection between workhouse schools and the rise of the national education system might be re-examined. The connection is particularly interesting with respect to church-state questions. Both the 1834 Poor Law Act and a supplemental act (7 and 8 Vict. c. 101) provided that the education of children in a religion other than that of their parents could not be authorized by the workhouse and that children should be permitted to receive instruction in their parents'

---

[55]Great Britain, Education Commission, Report of the Commissioners Appointed to Inquire into the State of Popular Education in England, 6 vols. (London: Eyre & Spottiswoode, 1861), 2:377.

religion.[56] But these statutes were without teeth--nothing in them compelled workhouse officials to observe them. In 1847 when the inspection of workhouse schools came under the jurisdiction of the Privy Council Committee on Education, none of the religious safeguards which applied to the Dissenting, Anglican and Catholic schools were applied to inspected workhouse schools.[57]

While Catholic periodicals exhibited an awareness of the fact that the Poor Law posed serious church-state problems for Catholics, the workhouse schools were not a major topic, as such, in the Catholic press, 1847-1852. The whole question of education under the Poor Law has been treated as a separate, specialized topic by historians, so its relationship to the main thrust of the education movement remains obscure. This is particularly unfortunate with regard to church-state history because workhouses were notoriously indifferent to religious rights of non-Anglican inmates.

Just as historians have treated workhouse education separately so have they isolated the ragged school movement.[58] This may be more justified as the ragged school movement was only a peripheral influence in Victorian education; moreover, the Ragged School Union received no state funds and was thus removed from church-state controversy. Ragged schools were casual operations providing off-

---

[56]Balfour, op. cit., pp. 63-65.

[57]That is, control over appointment of inspectors was not subject to sectarian approval.

[58]See C. J. Montague, Sixty Years in Waifdom, or the Ragged School Movement in English History (London: Charles Murray, 1904).

the-street activities for idle young ruffians. Whether they were ever intended to be serious educational institutions remains open to question, but it is clear that they were operated for proselytizing purposes by a circle of enthusiasts of whom the notoriously anti-Catholic Earl of Shaftesbury was the leader.

The Catholic concern over ragged schools stemmed from their presence in Irish slums. Of the papers surveyed for the present study, the Tablet provided fullest coverage and stoutly condemned ragged schools for encouraging apostacy and crime.[59] Awareness of these schools was evidenced in most other periodicals.[60] The Ragged School Union had been formed in 1844 and Catholics responded through the press long before the hierarchy controversy of 1851. Despite this we find a puzzling report in the May 31, 1851 issue of the Catholic Standard concerning Cardinal Wiseman's denunciation of the movement. The Cardinal reportedly claimed that the anti-Catholic character of the movement had been veiled up to the time of the Papal Aggression controversy when its hostile intentions became openly recognizable.[61] Since the 'no-popery' aims of the movement were well known long before that time it is fair to presume that the Cardinal had some motive for calling the matter to public attention in 1851. Whatever the explanation, Wiseman took an active interest in the matter and encouraged the formation of a

---

[59]Tablet, March 30, 1850, p. 203.

[60]Typical references include: Catholic School 1 (September 1849): 167-168; and Catholic Standard, December 18, 1852, p. 3.

[61]Catholic Standard, May 31, 1851, p. 9.

Catholic Ragged School Committee that year.[62]

The Catholic ragged schools were strictly imitative and competitive, which testifies to the Protestant influence in this area. In this respect a brief letter to the editor of the Catholic Standard, published November 6, 1852, condemning the use of the name "ragged schools" in connection with any Catholic institution, should be noted. The writer insisted that the term necessarily implied anti-Catholicism and should therefore not be adopted by Catholics. The author of the letter wanted the institutions to thrive but under a more respectable name.[63] As this really represented only a minor footnote to the coverage on ragged schools it would be a mistake to lay too much stress on the matter, but it does indicate a degree of resistance to such obviously imitative Catholic efforts in education which further substantiates Catholic awareness of the imitative character of their work.

The Catholic press assessment of Protestant day-schools is somewhat more problematic. It is not easy to determine whether Catholics were concerned about the appeal of Protestant schools or about the shortage of Catholic schools in poor Catholic neighborhoods; more likely these two dimensions of the question were two sides of the same coin. The sheer inadequacy of the Catholic mission to the poor in English cities was notorious long before the education movement gained momentum.[64] Reports of Catholic children

---

[62]Tablet, October 2, 1852, p. 630.

[63]Catholic Standard, November 6, 1852, p. 5.

[64]Kitching, op. cit., pp. 145-162.

attending Protestant schools were frequent but do not necessarily indicate that the parents of such children preferred Protestant schools where Catholic schools were available.[65] Answers to this question would require careful analysis of the distribution of Protestant and Catholic schools in Irish Catholic neighborhoods. Abundant reports about local Catholic schools in the press of this period would make such a research project possible, but that is well beyond the scope of this particular study. Still, until such research would be completed it would be indulging in mere speculation to say with any degree of definiteness just how competitive Protestant schools were. But interesting references to other aspects of the Protestant competition can be found which require some attention.

There are two Rambler articles which deserve special mention in this regard. The first, "Modern Almsgiving," (September 1848) was occasioned by the appearance of the first issue of the Catholic School. Written by John Moore Capes it reviewed the chief obstacles to Catholic educational progress, naming apathy, lack of information and awareness, and the teacher-shortage as the main ones. Capes strongly urged Catholics to compare their own efforts with those of Protestants and to repent their own "real niggardliness under the guise of frequent almsgiving."[66] The second article, "Wants of the Time," (June 1850) mercilessly compared

[65]A typical article concerning Protestant schools would be the following article attributed to Capes: "Duties of Catholic Journalists--Catholic and Protestant Education," Rambler 3 (January 1849): 328.

[66][Capes], "Modern Almsgiving," Rambler 3 (September 1848): 53-61.

Catholic and Protestant domestic mission work. Even if the statistical data provided is of the same questionable validity as most
Victorian statistical data, the author leaves absolutely no doubt
as to the generosity of Protestants as compared with that of
English Catholics. The Old Wesleyan Methodists, he said, spent
£75,000 on home mission work in one year--an amount equal to three-
fourths of the whole income of Propaganda; they spent £112,000 on
foreign mission work for the same period, which equaled the sum
collected by the missionary society of the whole Catholic Church
from all parts of the world for the same period. He described the
work of Congregationalists and Baptists in terms similarly devastating to any Catholic claim to generosity. Dissenters´ school
buildings were paid for, their periodicals were profitable, and
their output of cheap tracts was phenomenal.[67] Much of the information provided in this article is peripheral to the main theme of
this study, but it offers extraordinary proof of the relative
backwardness of Catholic activities, especially Catholic fund
raising. The Rambler was never hesitant to express disgust with
Catholic inaction and "niggardliness" and often pleaded with
Catholics to imitate Protestant efficiency. A little ironically
this same article admitted--with much relief--that all this
Protestant zeal produced results which were hardly impressive,
especially considering the enormous sums raised. Their efforts
were termed "hopelessly helpless" owing to their being lost in
error; still, to cite their zeal as a model to be imitated while

---

[67]Idem, "Wants of the Time," Rambler 5 (June 1850): 490-494.

condemning its results as hopeless seems an odd way to say "go and do likewise."[68]

Another reference to Protestant educational work appeared in the August 1850 _Rambler_ where Capes discussed the Protestant demand for the religious education of the poor. He explained that because "the aristocracy and gentry of England received no religious education themselves," their interest in the moral and spiritual training of the poor was a false concern stimulated not by genuine spiritual concern but by fear that the education of the poor would become a political threat to their power and wealth.[69] This suspicion concerning the motives underlying the aristocracy's insistence that education be religious was shared by the radicals, secularists, and many Nonconformists, whose educational goals were almost completely incompatible with those of the Catholics. This makes the argument all the more fascinating from the historical perspective. That such political opposites could have agreed that the Protestant demands for religious education lacked integrity says a great deal about contemporary assessments of Victorian religion and cannot be written off as mere sectarian polemics. Catholics believed that Protestants abandoned religious integrity when they abandoned the traditional means of guaranteeing the truth of Christian doctrine as passed from generation to generation; secularists, unconcerned with how such integrity was lost, were content to hack away at vulnerable spots, one of which was the use

---

[68]_Ibid._, p. 494.

[69]_Idem_, "Popular Education: Catholic Poor Schools and Middle Schools," _Rambler_ 6 (August 1850): 92.

of religious teaching to 'keep the lower classes in their place.' Both perspectives raise in an important way the question of how-- and whether--Protestantism can maintain itself as an integral part of civilization and show that this question worked itself out in the education movement.

It can be said in conclusion that the press coverage of Protestant activities indicates that the Catholic concern was part- ly rhetorical and partly real. Evidence suggests that Catholics feared their own failure as a cause of apostacy among the poor far more than they feared Protestantism as such. Catholic journalists tended to treat Protestant efforts primarily as examples to be emulated for their display of energy, generosity and organizational efficiency. Whether it stemmed from 'no-popery,' from conversion to Protestantism or from neglect by the Catholic Church, the apost- acy of the poor was seen as a single phenomenon, and it would seem that Protestant zeal was cited primarily for the purpose of shaming Catholics out of their apathy.

Catholic journalists reacted more strongly to the Protestant capacity to frustrate Catholic efforts by raising the 'no-popery' cry; there were two major examples of this during the 1847-1852 period. The first, noted in the previous chapter, concerned the Methodists' pressure on the Russell Government aimed at preventing aid to Catholics in April 1847. Later Catholics were subjected to more vociferous anti-Catholic feeling aroused by the restoration of the hierarchy. This had an impact on certain technical aspects of Catholic relations with the Privy Council Committee on Education and will be discussed below. But before turning to the technical- ities of Catholic troubles with the bureaucracy, the philosophical perspectives on education which were elaborated in the contemporary Catholic press should be considered.

The Nature of Education--Definitions

Much of the philosophical discussion over the nature and aims of education was reducible to the problem of definition. The question of the day was whether England wanted "education" or "instruction". In the general as well as the Catholic press, in the Houses of Parliament and in other public forums men discussed the church-state-education problem in these terms. To the extent that everyone claimed to want "true education" rather than "mere instruction" the debate was a false one; but in terms of what was at stake one finds genuine issues being talked about. Bishop Briggs described this debate at a Catholic educational meeting in York.[70] He said that the Latin term "educare" meant to develop the full faculties of man, both rational and spiritual, while the term "instruction" implied merely the training of the mind and the body, excluding care of the soul. Catholics, it was generally understood, could have nothing to do with mere instruction.

This debate made its way into most of the Catholic publications of the day in one form or another. It was given most serious attention in the Rambler and the Tablet, though the Catholic School contained one minor article on the topic, as did Dolman's Magazine; even the Catholic Vindicator made brief reference to this subject.

The Tablet, as a weekly, necessarily focused on specific news developments, but Lucas made the paper's position on this subject

---

[70]Tablet, April 10, 1850, p. 211.

clear even if he did not indulge in lengthy abstract debates. During the 1847 crisis over the Catholic Institute's fate the Tablet neglected philosophical questions and focused on the problem of power. This tendency remained characteristic of the Tablet throughout Lucas' editorship, but from time to time there were straightforward policy statements and discussions of first principles. Plainly stated, the Tablet's first principle was that men who have souls cannot be educated as if they had none.[71] In an editorial of November 13, 1847 the Tablet denied even the possibility of secular education, insisting that religious--or antireligious--assumptions penetrated all subjects. Variations on this theme can be found throughout Tablet reporting on educational developments. When the paper issued its first major appeal on behalf of the Catholic Poor School Committee that committee's policy of guaranteeing the religious character of Catholic schools was advertised as one of its chief merits.

The most thoroughly developed statement of the Tablet's position on this matter appeared in the April 17, 1852 issue in an article entitled "Popular Education."[72] The writer condemned the English for mistaking mere human knowledge for education and described the national educational theory as one which concerned itself with things "merely human" such as mere information, literary taste, and wealth. "It is not easy," the writer observed, "to contend successfully with this theory" which had a kind of easy

---

[71]Tablet, April 17, 1852, p. 250.

[72]Ibid.

appeal. That appeal was based on the assumption that the diffusion of knowledge was necessarily a blessing. The _Tablet_ denied that this was the case and claimed that in this matter the English confused ends with means. He went on to say, "education is surely not an end, but a means; and it depends on the use to which men turn it whether it be a blessing or a curse. Voltaire was an educated man; but there are thousands of souls who might be in a very different place had that wretch been unable to read or write." The article went on to note that the Catholic Inspector of Schools had recently made the following statement:

> The pursuit of Truth in whatever department is the common privilege of all who desire upon it, and there should be no limit assigned upon it but that of capacity and opportunity.

That, the writer insisted, was the theory of the state, not the theory of the Catholic Church. He went on to say that Catholics must understand that,

> . . . unless we can educate the human soul we had better let the matter alone; men become brutes in that case, but on the modern principle they will infallibly become devils.73

The _Tablet_ was much more concerned with actual power struggles than with philosophical debates, and its stand on this question will become even clearer when its coverage of specific policy problems will be treated in a subsequent section.

A somewhat novel contrast to the position of the _Tablet_ can be found in _Dolman´s Magazine_. The only article pertinent to our topic published in its pages focused on the English peasantry and was intended to suggest to proponents of sanitary reform that such

---

73_Ibid._

142

reforms, without national education, was a meaningless puff. The
writer said the real disease of the nation was that "moral
plague . . . which nothing can divert but the surgical hand of the
state and the humanizing beneficence of the clerical and political
schoolmaster." It is implied that religious and secular education
were needed, but that implication is obscured by the author´s
overwhelming hatred of ignorance and poverty, especially as it was
manifested in rural England. He described this plague of poverty
and ignorance as immoral, shameless and filthy, claiming that "the
true miasmata of contagion, the noxious pool and stagnant pesti-
lence, is in the mind . . ." One finds in these pages an almost
contemptuous attitude toward the peasants, and the whole thrust of
the article ignores the spiritual basis of evil, blaming all upon
the contemporary ignorance. The panacea proposed here was certainly not religious education, for which the writer had little regard,
as the following excerpt shows:

> If the present sample of provincial morality is the best
> that religious education can do for the well-being of
> society, it is surely time that the correcting influence
> of the State should interpose with the only panacea to
> the mischief--national education, based on intellectual
> and practical benefit.74

One might assume that the attack on religious education was
aimed at the Anglican failure to educate the peasants, since
Anglican control over rural schools was a cause of much controversy
during this period; regardless, the writer´s lack of interest in
providing spiritual correctives seems unusual in a Catholic

74"The Peasantry of England," Dolman´s Magazine (May 1849),
p. 11.

journal. This article must stand as the singular defense of state education, apparently based on rationalist principles, to be found in an English Catholic publication.

The Rambler treated the philosophical dimensions of the education question more seriously and more extensively than any other publication. Capes´ interest in social problems was very much tied up with the education question, and the Rambler reflected that interest. The themes developed here had to do with the impossibility of purely secular education, with the need to evaluate the way different theories would affect the preservation of religious truth, and with the need for a clearer understanding of first principles.

Capes touched briefly on the subject in a February 1851 review article, "Dr. Murray on Miracles and on Education," in which he complimented the Irish prelate for his theological exposition of Catholic educational principles but condemned the extent to which Murray gave credence to the idea of "secular education." "We hold secular education to be a simple impossibility," he said, elaborating upon the idea that religious truth was inextricably bound up with all subjects. In answer to the rhetorical question of the day concerning whether purely secular education would not be preferable to none he replied that it was a false question because "purely secular education cannot be."[75]

A later article claimed that the chief characteristic of the education movement had to do with the amount of secular instruction

---

[75][Capes], "Dr. Murray on Miracles and on Education," Rambler 7 (February 1851): 170-171.

being imparted to the masses.[76] Here Capes asked what intellectual and moral effects this would have. He dismissed the problem of intellectual effects by noting that so little time was being spent in school that there was hardly a danger of too much learning; thus he concluded the only real purely intellectual danger was intellectual superficiality. Moral and religious effects he viewed with greater anxiety, asking, "Will the generation of children that are being subjected to this kind of education turn out to be good citizens and Christians?" He feared that the mere memorizing of Scripture would never develop religion "in the hearts and affections of children" and that scholars would probably end up with "as little real knowledge as they have religion." He saw the movement fraught with grave dangers to the whole framework of society, and he reiterated the familiar theme about ignorant irreligious men being brutes and educated irreligious men being devils. The first he said were a generation of paupers and petty criminals, the second socialists and Red Republicans.[77] Capes concluded that it was the duty of Catholics to penetrate the education movement with a truly religious spirit, which could only be accomplished by making certain that religious instruction be given absolute priority and that it never be outpaced by secular instruction.

In the October 1851 issue the Rambler published a letter to the editor under the pen-name "Sacerdos." He asked whether Catholics sufficiently understood the first principles of Catholic education. Awareness of first principles, he said, was necessary

---

[76]Idem, "Popular Education," Rambler 10 (July 1852): 3.

[77]Ibid., p. 10.

if Catholics were to protect themselves against the popular de-

lusion of the day that:

> . . . the problem of human life, its happiness for this
> life, and the life to come, is to be solved by the acqui-
> sition of knowledge and by the labour of the school-
> master.78

Labeling this notion the "golden image of the nineteenth century,"

the writer criticized Catholics for feeling strongly but reasoning

little about their own philosophical assumptions which were neces-

sarily incompatible with such worship of mere knowledge.[79] The

same article discussed the appropriate education for the working

classes. There was great resistance among upper classes toward

working class education; it seemed related to the fear that workers

would abandon their subservient status and challenge the political,

social and economic status quo. This author seemed less concerned

with social and political questions than with the moral and

spiritual problem of generating both discontent and false expecta-

tions. He believed that the contemporary tendency to worship

knowledge in the abstract distorted understanding of reality. By

making knowledge an end in itself, isolated from the realities of

existence, educators were shunning their responsibility to society

and to the poorer classes.

Sacerdos did not believe that school-learning could immediate-

ly transform the lives of the poor, and he suggested that it was

scandalous--in the spiritual sense--to breed conceit, discontent

---

[78]"Correspondence: Catholic Popular Education," Rambler 8
(October 1851): 332-333.

[79]Ibid.

and "petty self-sufficiency" among the humbler classes. In short, he feared that education would endanger the souls of the poor by creating bitterness while at the same time failing in its material aspect to provide practical benefits. He cited both Greek and Christian tradition in support of the understanding that because mental faculties must be used for the exigencies of actual life children should all be trained for actual needs.[80] Though one might discern strands of anti-intellectualism in this argument it would be altogether inappropriate to dismiss the article on that basis, for the writer made a strong case against pie-in-the-sky rationalist idealism as the basis for national education. In the Burkean tradition this writer developed conservative thoughts about the relationship between education, society and religion.[81]

A final Rambler article requiring consideration outlined the "English Statesman's Idea and Plan of Popular Education" and contrasted it with that of the Catholic Church. Although this discussion focused mainly on the problem of authority in education it also developed certain assumptions which must be summarized. The pervading assumption was that education is absolutely dependent upon God because it treats of truth which comes from God. Theology and doctrine, which constitute human efforts to express truth, cannot be extracted from education that deals with truth, according to this writer in his letter to the editor. But English statesmen, he noted, wanted a "mixed education" which would separate theology

---

[80]Ibid., pp. 335-336.

[81]Ibid., pp. 336-337. Here the writer's reference to "religious common sense" is particularly in keeping with Burkean argument.

or doctrine from education; thus they would make education "independent of God in two ways": first by standing "aloof from God as an object of science," and secondly by failing to "mediate in the relation of friendship or enmity which may exist between God and man."[82] Such education would be fundamentally distorted; it would turn the mind loose on the subject of creation without imparting any understanding of the creator. The result would be intellectual and spiritual imbalance. The author, a priest, insisted that in the final judgment God views a man's whole life in both its secular and religious aspects. One judgment requires one education. Finally it is shown how Catholic education must be entirely dependent upon God: original sin left human life in a state of disorder, for which the only remedy is dependence upon God. Rationalists, it was said, presupposed an original perfectability of man which could be achieved by education. In all ways the author concluded the two systems were incompatible.[83]

In the remaining periodicals surveyed no comparable articles treating the philosophical problems in depth appeared. The Catholic Vindicator published only one article pertinent to this discussion, and it merely repeated the theme that knowledge without grace could never make men better or wiser. Education which failed to give religious teaching absolute priority over secular teaching

---

[82]"Correspondence: Popular Education--The English Statesman's Idea and Plan of Popular Education Examined as to Its Aim, Its Details, and Results, and Contrasted with that of the Catholic Church," Rambler 10 (July 1852): 76. Hereafter cited as "English Statesman."

[83]Ibid., pp. 72-82.

was denounced and the exclusion of doctrine or the separation of religious and secular instruction were clearly identified as disastrous Protestant errors.[84] In the Catholic School there was only one minor article on this subject, that written by an Italian priest, presenting substantially the same views. None of the other Catholic organs contained anything of note on this theme.

In summary it can be seen that with the singular exception of the article in Dolman's Magazine Catholic journalists defined education as an integrated whole requiring, by definition, the unity of religious and secular aspects. The Rambler, which published the most elaborate statements, developed thoughts which were clearly Roman Catholic in tone but were founded on Christian beliefs that crossed sectarian lines--beliefs about revealed religion, original sin, and man's dependence on God. All Rambler articles stressed the incompatibility between rationalist and Christian aims in education.

Certain ideas worked out in these few articles have considerable historical interest. From an ecumenical perspective it is significant that the chief object of Catholic attack was godless rather than Protestant education. Catholic writers generally made it clear that Protestantism's rejection of the principle of Church authority was ultimately responsible for the disunity which made it impossible for Protestants to develop a national system of Christian education, but such arguments were not aimed at Protestantism per se but at its historical outcome. Some writers

---

[84]"Catholic and Protestant Views of Education," Catholic Vindicator and Irish Magazine, March 13, 1852, p. 18.

were particularly careful to acknowledge the sincerity of many Protestant believers. Another aspect of these writings which is of historical interest is their tendency to paint things in primary colors; there was little concern with the details of sectarian squabbles; rather, the focus was on the confrontation between rationalism and belief in revealed religion. One comes away from these articles convinced that the authors understood that the rationalist perspective was becoming hitched to the power of the state, whence derived the critical character of the question of authority.

Authority

The whole problem of authority brings us to the main battle-field of the church-state-education conflict. Catholic press coverage of this problem was quite extensive in both theoretical and practical terms, so both representative theoretical statements and articles about practical problems will be considered.

There is little in the way of theoretical discussion in the Catholic press until after the Catholic Poor School Committee was formed and began applying for state funds. Then journalists began raising questions about whether Catholic authority in education was being protected adequately. If the cry about proselytizing was somewhat rhetorical, concern about the power of the state in education was very real. Protestant power was on the decline; the power of the state was very much on the rise.

As noted previously, modern historians have tended to conclude that the power of secularism in Victorian England was over-rated by contemporaries. It is generally implied that because Victorians tended personally to be believers or were at least outwardly pious, secularism was not a real threat.[85] The Catholic press treatment of this question, though representing only a minority viewpoint, sheds some light on the question.

English Catholics were exceptionally aware of church-state tensions because of their peculiar relations with a Protestant state which had branded their doctrines and priests as subversive and traitorous and severely penalized their religious practices. When the popular education movement rose to prominence Catholic Emancipation was in its infancy. English Catholicism suffered from internal division and struggled with changes brought about by emancipation, by Irish immigration, and in 1850 by the restoration of the hierarchy. This in turn resulted in a renewed persecution of Catholics. Yet despite internal division and a degree of external persecution, Catholic journalists were generally in agreement about the theoretical nature of the Church's authority in education. But when one moves away from theory into the realm of practical problems the area of agreement narrows. Thus it is helpful to examine how the articles which developed theoretical arguments were related to the reporting of actual confrontations over authority.

---

[85]See Best, "Religious Difficulties of National Education," pp. 155, 169; Adams, op. cit., pp. 150-160; and Maltby, op. cit., pp. 82-92. Perhaps it should be stressed that most writers of educational history have been educationalists rather than professional historians; even so, historians tend to accept the assumption that no one wanted secular education; see Woodward, op. cit., pp. 477, 479-484; and A. Victor Murray, "Education," in The New Cambridge Modern History (Cambridge: Cambridge University Press, 1962), pp. 184-185.

In a May 22, 1847 article entitled "The Beauties of Ignorance" the Tablet satirized the Protestant slogan: "Teach men to think and they will see the absurdities of the Roman creed." If Protestants believed this, the writer observed, they would encourage the Catholic education movement; he interpreted their resistance to it as testimony to the power of Catholic truth. This article was published in response to a Times article stating that the Catholic clergy was "possessed neither of the mind, the money nor the learning to educate Catholic youth." Admitting that Catholics lacked money the writer said Catholics were possessed of the one important "grand qualification" of an educator--unity regarding doctrine. He added, "and the great journal knows it."[86] The importance of Catholic doctrinal unity in this doctrinally divided nation was understood as were the grave obstacles to national Protestant education. The writer claimed that Protestants were unable to agree on education questions because there was a "screw loose in their system." Doctrinal division among the sects meant that national Christian education was an impossibility, and doctrinal division stemmed from the lack of authority in Protestant doctrine. This was the key to Catholic understanding about the relationship between truth and authority; because they were by nature inseparable the Protestant rejection of authority wrought confusion in doctrine and education alike.

Another line of thought presented in the Tablet dealt with the impact a national secular education system would have on the family as the basic unit of authority in society. In an article concern-

---

[86]Tablet, May 22, 1847, p. 321.

ing a Manchester meeting dominated by "a band of Orangemen" promoting secular education the Tablet writer, presumably Lucas, reiterated the theme that the Bible must be interpreted doctrinally if it is to provide the basis of religious education.[87] "Religion is either a dream or it must be pivotal," the writer asserted, and he predicted fatal social and religious consequences should a system of secular education be established. He cited conditions in Switzerland where families were prohibited from keeping a governess and were required to send even female children to government schools "or be subjected to the meddlesome infidel magistrates, with a posse of gendarmes." He foresaw the day when Englishmen would lose such social rights but admitted that in the measures being considered in Manchester local authority was being preserved. Still, he demanded that Catholics be more zealous in protecting not only the authority of the Church in education but of the family as well.

The clearest statement about authority in education was published in the Rambler article already cited, "The English Statesman's Idea and Plan of Popular Education." Here the two rival authorities contending for control over the schools are identified. The Church's only rival is identified as the secular state--not the Protestant churches. The state possessed both power and a plan which threatened Church prerogatives in a way no Protestant sects could. According to this writer that plan had not been made known in any straightforward fashion but was nevertheless discernible

---

[87]Tablet, April 6, 1850, p. 221.

from the policies already employed by the state. This author's concern about state education being independent of God has already been discussed. Quoting from Tocqueville he went on to describe the state's claim to the right to "repair every misery and assume the exclusive burden of the social welfare."[88] The Church, however, made similarly all-encompassing claims to authority, especially in the field of education.

The confrontation between the Church's plan and the statesman's plan was particularly confusing because the statesman deluded himself into thinking that the state could safeguard the Christian character of the nation while at the same time reserving to itself full power over education. In this context the correspondent identified the real trouble as stemming from the fact that the state itself was powerless to command belief or to guarantee the truth of any doctrine. The Church of England could not solve the problem because its clergy "too imperfectly comprehend the need of theology at all to trouble themselves about it." The author stressed his belief that the statesman discarded theology, not out of impiety but from the sheer impossibility of doing otherwise--he was the helpless victim of a system that had discarded the principle of authority in doctrine and was reaping the results in doctrine and in education. As for the Protestant insistence that the Bible would suffice to provide both a basis for Christian unity and the preservation of faith he said, "the Bible alone doesn't make man dependent upon God." That dependence must be an integral part of all life: the Bible must be interpreted and its meaning

---

[88]"English Statesman," pt. 1, Rambler 10 (July 1852): 75.

elaborated. That Protestants could not do. He concluded that education must be geared to one final judgment and therefore it must be one education under one administration; it was, in short, a work of authority.[89]

In the second part of this letter the correspondent asked whether it was possible for the Church and the state to work together. The answer, he said, depended upon who made the concessions. Much of this part of the letter dealt with questions of specific policy which will be mentioned below; here it is sufficient to point out that he once again stressed the view that the state's plan of education, which separated itself from the authority of God, exhibited confidence in and respect for "self alone." And he reiterated the argument that no such notion of self-sufficiency in human affairs was compatible with the tenets of revealed Christianity.[90]

In the leading article of the September 1852 issue Capes took a somewhat different view of state efforts:

> Time was when the Government left the whole burden of providing for the education of the people to the voluntary efforts of individuals; at present it offers assistance to all indiscriminantly, provided only that they will admit the visit of an inspector.[91]

The article predicted further attempts by the legislature to interfere more directly in school affairs; regardless, Capes contended that Catholics could refuse to cooperate with the state only at the

---

[89]Ibid., pp. 75-79.

[90]Ibid., pt. 2, Rambler 10 (August 1852): 161-167.

[91][Capes], "Popular Education," Rambler 10 (September 1852): 169.

risk of imperiling the progress of necessary expansion, and he insisted that Christian priorities were being maintained in church-state relations. Though Capes´ main concern here was not philosophical, he was extremely anxious about the theoretical concerns which accounted for so much Catholic reluctance to apply for state grants.[92]

The Tablet´s coverage was devoted almost exclusively to specific aspects of the Catholic Poor School Committee negotiations with the state, but a few articles treated the conflict of authority in more general terms. Lucas was ever suspicious of state initiatives because he believed the Government´s aim was the subjection of the spiritual to the civil power.[93] He chided Catholics for lacking skill in negotiating with the state and for being gullible with regard to the Privy Council Committee´s intentions. He said the Committee on Education alone presented a "clear and practical solution to the difficulties" but its solution was incompatible with Catholic principles. The English, he insisted, prided themselves on practicality "to the exclusion of all the considerations which derive their value from the distinction between right and wrong."[94] If the pragmatic Englishman hated difficulties he hated principle "quite as profoundly." And Lucas urged Catholics not to be snared by the appeal of pragmatic solutions.

If theoretical discussions presented in the Catholic press

---

[92]Ibid., pp. 170-172.

[93]Tablet, August 18, 1849, p. 521.

[94]Ibid.; and ibid., January 5, 1850, p. 9.

exhibited fundamental agreements among Catholics, that situation changed as journalists considered actual church-state-education problems.

The Church-State-Education Chronology, 1847-1852

After the 1847 formation of the Catholic Poor School Committee the Privy Council Committee on Education set about preparing Minutes to govern state aid to Roman Catholic schools. The Minute of December 18, 1847 established the following conditions: (1) the Catholic Poor School Committee became the recognized agency for communication between Catholics and the Committee on Education, (2) aided schools were to be open to inspectors whose appointment was subject to the approval of the Catholic Poor School Committee and the bishops, and (3) no one in Holy Orders was to be permitted to receive schoolmasters' or teacher-assistants' stipends. The Committee on Education reserved the right to make exceptions to the last conditions where normal schools or model schools were involved.[95] Another general Minute of the same date provided funds for purchasing books and maps, and while this Minute did not apply exclusively to Catholics, it broadened the scope of state aid for which they could apply. There was considerable delay before Catholic schools actually began receiving state funds. The new Minutes did not go into effect until Parliament approved the annual education appropriations; that approval was forthcoming in 1848. Meanwhile the Poor School Committee had to struggle with the Privy Council Committee which had, in the interim, imposed more elaborate

---

[95]"Education," Catholic School 1 (August 1848): 7.

conditions on building grants.

Catholics were not experienced in government negotiations, and there were disputes over nearly all aspects of the government program, some of which merely stemmed from bureaucratic obfuscation of policy. Negotiations over building grants were most troublesome because the government advised Catholics of new conditions after the original terms had been settled, and those new conditions were exceptionally Protestant in character. This struggle has generally been called the "management clause dispute." It had to do with the demand of the Privy Council Committee on Education that school trust deeds contain clauses defining the structure of school management in such a way as to give the laity predominance. A principle more in conflict with current Catholic practices could hardly have been constructed. The Privy Council Committee efforts to impose this policy unconditionally on Catholic schools extended negotiations into 1852, the fifth year after aid to Catholics had been officially approved by Parliament.

Other confrontations with the government were of shorter duration and lesser intensity. The more important ones involved conditions governing the assignment of pupil-teachers, and the selection of materials which could be purchased with book grants. There were also internal disputes among Catholics; the most important involved the management clauses and the principle of inspection. Lesser troubles concerned the certification of teachers and the character and quality of books purchased through the government grant system.

The chronological framework in which these disputes worked themselves out was highlighted by the 1847 formation of the Poor School Committee, by the official appointment of the Catholic inspector in December 1848, by the beginning of the first minor grants to Catholic schools in 1848, by the renewal of the ´no-popery´ cry generated by the restoration of the hierarchy, and by the 1851 Ecclesiastical Titles Bill which made it illegal for Catholic prelates to call themselves bishops or archbishops.[96] During this period there were also a number of educational bills introduced in Parliament which could have posed grave problems for Catholics had they passed. Certainly these proposed measures touched on church-state questions, but it must be remembered that this was the era of executive control in education. It had become customary for the Privy Council Committee on Education to maintain initiative with respect to educational policy, and Parliament´s role was restricted to budgetary approval. Thus it was only during the general supplies debates that the English educational question was generally debated. Parliament´s only means of seizing the initiative which it desired lay in the passage of legislation, but so long as chances for that were slim the bills introduced failed to arouse serious concern.

The pre-1847 character of the inspection problem has already been treated, and the broad outlines of the management clause

---

[96]This "Act to prevent the assumption of certain ecclesiastical titles in respect of places in the United Kingdom" was in a sense an elaboration upon the restrictive clause in the 1829 Catholic Emancipation measure prohibiting Catholic prelates from assuming the titles of ancient sees; see B. Ward, The Eve of Catholic Emancipation, 3 vols. (London: Longmans, Green & Co., 1912), 3:257. The Ecclesiastical Titles Bill made it illegal for Catholic bishops to assume titles of bishop and archbishop in the United Kingdom; thus they were refused the right to call themselves bishops of ancient sees or any other "pretended sees." W. Ward, Wiseman, 2:533-535, published the text of the bill.

disputes can be found in any general history of English education. Still, it should be noted that Anglican resistance to the management clauses was more serious than writers of educational history have acknowledged. The establishment of the principle of lay control was probably the most important state achievement prior to 1870, and it deserves more balanced attention from historians. The leading Anglican opponent of the management clauses was George Anthony Denison who claimed that the clause introduced de facto separation of the religious and secular components of education.[97] It was his belief that the state would not settle for an independent Anglican school system enjoying state support and that the state could not establish a national system completely independent of the parish network; therefore, he believed--and his arguments were substantial--that the state intended to appropriate the parish schools by gradually transforming them into "national" parish schools--featuring "mixed education." He was convinced that the management clauses constituted a critical element in that design.[98] It is not clear just how or when this Anglican resistance was overcome, for educational historians have minimized the significance of these disputes with casual reference to Anglican obstructionism.

The Catholic Press Assessment of Specific Disputes

The Catholic press treatment of these church-state relations is best approached by taking up the more important disputes separ-

---

[97]For a discussion of the Tablet's response to Denison's position see pp. 165-167 below.

[98]Denison, op. cit., pp. 96-115.

ately and concluding with some analysis of the way the various publications analyzed the work of the Poor School Committee as a whole.

Management Clause Disputes

The Tablet first mentioned the management clauses on November 20, 1847 and described them as dangerous in that they threatened to destroy clerical control over schools. Here Anglicans were reported as being "up in arms" over the matter, and Kay-Shuttleworth's method of imposing such conditions was condemned as dishonest and devious.[99] Further mention of the matter does not appear until 1849.[100]

By this time the fact that Catholics were still not receiving state funds had become irritating to many, and the Catholic Poor School Committee became defensive, as an article in the Catholic School indicates:

> We have been sometimes asked, not without a slight curl of the lip, "Well, and what have you got from the Government?"

The writer, Scott Nasmyth Stokes, pleaded for patience, explaining that matters had been held up by trust deeds negotiations and assuring readers that it was better to delay than to accept unfavorable terms.[101]

The Tablet soon took up this subject, attacking the Govern-

---

[99]Tablet, November 20, 1847, p. 737.

[100]Ibid., July 28, 1849, p. 472.

[101][Stokes], "Government Aid," Catholic School 1 (May 1849): 83.

ment's lay management policy. Acknowledging that Catholics had not yet yielded on the matter the writer charged that the Poor School Committee had already conceded too much when it offered to let the Catholic inspector be a party to the settlement of appeals which should be solely under episcopal authority.[102] Such an arrangement, he insisted, would contribute to the subjection of the spiritual to the temporal authority; the following excerpt from the Privy Council Committee correspondence with the Poor School Committee was cited as proof that this was the Government's aim:

> It is not consistent with the principles on which the Committee of Privy Council on Education have invariably administered the Parliamentary grant, to allow the spiritual authorities of any denomination an absolute control over the schools aided from that fund.103

The Committee of Council had claimed to provide for the "due influence of the spiritual power." Of that the writer said, "in the mouth of secular men 'due influence' means no influence at all . . ." Privy Council officials had also suggested that nothing prevented Roman Catholic laymen from implicitly deferring to the spiritual authority of the Church, which the Tablet answered by noting that if all Catholic laymen "were devout enough to defer implicitly to the spiritual authority of their Church" no provisions for settling disputes would be required.[104] The theme of the argument was simply that Catholics must guard against binding agreements which would protect rebellious Catholic laymen in positions of authority in Catholic schools from the proper author-

---

[102]Tablet, July 28, 1849, p. 472.

[103]Ibid., August 18, 1849, p. 521.

[104]Ibid.

ity of the Church. A provocative hypothetical example was presented:

> In time to come we may have a Catholic Inspector who is
> better treated in Downing Street than in Rome and who may
> think it his duty to thwart the bishops and to extend the
> influence of the State.

In summary it was recommended that:

> Our true course is to insist upon our own terms, to
> refuse everything which requires in writing any con-
> cession . . . The state must give way as it did in the
> matter of the veto.105

This reference to the veto controversy[106] provides a key to
Lucas´ historical understanding of what Catholics could realist-
ically insist upon. Catholics had been able to obtain uncondi-
tional emancipation in 1829 because England feared Ireland. If the
connection seems remote, it must be remembered that Lucas was
exceptionally interested in and informed about conditions in
Ireland. He understood the English fear of Ireland and believed
that if English Catholics had the sense to harass English politicians with the Irish question they could dictate their own terms.
In short, he was arguing about what he viewed as real political
possibilities, not abstract principles. It may be that he was less
realistic about the character of English Catholics. Those who
disagreed with the Tablet saw things differently; as loyal
Englishmen they shied away from the Irish question, but without
that political card they certainly played a weaker hand. This may

---

[105]Ibid.

[106]See B. Ward, The Dawn of the Catholic Revival, 2 vols.
(London: Longmans, Green, 1909) 2:215-217; idem, Eve of Catholic
Emancipation, 1:49-82, 107-113, 133-138, 142-145; 2:10, 28-36, 71-
84, 135-154.

explain why they were willing to settle for terms less rigorous than Lucas called for.

In August 1849 the Catholic School published a more moderate account of the management clause problem, giving benefit of the doubt to the state:

> It must not be forgotten that the funds administered by the Government are public property. The Committee of Council is but the trustee appointed to manage the money of others. As trustee, then, the committee is morally bound to exercise a careful discretion . . .107

The article went on to observe that since the Committee of Council had to account to Parliament for the way its funds were spent it had the right to inquire into the principles upon which state-assisted schools were conducted. Experience with poorly constructed schools and unsecured deeds had proved the necessity for such a policy.[108]

The crucial question was whether the state's right to be assured that its funds were spent properly necessarily implied the right to dictate the principles upon which such schools were conducted. Opposition to the state's effort to impose management clauses derived from the belief that accountability could be achieved in other ways requiring considerably less state interference in school management. It must have interested and pleased Privy Council officials to find Catholic authorities defending the state principle in the Catholic Poor School Committee's official

---

[107]"Conditions of Government Aid," Catholic School 1 (August 1849): 133-134.

[108]Ibid.

magazine--and defending that principle in moral as well as pragmatic terms.

The article listed conditions which the Poor School Committee demanded with regard to the management clauses: (1) that the charge of religion and morals, and everything connected with either or both be under the authority of the priest, (2) that matters purely secular, e.g. finance, be controlled by a committee partly lay and partly clerical, with an appeal, in case of dispute, to two arbitrators, one appointed by the Bishop, the other (who must be a Catholic inspector) by the President of the Council, (3) that if it be doubted whether any questions in dispute do involve religion or not, the bishop shall decide. In all cases the managing committee was to be bound by the deed to carry out the decision of the bishop.[109] Poor School Committee officials insisted that these conditions thoroughly safeguarded ecclesiastical authority; they said the Committee of Council's refusal to accept these conditions derived from a reluctance to give bishops so much authority.

About this same period (mid-1849) the Tablet and the Catholic School came into conflict over the Anglican position on the management clauses. At the June 1849 meeting of the National Society Denison and his supporters introduced a resolution rejecting the management clauses as unacceptable to the society and stating that the only conditions acceptable included legal tenure of the school site and the right of inspection as defined in 1840.[110] In the

---

[109]Ibid., p. 134.

[110]See Purcell, op. cit., 1:424-434; and Adams, op. cit., pp. 139-144.

course of this meeting the Anglican Archdeacon Henry Edward Manning was persuaded by Denison's opponents to introduce a compromise measure which would have been less offensive to the Government. Though Denison eventually acquiesced in the Manning substitute, he always blamed Manning for effecting an unnecessary compromise.[111] Years later Denison wrote to Manning's biographer confirming his earlier judgment that Manning's move had been the "beginning of the surrender of the Church school into the hands of the civil power." Of Manning's responsibility for this he said, "All I know is that it was first by his hand that the Church School in England was destroyed."[112]

The _Tablet_ reported this meeting on June 16, providing sensitive commentary on the question. The article depicted Denison and his "party of movement" as pitted against the "Bishops generally, and all the grave and ´revered laymen´ who have raised themselves high by the extreme caution and prudence of their behavior." It was said that these "safe men" together with the Evangelicals and the "men of no principle" were pursuing a policy of peace and utter subservience to the government. Denison's resolution was praised for its firmness while Manning's compromise was judged a mistake; so long as the National Society had the power to pass the firm resolution it acted unwisely in not exercising it. The writer argued that defeat would have been better, for "timid or judicious friends who come forward as mediators, have never succeeded in

---

[111]Purcell, _ibid._, 1:426.

[112]_Ibid._

anything but mischief."[113]

Kay-Shuttleworth was condemned for moving quietly and for duplicity in imposing new conditions after the 1840 agreement had been reached; at first they were posed as mere suggestions which evidenced good will; then as they were accepted from time to time and the committee's power grew, the Committee of Council's secretary worked to make such conditions obligatory. The writer, who could hardly have been anyone but Lucas, said that however much Catholics opposed Anglicanism, they should not rejoice in the schemes of Mr. Kay-Shuttleworth:

> It is very true that the Established Church has influence and wealth, and that it is desirable to destroy it; but it is not desirable to bring it to nothing by means that are so transparently unjust.[114]

Moreover, he warned Catholics against over-estimating the power of the Established Church to resist the civil power:

> The Church of England is an unpopular and divided body; it has no fixed principles, and many of its professing members profess among other things a vehement wish to see it destroyed. Its bishops are unwilling to be on bad terms with the Government, and the expectant Bishops would think such a state of things one of mortal sin.

Catholics were thus warned against being blinded by the thought that anything which undermined Anglicanism would help Catholicism:

> We must not shut our eyes to the real meaning of this aggression on the part of the State. The aim is to bring all education into secular and civil hands . . . The terms imposed on the established religion will be imposed by degrees on others.

Finally, Lucas urged Catholics to be wary of patriotic compromise:

> English Catholicism is given to compromise, and has never

---

[113]Tablet, June 16, 1849, p. 376.

[114]Ibid.

been--at least since the conquest--too loyal to the Holy
See; Protestants have observed this fact, and we believe
are prepared to turn it to their own account. We have a
strong tendency to worship the sovereign and to have
amicable relations with the Supreme Pontiff. At our
public dinners we drink the Queen's health and then the
Pope's, by which we greatly insinuate that the spiritual
is inferior to the temporal power, and that we are
Englishmen in the first place, and in the second place--
sensible Catholics.115

This is a surprisingly penetrating analysis of the Anglican

position at a time when anti-Anglican rhetoric focused on the

strength of parish schools rather than on their vulnerabilities.

Lucas' capacity to measure the growth of state power in education

by its ability to dictate to the Church of England represented a

political astuteness shared by few other Catholics, and it is

interesting that this analysis was substantially the same as the

judgments of both Denison and Francis Adams, who chronicled events

from different perspectives many years later.116

In its August 1849 issue the Catholic School published its

side of the debate and denied that there was any comparison between

the High Church and Catholic positions. It was argued that spir-

itual authority with the Anglicans was "but a name," that Anglicans

could never hope to prevail against the state, while with Catholics

it was a "real power" which history showed could indeed resist the

state. It was also asserted that the Anglicans had "no real case"

as three-fourths of their people did not object to the management

clauses and their schools were accepting "the lion's share of the

grant." Finally, it was said that the Anglican position differed

---

115Ibid.

116Adams, op. cit., pp. 139-145.

most materially from the Catholic in its internal disunity:

> If the turbulent party in the National Society can, in opposition to its leaders, the Bishops, carry its point with the Committee of Council, we shall not regret it. But we do protest against any abandonment of our own peculiar ground, which is a high and tenable one, for the sake of a coalition with those whose cause on this and all other subjects is scouted by the common sense of the nation.[117]

The Catholic Poor School Committee position had much to recommend it and revealed a realistic appraisal of Anglican vulnerabilities. But it failed to show how the Catholic position vis-à-vis the management clauses protected Catholic schools from similar problems. So the Tablet continued to compare Catholics with Anglicans and suggested that the latter better understand the need to resist the "creedless bureaucracy."[118]

Though the January 1851 Catholic School published the model trust deed which was agreed to in November 1850,[119] this matter was not prominent in the press during the height of the Ecclesiastical Titles Bill debates. Finally in October 1851 the Tablet reported the settlement of the dispute, quoting from the Catholic Poor School Committee annual report.[120] The management clause (a copy of which is provided as an appendix) gave control over matters of faith and morals to the Church but reserved all "questions of management properly so called" to the lay committee on which the

---

[117]"Education" Catholic School 1 (August 1849): 134.

[118]There were numerous articles referring to this problem in the Tablet; see especially that of May 8, 1852, p. 297.

[119]"Privy Council Building Grants," Catholic School 2 (January 1851): 92-94.

[120]Tablet, October 4, 1851, p. 633.

priest sat as chairman; in case of deadlock he had a second vote. The _Tablet_'s chief complaint was that the settlement achieved practical separation of the religious and secular elements of education--a principle against which the Holy See and Ireland were fighting. The writer protested that not even the Anglicans had surrendered this.[121]

It is significant that in this final settlement the conditions originally agreed to by the Poor School Committee concerning the Catholic inspector's participation in an appeal process were altogether excluded. Whether this could be attributed to the furor Lucas generated over the matter cannot be determined, but his position certainly won out in substance, for the ecclesiastical authorities were given full power over appeals having to do with religious matters. Moreover, the _Tablet_ expressed skepticism about the wording of these provisions, noting that the priest could not remove teachers or object to books except on strictly religious grounds. "We know," the writer continued, "how narrow these grounds may appear in the eyes of laymen when they are disposed to thwart the priest."[122] The wording of the deed does appear to have given great leeway for clerical control over purely religious matters. For example, it gave the priest power to dismiss schoolmasters on religious grounds, requiring a written statement to that effect by the priest. Final judgment was deferred to the bishop. In a preceding section, however, the deed gave power over dismissal of schoolteachers to the lay committee. The most obvious and pro-

---

[121]_Ibid._

[122]_Ibid._

Catholic construction of the deed would certainly be that the highest ecclesiastical authority in all cases would bind the lay committee. But there is room for doubt. And the concern expressed in the *Tablet* reflected Lucas´ view that it was necessary to guard against the least charitable construction possible rather than rely on the most charitable construction possible.

Langdale replied to the *Tablet*´s objections in a letter to the editor published on October 25. Though he admitted that the Catholic Poor School Committee never basically approved the idea of a lay management committee, he insisted that ecclesiastical author- ity had been safeguarded. In support of his position he appealed to the authority of the bishops who had approved the settlement and to the fact that the priest appointed the original members of the committee.[123] He continued:

> The Poor School Committee has insisted on retaining to the priest alone, and to the Catholic ecclesiastical authority alone, the entire right of objecting to any book or any master simply stating that in his judgment religion was therein concerned.[124]

In response to the *Tablet*´s constant harping about the Anglican position he said that the Church of England officials were always complaining that Catholics were able to secure safeguards the Committee of Council refused to grant the Establishment. Nothing was mentioned about the separation of religious and secular educa- tion or about the issue of state motives.[125]

---

[123]*Ibid.*, October 25, 1851, p. 682.

[124]*Ibid.*

[125]*Ibid.*

In the same _Tablet_ Lucas answered Langdale, quoting directly from his letter to show that what Langdale viewed as safeguards were by virtue of his own statements concessions. Both had strong grounds for their positions, but it would seem that Lucas´ demand for security against a hostile construction of a Catholic document was well justified in 1851.

The December 1851 _Catholic School_ let the matter rest with the republication of Langdale´s letter to the _Tablet_. Though it is somewhat difficult to assess the technical arguments involved, it is clear that the Catholic Poor School Committee refused to address itself seriously to the assumptions underlying the _Tablet_´s opposition. Had the matter been one affecting only formal debate that refusal would have been understandable. On the contrary, the real opposition which the Poor School Committee faced came from parish priests who for good or ill rather obviously agreed with Lucas and refused to deal with the government. The power of Lucas´ arguments--which could not be easily dismissed--was only part of the picture, for the _Tablet_´s position represented a substantial body of clerical opinion, especially among Irish priests in England--the very priests whom the Poor School Committee should have been most concerned with because they served those missions most in need of poor schools.

The basic disagreements proceeded from two incompatible sets of assumptions about the political aims of the Privy Council Committee on Education and the way to cope with them. Lucas assumed that the Privy Council Committee would oppose ecclesiastical authority with all its might and with every device available-- including careless wording of any official documents. The Poor

School Committee evidenced greater confidence in the government and trusted the bishops to safeguard their authority. It is not an easy matter to judge who was right--and in any event that judgment would have to rest upon historical events which well exceed the scope of this study. Even if the conflicting views about the importance of the Anglican position were only peripheral to the main controversy, it should at least be noted that the Poor School Committee--as evidenced by commentary in the Catholic School-- missed or ignored Lucas´ whole argument: that the state´s attacks on the Established Church were indicative of a growth in state power which would as easily be turned against Catholics.

The November 1850 agreement on the management clauses which produced the model trust deed discussed above did not conclude the dispute, for passage of the Ecclesiastical Titles Bill interrupted promulgation of that settlement.

Catholic press coverage of the ´no-popery´ agitation during 1850 and 1851 was much too extensive to permit detailed study here, but a serious effort has been made to scan that material to determine the relationship between this controversy and the educational situation. Only the Rambler and the Tablet indicated that there was any connection between the two issues.

As usual the Tablet´s coverage was most extensive. This is easily explained by Lucas´ long-established hostility to Lord Russell. When Russell´s attitude toward Catholics was thoroughly unmasked in 1851 Lucas was the last man to be surprised, and he relished culling from Russell´s past whatever could be used against him in the Titles Bill struggle. One of the items in the Tablet´s arsenal was Russell's record on Catholic educational aid.

On November 16 the Tablet published a model article entitled "The Whig Apostle of Bedlam Broke Loose." In it Lucas attacked Russell's claim that he had supported Catholics on the education question in the past, calling the assertion "fraudulent."[126] The same theme was repeated in other articles, and as the temperature of the debate rose the color of Lucas' commentary about Russell and the godless and faithless Whigs became ever more vivid. Finally, on June 12, 1852, the Tablet published the correspondence between the Committee of Council and the Poor School Committee concerning the management clause conflict.[127] This showed that in May 1851 the Poor School Committee presented a model trust deed to the Privy Council Committee, based on the earlier settlement of the question; the Committee of Council replied on November 28 advising Langdale that the delay had been caused by difficulties related to the Ecclesiastical Titles Bill. Because the model deed employed the terms "Roman Catholic Bishops" the matter had been submitted to the law officers of the Crown for a determination as to whether those terms were contrary to the new law; they had been advised in the affirmative and were consequently suggesting that a substitute wording be used. In place of the terms "Roman Catholic Bishops" the Poor School Committee was advised to insert: "officiating as a Bishop of the Church of Rome, and as the Ecclesiastical Superior of

---

[126]Ibid., November 16, 1850, p. 729.

[127]Ibid., June 12, 1852, p. 371.

the persons in communion with that Church within the district."[128]

This substitute was rejected summarily by the Poor School Committee. Subsequently there were other exchanges between Langdale and the Privy Council Committee which resulted in a new settlement. It is not clear whether the new settlement was based upon a minor alteration in the wording or whether the Committee of Council simply determined to ignore the advice of the law officers of the Crown. The Committee on Education's Secretary, Ralph Lingen (who succeeded Kay-Shuttleworth), stated in his February 16 letter to Langdale:

> My Lords, however, have no motive for preferring the description suggested by the law officers of the crown to any which may equally satisfy the letter and spirit of the law.129

He went on to say that another draft deed from St. Chad's, an important school in Manchester, had been received by the Committee on Education and that the Committee had decided to accept it. The wording of the new deed mentioned the bishop by name as "The Right Rev. William Turner, DD., Roman Catholic Bishop," or as "said Roman Catholic Bishop, or his successor for the time being."[130] Presumably the acceptable distinction had to do with the fact that the bishop was not named as bishop of a specific district or see--but the distinguishing characteristic was anything but obvious. Langdale's reply revealed a little puzzlement over such trifling

---

[128] Ibid.

[129] Ibid.

[130] Ibid.

points, but he was satisfied.[131] Thus with this obscure but eminently practical determination on the part of the Lords of the
Privy Council the matter was formally settled at last.

The only other periodical to notice the matter at all was the
Rambler. In its March 1852 "Ecclesiastical Register" column there
was a brief account of the affair written by Stokes in the form of
a letter to P. H. Howard, M. P. Howard had asked Stokes for information about Catholic attitudes concerning Committee of Council
dealings with the Poor School Committee, and Stokes replied by
outlining the latest troubles which the Ecclesiastical Titles Bill
had produced. The letter merely traced the details discussed
above, though excluding the final details which were worked out
after the letter was written in January 1852.[132] It may be significant that the Rambler never reported the outcome--but by this time
surely the matter had become so tedious to all concerned that one
could hardly blame a lively journalist like John Moore Capes for
letting matters stand.

Inspection

Inspection, as a condition of participation in the state
program, was the second most prominent school controversy among
Catholics. Discussion about the desirability of having Catholic
schools inspected by a civil servant--even a Catholic civil
servant--began to appear in print in 1849. Though Catholics had
agreed to the inspection principle in 1847 the first Catholic

---

[131]Ibid.

[132]"Ecclesiastical Register," Rambler 9 (March 1852): 250-252.

inspector was not appointed until the end of 1848.[133] The first hint of controversy came in a series of letters exchanged between Daniel O'Gorman and Her Majesty's Inspector of Catholic Schools, T. W. Marshall.[134] As it proved, O'Gorman had been removed from his teaching post under questionable circumstances, and his attack on inspection had a personal dimension to it; when this became apparent the Tablet refused to publish further exchanges. By mid-1849, however, Tablet editorials began questioning the inspector's powers.

Lucas' chief concern stemmed from the inspector's allegiance to the civil power. It has already been noted that he objected to the proposal that the inspector take part in settling appeals. As a lawyer Lucas envisioned numerous hypothetical difficulties which might stem from the fact that inspectors derived full authority from the state rather than from the Church--whether or not they were conscientious Catholics. He was quick to admit that such hypothetical troubles might never develop; all the same Lucas insisted that the Poor School Committee must guard against their eventuality. By way of example he said,

> In the course of time we may have Catholic inspectors like the officer of the Grand Duke of Tuscany who super-intends the Pastorals of the Bishops, and calls himself a Catholic; when he is ex officio excommunicated.135

By 1850 the Tablet was taking an even harder line and saying that

---

[133]Ibid.

[134]Tablet, March 17, 1849, p. 163; ibid., March 24, 1849, p. 179; ibid., March 31, 1849, p. 195; ibid., April 7, 1849, p. 209; ibid., April 14, 1849, p. 26.

[135]Ibid., July 28, 1849, p. 474.

the Poor School Committee had yielded too much by admitting inspectors into Catholic schools.[136] Hereafter the paper regularly
reported anything done by Marshall, at that time the only Catholic
inspector, which varied in the least from the restriction that only
secular aspects of schools and instruction be discussed by that
official. At one point Marshall was criticized for praising a
priest's handling of religious instruction on grounds that the
power to praise implied the power to blame.[137] There were a number
of similar reports, and it appears that many of Lucas' objections
to inspectors may have been objections to Marshall's work in particular.

The Tablet's critical attitude toward Marshall undoubtedly had
two sources. In the first place the inspector took altogether too
much delight in being a civil servant for Lucas' taste, and he was
full of praise for the benefits--moral as well as technical--to be
derived from cooperation with the government. At one point
Marshall said that Catholics must overcome prejudice against dealing with the state, which he attributed to a "total misconception
of the real intention of the Committee of Council on Education."
To this Lucas answered:

> In the face of all that state interference has done in
> France and Belgium, it does astonish us to be told that
> the Catholics of England see with pleasure the Government
> assuming the functions it has too long abdicated, and
> that we unfortunately are without the blessings of a
> Minister of Public Instruction.138

---

[136]Ibid., January 5, 1850, p. 9.

[137]Ibid., August 17, 1850, p. 523.

[138]Ibid., August 17, 1850, p. 523.

The editor´s perspective was also undoubtedly influenced by the consistent refusal of the Christian Brothers to deal with the state. After the _Tablet_ was moved to Dublin Irish prejudice against dealing with the English government would have had an impact. This same influence was undoubtedly responsible for much of the Christian Brothers´ stance.

Finally, the _Tablet_ was critical of inspection because it would undoubtedly place greater emphasis on secular learning. So long as inspectors awarded secular learning, pupil-teacher appointments stressed that, and if teachers prepared for inspections on that basis the general outcome would be the practical disparagement of religious knowledge as such.[139] This represented another form of argument against the separation of religious and secular instruction, but it was not stated in that way.

Naturally the _Catholic School_ defended the Poor School Committee commitment to the inspection system; it also defended the inspector. It was argued that the inspection system encouraged teachers in their work and assisted school committees in organizing schools. The Catholic Poor School Committee´s acceptance of inspection in principle was defended on two grounds: (1) because the bishops had approved the scheme it was assumed to be compatible with Catholic interests and principles, and (2) the Catholic inspector was honorable and trustworthy and was always appointed with the bishops´ full approval.[140]

---

[139]_Ibid._, April 3, 1852, p. 218.

[140]"The Catholic Poor School Committee," _Catholic School_ 1 (August 1848): 3-11; "Conditions of Government Aid," _ibid_. (August 1849): 131-137; "Pupil Teachers," _ibid_. (November 1849): 179-183;

Although the <u>Rambler</u> published three articles touching on this subject, its coverage provided no detailed analysis. One writer observed that the inspection question was a "controverted" one into which it was "almost bootless to inquire" because Catholics were "not independent of aid which the public funds supply." He said that inspection was not a condition on which Catholics had been "singled out for any special or peculiar oppression," and that Catholics had a right to share in the public funds. He was critical of the Christian Brothers´ refusal to admit inspection and urged that this policy be changed. The same writer defended the government´s right to see that its money was spent properly. Then he went on to say that there was nothing in the arrangements to which Catholics had agreed which compelled them to pay the slightest attention to the inspectors.[141] This was a most intriguing suggestion, and it is not clear whether it was based on shrewdness or ignorance. It would appear that Catholics had turned the Irish national schools into Catholic schools by doing pretty much what this writer recommended, but this article does not evidence much awareness of technical or political realities of educational politics, which suggests that the statement may have been based more on ignorance than on political astuteness. Nevertheless, the article as a whole favored the inspection system for reasons very similar to those held by the Privy Council Committee.

Capes´ September 1852 article appealed to practical considera-

---

and "Christian Brothers," <u>ibid.</u>, 183-184.

[141]"Correspondence: Catholic Popular Education," <u>Rambler</u> 8 (October 1851): 329.

tions and urged Catholics not to shun state aid. In this context
inspection was mentioned as the "only" condition of state aid; in
view of the haggling over trust deeds which was still going on at
that time this statement revealed the editor's lack of familiarity
with the situation. The tone of the article indicated the editor
to be generally in favor of inspection, but it is clear that Capes'
understanding of the details was quite limited.[142] This is especially interesting in light of the Rambler's very strong theoretical statements about the need to guard Catholic interests in education.

Little else of substance was published about this subject
during the 1847-1852 years, but many priests and local school
committees continued to resist inspection, so the subject was far
from closed.

Curriculum

The curriculum problem arose because state grants for book
purchases could only be applied to materials approved by the Privy
Council Committee on Education. Only the Tablet and the Catholic
School took much note of this difficulty which was not extremely
important in comparison to others, but since curriculum is such a
significant test of whether Catholic education is in fact Catholic,
the topic requires some attention.

In October 1848 the Catholic School called for publication of
a whole series of Catholic school books. The article acknowledged

---

[142][Capes], "Popular Education," Rambler 10 (September 1852):
169-179.

that the Christian Brothers´ books were good but added that the books issued by the Commission of National Education in Ireland were more highly recommended. They were, the article contended, "the best educational course procurable in the English language."[143] The Poor School Committee defended the Irish Commission books throughout the period for the very understandable reason that they could be obtained cheaply through the Privy Council grants. But the Poor School Committee, through its reports and in the pages of the Catholic School also defended the books on their own merits and insisted that they were better than the Christian Brothers´ books.

The Tablet took less kindly to the Irish books which it said were "national" rather than Catholic and lacked "Catholic sentiment--not to mention meaning." The editor deplored their supposed merit of conveying the "blessings of sound and impartial education . . . unalloyed by the taint of proselytism or sectarian prejudice."[144] "In the slang of the godless everybody knows what impartial education and the ´taint of sectarian prejudice´ mean," said Lucas, and he went on: "they mean the education of Catholic children should be no more Catholic than Protestant."[145] The Tablet called for Catholic schools to use the Christian Brothers´ books. Finally, in the face of continued criticism, the Poor School Committee secretary eventually admitted in a letter to the

---

[143]"School Books," Catholic School 1 (October 1848): 27.

[144]Tablet, January 17, 1852, p. 41; ibid., January 24, 1852, p. 58.

[145]Ibid., January 24, 1852, p. 58.

editor of the _Tablet_ that the Committee had also preferred the Christian Brothers´ books. Stokes explained that an unsuccessful effort had been made to have them listed by the Committee of Council; he then appealed to practicality by pointing out that schools simply didn´t have book funds. Thus, he concluded not getting the Irish books meant not getting any books.[146]

There is no need to go into these details further or to quote discussions condemning one book and praising another. The dire financial needs of most poor schools undoubtedly left them with little choice but to use the Irish national books; in this it seems they were not alone, for the Irish books were used widely in non-Catholic schools throughout England for the same reason.[147] Yet this is certainly another example of the way state influence worked--a reminder of the fine line between permissive and compulsory influence. Schools were not officially obliged to participate in any state curriculum program; by circumstance they found themselves forced to do so.

General Assessment of the Catholic Poor School Committee

Outside the area of technical controversies the Catholic press coverage of the Catholic Poor School Committee was more widely distributed among the various Catholic publications. Even so, evaluation of the Poor School Committee derived from a detailed understanding of its work remained the exclusive province of the _Tablet_. Certainly the _Catholic School_ understood the issues, but

---

[146]_Ibid_.

[147]Hurt, _op. cit._, pp. 78-82.

as the official publication of the committee its point of view can hardly be considered disinterested.

Reviews of the Catholic School appeared in most Catholic periodicals; these sometimes served as the only notice given to the work of the school committee. Such reports seldom revealed much familiarity with Poor School Committee efforts and occasionally contained misinformation. Dolman's Magazine reported favorably on the Committee's work but only in a general way. Perhaps the only sensitive comment in its pages showed an awareness of the difficulty the committee had persuading parochial clerics to work with the government.[148] The Rambler was also complimentary in a general way, congratulating the Poor School Committee for its ability to "steer clear of the shoals which have hampered the progress of other kindred institutions," for its "united caution and energy," and for its firmness in resisting the "anti-Catholic devices of the government."[149] Two or three other articles pleaded with Catholics to support the committee, but the Rambler evidenced no particular awareness of the difficulties the committee encountered or of church-state confrontations. Similarly, the Dublin Review--which barely touched the education question at all--published only one review of the Catholic School, and that was singularly uninformative.[150]

The Weekly and Monthly Orthodox Journal paid little attention

[148]"Catholic School," Weekly Register [continuation of Dolman's Magazine], August 11, 1849, p. 38.

[149][Capes], "Popular Education," Rambler 6 (August 1850): 104.

[150]"Notice of Books," Dublin Review 27 (September 1849): 251.

to the Catholic Poor School Committee's affairs during its brief existence, though we find one review of the Catholic School which particularly recommended that rural clergy study that periodical and suggested that they suffered from a lack of understanding of either organizational techniques or teaching methods.[151] About the only other pertinent comment in this journal had to do with the Poor School Committee's first annual report. An article appeared on March 31, 1849 which discussed that report, but the writer found himself distracted by accounting problems; it seems he could not determine from the report what had happened to the furniture which had been owned by the old Catholic Institute.[152] That this was the only substantial question raised about the Poor School Committee report indicates the level of editorial concern with the church-state-education question, and if this initial article got lost in triviality its successors became ridiculous. Apparently no one ever did find out what happened to the furniture.

During this period the Catholic Standard contained virtually no editorial commentary on the church-state-education question, though it published abundant material on local poor schools. There were occasional references to Poor School Committee reports, but it is not possible to discern an editorial policy.

Of the Tablet's position enough has already been said to give an understanding of overall views on the committee's work as it was treated in this newspaper. That Lucas was extremely interested and

---

[151]"Catholic School," Weekly and Monthly Orthodox Journal, (July 21, 1849, p. 40.

[152]"Association of St. Thomas of Canterbury," Weekly and Monthly Orthodox Journal, April 4, 1849, pp. 281-282.

informed about the committee's efforts cannot be doubted, and the Tablet's careful coverage of educational questions was an important fact in itself. Its chief criticism of the committee was that it failed to demand sufficiently favorable terms for Catholics. It is difficult to determine whether the Tablet's role was essentially negative in its effect upon the Poor School Committee. A statement by Marshall suggests the Tablet's reporting was not altogether unappreciated:

> Do not suppose, however, that I wish to remonstrate either against your article upon the connection of the Catholic schools with the Government, which is a very proper question to be handled in a journal such as yours, or against your remarks having special reference to myself and my office. No one who knows you can doubt that, whether you speak about principles or individuals, you are influenced only by the desire to promote the welfare of religion and of the Church.153

It is important to stress the fact that the periodicals which objected to the Tablet's editorial policy concerning poor schools failed to provide anything approaching serious answers to the questions raised by Lucas. Thus they failed to defend the Poor School Committee against charges made in the Tablet. The questions raised by the Tablet had to do with how well the Poor School Committee negotiators understood the politics of the day, how well they were prepared to deal with the guile of the 'godless' Whigs, and how accurately they assessed the shrewdness and the aims of the Privy Council Committee. The defense of the Poor School Committee as presented in the Catholic School tended to rest primarily on two points--the desperate need for funds and the authority of the

---

153Marshall, "Letter from Marshall," Catholic School 2 (May 1852): 238.

bishops, but it must be admitted that such a defense was in fact a straightforward justification of existing policy rather than a means of providing substantive answers to challenges formulated in the Tablet.

In addition to the problems already discussed there was a problem which might be called the "undefined resistance" of many clerics and school committees to any cooperation with the government. Catholic School articles were constantly reiterating procedures, advertising the benefits to be got from the government, and urging local schools to apply for state monies. Even Cardinal Wiseman mentioned a "narrow feeling" which resisted the work of the Catholic Poor School Committee.[154] Wiseman was apparently referring to localism--the reluctance to turn affairs over to any centralized body--but there was also evidence that the Irish priests in poor Irish neighborhoods stoutly resisted all dealings with the government. The small number of applications for state building grants substantiates the strength of this resistance,[155] yet its exact nature is not specified in the contemporary Catholic press.

A possible explanation is suggested by Wiseman's 1852 pastoral describing the membership of the Catholic Poor School Committee, which, he said, consisted of a priest and "two gentlemen of high character and position" from each district. It was stressed that

---

[154]Nicholas Cardinal Wiseman, "The Cardinal Archbishop's Pastoral Letter in Behalf of the Poor-School Fund," Tablet, June 26, 1852, p. 402. It should be noted that the Tablet regularly published pastoral letters of the bishops, and Wiseman's annual letter in behalf of the committee was an important expression of support.

[155]Ibid.

all negotiations with the government had been carried on with

dignity and that the

> . . . patient perseverance and calm prudence of the com-
> mittee have conquered every difficulty and obtained terms
> which more influential religious corporations have com-
> plained they could not procure. And all this has been
> done in the most unostentatious way, without meetings, or
> speeches, or letters, or appeals to public feelings.156

Perhaps the Cardinal should have added that the committee's work

also proceeded without the wholehearted endorsement of the clergy.

Though such dignified methods appealed to upper class

Catholics it is hard to believe that they appealed equally to Irish

priests or the Irish poor. The great void in the history of the

Catholic Poor School Committee has to do with the committee's

dealings with the parochial clergy and their poor relationship with

the Christian Brothers.

One or two exchanges published in the Tablet do tell something

about the committee's relations with the clergy. In February 1851

the Tablet published an exchange between Henry C. Maxwell and two

members of the committee. Maxwell's letter admitted that the

committee and the bishops had proceeded on good intentions but

insisted that the safeguards they had relied upon had proved very

inadequate in other countries:

> Considering the long series of treacherous policy by
> which this country has sought to undermine the religious
> education in Ireland . . . we should not hesitate to
> distrust and canvass the motives which prompt any inter-
> ference . . .157

Both C. J. Pagliano and James O'Neal responded, and both argued

---

156Ibid.

157Tablet, February 1, 1851, p. 74.

that the committee had not trusted blindly to government assurances and that Protestant influence in the schools was impossible; but neither reply revealed any real understanding of the mentality of suspicion which pervaded Maxwell's letter and much of the Tablet's coverage.[158] Poor School Committee members could hardly have denounced the government as the enemy one day and carried their requests for aid to the Lords of the Privy Council the next, but they seemed to bend over backward to defend the good intentions of the Lords. Had their ranks contained only "respectable" upper class Englishmen such a policy might have been a winning one; under the circumstances it seems likely that this posture cost the committee the trust of many Catholics--not a few of them priests working in the poor schools most in need of funds.

Thus appears that ever-present problem of English history--the Irish problem. There is no denying that there was a great gulf separating English Catholic missions and those serving the poor neighborhoods concentrated in industrial cities, nor that this situation posed serious pastoral problems. Poignant evidence of this condition is to be found in an 1852 letter written by Wiseman to Frederick Faber concerning the Cardinal's desire to expand missionary efforts among the London poor. This letter has been published elsewhere[159] so there is no need to reproduce it here, but it is well to summarize its chief points. Wiseman described his previous efforts to secure missionary communities of religious

---

[158]See especially ibid., February 8, 1851, p. 90; and ibid., March 1, 1851, p. 132.

[159]W. Ward, op. cit., 2:115-153.

for this purpose and explained that Jesuits, Passionists, Redemptorists, Marists and Oratorians alike had come to London at his invitation and for this purpose only then to discover technical reasons making it impossible for them to work among the poor. Those technical reasons always had some relationship to their rules, which Wiseman never questioned, but he went on:

> Now look at the position in which I am. Having believed, having preached, having assured Bishops and clergy, that in no great city could the salvation of multitudes be carried out by the limited parochial clergy, but that religious communities alone can, and will, undertake the huge work of converting and preserving the corrupted masses, I have acted on this conviction, I have introduced or greatly encouraged the establishment of five religious congregations in my diocese; and I am just (for the great work) where I first began; not one of them can (for it cannot be want of will) undertake it. It comes within the purpose of none of them to try. Souls are perishing around them, but they are prevented by the rules, given by Saints, from helping to save them--at least in any but a particular and definite way! But what makes it to me more bitter still, from them comes often the cry that in London nothing is being done for the poor.160

It was in this context that Wiseman wanted Manning to establish the Oblates of St. Charles--thus one wonders how much of the Cardinal's appreciation for Manning related to Manning's social concerns. But this is to venture beyond the immediate topic. Wiseman clearly understood that the mission to the poor required a special approach, an understanding which failed to penetrate the work of the Catholic Poor School Committee.

160Ibid., 2:117-118.

CHAPTER IV

CHURCH-STATE-EDUCATION PROBLEMS, 1853-1858

The prominence of Parliamentary concern with the education question and the growth of the Manchester-based secular education movement would seem to suggest that church-state issues were central during this period, and yet it is not easy to discern whether this was the case. Few important measures affecting denominational day-schools were implemented, and none of them had any major impact on church-state questions which remained relatively stable. Even so, it would be a mistake to lay too much stress on that apparent stability. The purpose of this chapter is to describe and evaluate the Catholic assessment of these years of apparent calm.

The Privy Council Committee's innovations of 1846 and 1847 represented an acceptance of denominational control in English education, and although state aid made possible a significant expansion of the existing system there were few innovations in principle. This meant that the increase in the number of schools extended the influence of the religious bodies, especially the Church of England, which controlled the largest percentage of schools and received the greater part of the state funds. This arrangement, which divided influence between the religious bodies and the Committee of Council, dated from 1833; however, it was not regarded as permanent, and the first substantial signs of its disruption appeared during the 1850s.

Independent executive authority and the growth of denominational control in education were at odds with fundamental characteristics of the age: democratic sentiment calling for Parliamentary supremacy manifested itself in the cry for a Parliamentary solution to the education question; that cry was most often expressed in terms of the need for one "national" school system. This is the aspect of educational history which has received the most attention by historians. At the same time political anticlericalism and mid-Victorian intellectual trends militated against Anglican parish schools and undermined commitments to religious education. More importantly, the exasperation of sincere Christians with what appeared to be the petty obstructionism of sectarianism contributed to the increasing willingness of many to eliminate the religious difficulty by eliminating doctrinal instruction altogether.

The 1850s were years of confrontation between executive and parliamentary forces in general, and this applied to educational politics as well. Because the preliminary tests of authority produced no definitive results these years constituted something of a calm interlude. Historians have often described the third quarter of the nineteenth century as a period of balance, and this description is appropriately applied to the educational situation. Intellectual influences which would eventually have some impact on the general understanding were in a fairly quiet state of equilibrium. The power of the Oxford Movement and Church renewal were on the decline; the height of the Evangelical spirit had passed, and certainly the influence of Benthamites had seen its peak. On the other hand Darwinism, Positivism and the impact of Biblical criticism were yet in the future. In religious politics the battles against church rates were continuing in the vestries, and outbursts of ´no-popery´ could be found here and there, but church-state problems had become less prominent.

Beneath the surface fundamental changes were underway. Dissenters were realigning their forces, moving into local politics and developing their political bases in municipal corporations.[1] Although a substantial segment of Dissent had withdrawn into Voluntarism, Voluntarists were not necessarily politically inactive. It might even be said that this was merely a short term policy which was discarded as soon as Nonconformists felt secure enough in local politics to assert themselves. Much historical research remains to be done on this general problem, but we can say that Voluntarism was still very much present during the 1850s, which was no small factor in accounting for a state of apparent equilibrium in education.

The Crimean War contributed to the mid-Victorian balance by shifting political preoccupations away from domestic issues. Throughout the Palmerston years this emphasis on foreign affairs continued to characterize English politics. However one explains the mid-Victorian balance it is clear that the time was not at hand for either political or educational reform. Despite this there

---

[1]For an example of the way this was done see Welch, op. cit., which treats the work of the Birmingham reformers as it related to the national movement for popular education, 1840-1877.

were several substantial attempts to achieve a Parliamentary settlement in education, and a few important measures were actually passed which touched on peripheral educational questions--reformatories and industrial schools.

During these years, specifically 1853-1858, the Catholic press continued to publish general theoretical discussions about educational policy. At the same time that press presented debates over the management clauses, inspection, and curriculum, and it evidenced increasing concern over the probability of a major Parliamentary move. Consideration of the Catholic press assessment of 1850-1852 legislative proposals was omitted from the preceding chapter because that response was only minor and because the measures discussed belonged more appropriately to the period presently under review. Since the major educational developments of the 1850s were directly or indirectly related to proposed legislation, a quick review of those measures as seen by the Catholic press will help define the chronology of the period.

Before examining the press coverage of these measures it is helpful to make a few preliminary observations about the periodicals and newspapers under study. Necessarily this discussion will concentrate upon the Tablet, the Catholic Standard (which became the Weekly Register and Catholic Standard in May 1855), and the Dublin Review. The Rambler did not treat pertinent legislation during this period, though its approach to related questions will be characterized. The Catholic School ceased publication in September 1856 and cannot be said to have given extensive coverage to legislative questions. Brief references must also be made to a

Liverpool publication, the Catholic Institute Magazine.

Three of these publications underwent major editorial changes during the period--the Tablet, the Catholic Standard and the Catholic School. The Rambler too experienced editorial transitions during these years which have been discussed elsewhere and had little to do with the education question except perhaps to decrease editorial interest in the subject.[2] T. W. Allies became editor of the Catholic School as of August 1853, the date of his appointment as secretary to the Catholic Poor School Committee.[3] There is no evidence that Allies had had an overriding interest in popular education, but he was an Oxford convert without a living and the Poor School Committee post was salaried. More will be said about his attitude toward the job below.

The Catholic Standard changed hands twice during these years, first in mid-1853, and then again at the close of 1854. Though almost nothing is known about the 1853 development[4] it is certain that Henry Wilberforce assumed control in 1854 and held his post until 1863. He had long been an associate of Manning[5] and was a

---

[2]Altholz, op. cit., pp. 7-82, treats this period of the Rambler's history. See also McElrath, Richard Simpson: 1820-1876, a Study in XIXth Century English Liberal Catholicism (Louvain: Bibliothèque de L'Université, 1972), pp. 53, 58, 63; and the Wellesley Index, 2:734-737.

[3]Mary H. Allies, Thomas William Allies (London: Burns and Oates, 1907), p. 83.

[4]Catholic Standard, June 4, 1853, p. 4. This is the issue in which this particular editorial change was announced, but of course no names were provided.

[5]David Newsome, The Parting of Friends: A Study of the Wilberforces and Henry Manning (London: John Murray, 1966), pp. 220-221.

friend of Newman, but his place in Catholic circles must yet be pieced together from the various letters and diaries of the period.[6] One fact of importance here is that Manning and Wilberforce were active in Anglican educational expansion as far back as 1838 when they helped form diocesan organizations to promote schools. Since Wilberforce was in Ireland for two years before his acquisition of the Catholic Standard[7] he cannot have been intimately involved in the English Catholic educational developments. But, as will be seen, he used his newspaper to bring the whole question more vividly before the attention of English Catholics after 1854.

The most important change of personnel in Catholic journalism, however, resulted from the death of Frederick Lucas in 1855.[8] Large sectors of the Catholic population had resented his Irish politics and his inclination to engage in personal invective, but Lucas had been a powerful influence on the Catholic press and an energetic and perhaps unequalled Catholic Member of Parliament. His loss was deeply felt, as J. G. Snead-Cox suggests:

---

[6]Except for Newsome, ibid., there is little biographical material on Henry Wilberforce. It would be especially interesting to know what his relations with Wiseman and Manning were during the 1850s, given their mutual interests in social questions.

[7]Dessain, Letters and Diaries of Newman, 21:569. In Dublin Wilberforce served as secretary to the Catholic Defence Association.

[8]Because the influence of Acton and Simpson on Catholic controversies during this period was so prominent it would seem that the Rambler editorial changes might be considered as equally important, but neither the Rambler nor its editors enjoyed the wide base of support which Lucas enjoyed. Moreover, Lucas' Parliamentary career extended his influence. As a Catholic M. P. Lucas had no rivals during this period, which fact was even acknowledged in the Rambler.

> For fifteen years he had fought their battles with a
> courage which had taken their breath away, and an ability
> which had compelled their reluctant admiration; and, in
> spite of his violence, and in spite of his absorption
> during the later years in purely Irish politics, he
> remained the man they were proudest of. His death left a
> great blank.9

Lucas had devoted special attention and energy to the education questions of the day--both in England and in Ireland--and his absence from the columns of the Tablet and from the debates in Parliament was a misfortune for the cause of Catholic education. His successor was J. E. Wallis; though he was perhaps a man of lesser talent, Wallis had a certain interest in education and carried on the Tablet's tradition of attending carefully to educational problems.10

Proposed Legislation and the Catholic Press

It would be difficult to separate the proposals of this period from the educational movements which originated in Manchester. There, in 1847, the Lancashire Public School Association was formed for the purpose of establishing a system of secular education in that county.11 The association's aims were to replace central control with local political control, to provide aid on the basis of need rather than on the basis of the local capacity to raise

---

9J. G. Snead-Cox, The Life of Cardinal Vaughan (London: Herbert & Daniel, 1910) 1:187.

10Wallis' acquisition of the Tablet was announced in the issue of March 22, 1856, p. 184. It is interesting that the Tablet of April 9, 1853, p. 229, stated that Wallis was one of the candidates for the post of secretary to the Poor School Committee, which post Allies assumed in August of that year.

11Maltby, op. cit., pp. 67-75.

funds--a Privy Council policy which was viewed as self-defeating--
and to provide schools for those not connected with the denominations. Local political control over schools was to be established
and those schools were to be free from all creeds, and therefore
free from the hopeless disagreements which characterized Victorian
denominational squabbling.[12] It was characteristic of Manchester
politics during this period that the movement attracted the interest of prominent Members of Parliament.[13] Though the secular
principle of the association was successfully challenged in 1849,
that policy had been secured by 1850 when the scope of the movement
was expanded. The name was changed to the National Public School
Association, and its proclaimed intention was to formulate legislation for a national secular education system. By this time
interest in the movement had increased and Richard Cobden had
become one of its chief proponents.[14]

In 1851 another Manchester committee was formed to counter the
secularist schemes of the National Public School Association. Encouraged by the former secretary of the Privy Council Committee,
Kay-Shuttleworth, a group of Manchester citizens founded the
Manchester-Salford Committee on Education. Its program also called
for local school taxes (rates), free education, and assistance on
the basis of need, provisions which were in agreement with the
National Public School Association proposals. But the Manchester-
Salford Committee objected to secular education in principle and

---

[12]Ibid., pp. 67-81.

[13]Ibid.

[14]Ibid., pp. 75-80.

proposed to apply school taxes to existing denominational schools.[15]

In all this discussion about secular education one must keep in mind that prominent historians have reminded their readers that most of its proponents were Christians, not a few of them ´ministers of religion.´ There is little reason to dispute such claims, but they are generally intended to suggest that those attacking the so-called "secularists" were unfairly attributing anti-Christian or antireligious motives to the work of respected Christians. There was a degree of this, for in the realm of public debate abuses are ever present. But it will be shown that Catholic journalists were not engaging in mere rhetoric when they attacked proposed schemes as furthering the cause of secularism. It cannot be forgotten that defenders of certain secular schemes were always eager to dissociate themselves from purely secularist intentions, and a fair historical evaluation of their intentions is surely called for--but that should be complemented by an accurate estimate of the character of their schemes. Since Catholic journalists were among the most outspoken critics of secularism, their judgment cannot be taken as a sufficient test of historical truth, but we will see that their willingness to credit the proponents of such schemes with honorable--even Christian--intentions did not affect their judgment that the proposals themselves would prove harmful to the Christian basis of English civilization.

In view of the importance of the Manchester movement one might

---

[15]For a discussion about the Manchester-Salford Committee on Education see _ibid._, pp. 82-94.

expect to find considerable press coverage of the movement, but the
extent to which Catholics--even in Manchester--were concerned with
this movement is not clear. What is clear, however, is that
Catholics feared that the schemes originating in Manchester might
make their way into the statute books.

A rather substantial number of education bills were submitted
for Parliamentary consideration in the years 1850-1858, and it is
impossible to detail each and every proposal here, but it is necessary to discuss the first in this series of proposals, that introduced by William J. Fox on February 26, 1850. Although he was a
vice-president of the Lancashire Public School Association, his
bill was neither supported nor opposed officially by that organization. It provided for educational expenses to be paid out of the
local rates and gave locally elected school boards power to determine what religious instruction would be supplied.[16] The Tablet
reported on the bill briefly on March 16, identifying it as the
work of the Radicals, denouncing it for excluding doctrinal instruction, and comparing the Radical movement in England with the
Irish ´godless colleges´ movement.[17] At this time Bishop
Ullathorne issued a pamphlet, Remarks on the Proposed Education
Bill, which attacked the Fox bill for divorcing education from
religion. Although the bishop said it was scarcely possible that
the measure would pass, he used the occasion to pronounce his views
on secular education. The pamphlet was reviewed by the Tablet, the

---

[16]Adams, op. cit., pp. 152-154.

[17]Tablet, March 16, 1850, p. 169.

Rambler, and the Catholic Standard;[18] all agreed with its supposi-
tions, but neither the bill nor the pamphlet produced much Catholic
reaction. This can also be said for bills introduced throughout
1850 and 1851.

The Tablet was the only paper to pay attention to the
Manchester education movement as such, but reporting on this was
generally tucked away in provincial notices concerning diocesan or
other local news. There was some discussion of the work of the
Manchester-Salford Committee because the Catholics of the diocese
made an attempt to work with that committee. When it failed the
Catholics of Manchester and Salford issued a declaration, signed by
bishop and clerics alike, explaining their withdrawal from the
effort. This declaration, published in the Tablet and the Catholic
School, blamed the committee for discriminating against Catholics
and violating their rights of conscience.[19] One of the "obnoxious
elements" in the scheme was the requirement that the authorized
version of the Holy Scriptures be read in all schools; other bases
for complaints involved technical details which were said to operate unfairly with respect to Catholics. Neither publication provided editorial comment on the matter, and it was not discussed
further.

The 1851 and 1852 bills need not be described in detail since
there was hardly any chance of their passing and the Catholic press

[18]Ibid., March 23, 1850, p. 185; Catholic Standard, March 30,
1850, p. 7; and "Short Notices," Rambler 5 (May 1850): 476-477.

[19]Tablet, May 31, 1851, p. 338; "The Manchester Education
Scheme," Catholic School 2 (December 1851): 209-211; and see ibid.,
pp. 211-214, for background information and the committee's response.

paid no attention to them.[20] What does need to be said is that the
bills embodied the principle of local rating and introduced means
for different forms of local control. The fundamental aims of the
Manchester-Salford bills involved the safeguarding of denominational control over education; this would have perpetuated religious
pluralism in the schools. The chief aim of the National Public
School Association proposals was to secure a so-called "national"
system whereby children of different denominations would be brought
into one school. Thus there was agreement over the desired means
of financing by local taxation but basic disagreement over the
employment of the funds. The character of the quarrel remained the
same, though its scope extended throughout England, until the
passage of the 1870 education act.

It is no exaggeration to state that the history of "national
education" in England has only reflected one side of the story. It
is generally said that everyone more or less agreed upon the desirability of having all the children in the same school but that
squabbles over religious government of the schools got in the way.
The problem is that there is altogether too little evidence to show
that everyone did more or less agree that all children should sit
in a single school. The struggle over religion was a struggle to
preserve the identity of the distinctive denominational positions.
Sometime during the mid-1860s alignments in that struggle changed;
how and why that happened is not clear. But during the period
under consideration here the identity of denominational peculiar-

---

[20]See Maltby, op. cit., pp. 82-94.

ities in the schools was a major issue. This fact has not been sufficiently acknowledged.

The Catholic press coverage of the proposals put forward during this period shed some light on these general questions, but only indirectly. In general it may be said that the press opposed all the measures put forth on one of two grounds: that such measures would, directly or indirectly, cause secular subjects to predominate over religious subjects, and that the freedom to teach Catholic doctrine was threatened. There was also strong resistance to efforts to extend Anglican influence in education, but the other two factors were more influential.

Perhaps more important is the fact that the press coverage of this legislation reveals the details of these measures to have been complicated in much the same way as the reform bill of 1832 was complicated. For years historians overemphasized the uniform franchise established by the Great Reform Bill until Norman Gash showed that the complex schedules not only failed to provide anything like a uniform settlement but in fact secured in ingenious ways the maintenance and even extension of control by the existing representative interests which governed England.[21] One encounters a similar kind of difficulty with respect to educational history. Historians who bother to review the legislation proposed during the 1850s stress the fact that local taxation and local political control were the fundamental provisions; the result is that a kind of uniform momentum is pictured. When the bases of local taxation

---

[21]Norman Gash, Politics in the Age of Peel (London: Longmans, Green, 1953), pp. 3-33.

as discussed in the Catholic press are examined one measure is found to have given the taxing power to the Poor Law Unions, another to the vestries or the town councils, while others would have created new bodies to manage education and collect the education rates. It becomes extremely clear that the specific political boundaries defining the bases of taxation also affected the character and religious composition of the local body which would govern the schools. The extent to which the press coverage focused on such details suggests the need for exhaustive comparative legislative analysis.

In 1853 Lord John Russell introduced a government education bill, generally referred to as his "borough bill," but he made no real attempt to have the measure passed. Russell's bill provided that boroughs could extend aid to existing schools out of the rates in order to pay school fees. The Catholic Standard and the Tablet hardly noticed the measure, and it received no attention elsewhere in the Catholic press. The Standard issued a pro-Whig editorial on the bill in April, noting that Russell intended to leave the existing school system intact and expressing great respect for him.[22] The Tablet gave no editorial space to the matter and confined its coverage to a description of the bill's thirty-three sections.[23] The Tablet's failure to provide editorial discussion seems rather

---

[22]Catholic Standard, April 9, 1853, p. 8. One interesting aspect of this editorial is its inclusion of somewhat simplified discussion about the National Society and the British and Foreign Schools Society, which suggests either that the editor was just learning about these organizations or thought most Catholic readers were unacquainted with their work.

[23]Tablet, April 16, 1853, p. 245.

surprising given Lucas' usual inclination to attack Russell's educational policy.

During 1854 both the Tablet and the Catholic Standard showed great concern over two bills providing education for juvenile vagrants and criminals, both of which passed into law. Despite the fact that such measures are not generally discussed as part of the popular education movement, it is clear from what was published in the Catholic Standard and the Tablet that Catholics believed these measures were central to Catholic concerns about education. It will be helpful, then, to examine briefly the press response to the industrial schools and reformatories bills in 1854 and in subsequent years.

The two measures passed in 1854 were alike in many respects, the major difference between them being that one was a private measure affecting only Middlesex while the other was a general bill affecting all of England. Coverage in the Tablet and the Catholic Standard was complimentary; where both papers published the same correspondence, as was often the case, it was identical. The Tablet, however, called the matter to the public attention as early as September 1853,[24] while the Catholic Standard did not notice it until the following year. In 1853 the Tablet predicted that if war could be prevented reform and education would be major topics in the forthcoming Parliament; at the same time the Tablet pointed out the importance of the forthcoming bill concerning the education of

---

[24]Tablet, September 24, 1853, pp. 617-618. This was an editorial which referred specifically to Adderley's Juvenile Offenders Bill and described the background of it.

juvenile offenders, to be introduced in Lords by Lord Shaftesbury and in Commons by Sir Charles Adderley respectively.[25]

War did interfere with the general debates on education, and the progress of parliamentary reform was delayed as well, but still the reformatories and industrial schools bills became important topics of controversy. Most of the information to be found in the Tablet and the Catholic Standard can be related in some way to the efforts of John Kyne, a priest in the Clerkenwell district of London, though Kyne himself claimed Lucas had alerted Catholics to the need to monitor these proposals.[26] Practically nothing is known about Kyne, but his letters were prominent in these papers over many months and occasioned numerous editorials concerning the industrial schools and reformatories bills before Parliament. The letters described the bills, analyzed their probable effects and showed how these measures had been engineered to "bring about a wholesale and legal perversion of Catholic children of the poorest class."[27] Kyne admitted that this was by no means the only intent underlying the movement, but he insisted that Lord Shaftesbury's connection with the affair and the publicity of the Ragged School Magazine proved the anti-Catholic intentions of many supporters.

Kyne attacked the way destitution was equated with crime as a pretext for confining destitute children to reformatory institutions. At the same time he complained that the two Catholic mem-

---

[25]Ibid; and ibid., November 12, 1853, p. 730.

[26]Catholic Standard, April 15, 1854, p. 2; and Tablet, May 20, 1854, p. 308.

[27]Ibid., January 7, 1854, p. 4.

bers of the Parliamentary committee considering the general bill
had not even attempted to have priests or Catholic laymen testify
before the committee or to secure safeguards for Catholic
children.[28] In February, when the committee's formal resolution
became known, Kyne expressed the fear that Catholics little understood the important practical terms of the bill.[29] The committee
was proposing three different types of institutions: penal reformatories for criminal children convicted of serious crimes, non-
penal reformatories for educating and correcting children convicted
of minor offenses, and district pauper schools. The penal reformatories for convicts were to be entirely under state control; the
non-penal reformatories for convicts were to be supported by state
and local funds, while the pauper schools were to be supported and
controlled by the Poor Law Guardians. All were to be under
Anglican control insofar as religious instruction was concerned.
This would have meant that all Irish Catholic children brought
within the scope of this law would have been subjected to
Protestant indoctrination, and Kyne quoted from the testimony of
numerous witnesses to show that this was not an accidental by-
product of the committee's efforts. Two factors worked to produce
this state of affairs: the belief--supposed or real--that the Irish
street children were virtual heathens was the stated justification
for such proselytizing, and the deliberate anti-Catholicism of men
like Lord Shaftesbury contributed to the formulation of policies
which would assure Protestant control. Kyne admitted that many

---

[28]Ibid., pp. 4-5.

[29]Ibid., February 11, 1854, pp. 82-83.

Protestants sincerely believed that poor 'hoodlum' children were heathens, but he insisted that they were unable to understand the extent to which religious zeal and apostacy could thrive side by side in the crowded slums, and he called on Catholics to protect these children from proselytizing institutions.[30]

By mid-April Kyne had turned his attention to the Middlesex Industrial Schools Bill which also disregarded the rights of conscience of Catholic children.[31] The specific means whereby Catholic children were discriminated against in this measure were clever. On the one hand the bill provided that parents not wishing their children to receive religious indoctrination by Protestants were required to make special requests exempting them from the religious instruction; this provision, Kyne noted, differed significantly from existing provisions of the Poor Laws whereby the children themselves, their guardians, or their parents could make such requests. On the other hand the bill conferred upon magistrates the power to oblige parents to pay part of the upkeep expenses for their confined children. Of course the latter provision all but guaranteed that poor parents would not make special requests concerning the religious education for their children.[32]

The other dangerous provision had to do with the bill's definition of the offenses which could result in arrest and confinement. Since it applied to children arrested for vagrancy it meant

---

[30]Ibid.

[31]Catholic Standard, April 15, 1854, p. 2; and ibid., April 29, 1854, p. 6.

[32]Ibid., May 6, 1854, p. 5.

that minor technical infractions of police regulations could result in several years' incarceration.[33] These so-called "vagrants" included hundreds upon hundreds of poor children who made their livings in the streets, selling flowers and wood or engaging in other kinds of street commerce so characteristic of the period. Because of the prominence of the Irish among this street population and because of the support given this measure by Lord Shaftesbury and the Protestant Alliance, Kyne was convinced that the bill was intentionally aimed at the Irish poor.[34]

Due to Kyne's appeals three Catholic priests--Kyne himself, Frederick Oakeley, and a Jesuit, James Rowe,[35] testified before the committee considering the Middlesex bill. They obtained certain concessions from the committee, but these were lost in the House of Lords; and both this bill and the general bill went through Parliament containing provisions believed to be extremely damaging to Catholic interests.[36]

During July and August of 1854 the Tablet published another series of articles on the reformatories question, this time written by William Anthony Hutchison, a priest of the London Oratory.[37]

---

[33]Ibid. See also ibid., April 29, 1854.

[34]Tablet, January 7, 1854, pp. 4-5; and ibid., May 6, 1854, p. 276.

[35]Ibid., May 13, 1854, p. 292.

[36]Ibid., May 20, 1854, p. 308; ibid., July 8, 1854, p. 424; and ibid., July 15, 1854, p. 441.

[37]Ibid., July 8, 1854, pp. 424-425; ibid., July 15, 1854, p. 441; ibid., July 22, 1854, p. 457; and ibid., August 5, 1854, pp. 489-490.

In his first letter Father Hutchison quoted extensively from a letter by Henry Pownell, M. P., published in the Ragged School Magazine and proving that the Middlesex bill was aimed at Catholic children and intended to counter "inroads" Roman Catholics had been "trying to make in our prison arrangements."[38] Pownell had predicted that the concessions won by Catholics in committee giving priests certain privileges in attending children in the reformatories--including saying Mass--would be struck down in Lords; Pownell had also argued that nothing so revolutionary as allowing priests to say Mass should be introduced in a private bill. Father Hutchison pointed out that this was inconsistent with Pownell's being so anxious to gain Parliamentary approval, for the first time, of the "much more novel principle" of establishing reformatory institutions via private legislation.[39]

Hutchison's second letter reported that the Lords had rejected the clause protecting Catholic interests and the bill had been passed. The chief thrust of this letter had to do with the way the measure threatened innocent children who could thus be summarily placed in institutions for one to three years where they would be deprived of their religion. Protestant philanthropists were to blame, he said, for speaking of poor Catholic children in universal terms, as though all "without exception, are sunk in one universal slough of vice and ignorance." The author pleaded for a greater public awareness of the many innocent and virtuous children who lived in the slums but who could easily become involved in

---

[38]Ibid., July 8, 1854, pp. 424-425.

[39]Ibid.

minor infractions of police regulations--without having any moral
guilt or committing any really serious offense.[40]

The reformatories and industrial schools question continued to
concern Catholics over the next few years, and the Catholic press
took a considerable interest in the matter. During 1855 both the
Tablet and the Catholic Standard, which became the Weekly Register
in May, reported faithfully all Catholic efforts to establish
reformatories or industrial schools of their own; these efforts
were quite substantial.

Perhaps the most helpful article on the subject appeared in
the December 1855 Dublin Review.[41] Written by R. J. Gainsford, the
article summarized the provisions of the general bill passed in
1854 (17 and 18 Vict., c. 86), and a supplementary measure passed
the following year (18 and 19 Vict., c. 87). The manner in which
the act empowered magistrates to sentence youthful offenders to
reformatory institutions has already been noted. Gainsford clarified the provisions as they affected religious rights and stressed
the permissive character of the law. It allowed voluntary agencies
to establish reformatories and industrial schools, subject to certification by the government inspector of prisons. This meant that
Catholics could establish their own reformatories, and they began
to do so. Those schools were to be initially approved by the
prisons inspector and then open to the schools inspectors who were
empowered to visit such institutions from time to time and to

---

[40]Ibid., July 15, 1854, p. 441.

[41]Robert J. Gainsford, "Catholic Reformatory Schools," Dublin
Review 39 (December 1855), pp. 312-328.

recommend the withdrawal of any institutions already certified.[42] Although the government would not build or contribute to the building of such institutions, it was empowered, should Parliament approve, to pay the costs of maintaining and training the inmates, up to five shillings a week per child.

The religious difficulty stemmed from the power of the magistrates to detain offenders in any reformatory. Catholics feared that the magistrates would send Catholic children to Protestant institutions. The Home Secretary, however, had the authority to order the transfer of any inmates to other institutions certified by the government. Still, the protection of Catholic children was subject to the good will of either the magistrates or the Home Secretary. Gainsford expressed some hope that the matter would be executed fairly, but on the whole his article revealed deep distrust of the magistrates on the one hand and the Home Secretary´s bureaucratic machinery on the other.[43]

The one aspect of the act which received Gainsford´s whole-hearted approval was its underlying principle of extending aid to education in proportion to real need; this he described as an immense improvement over the Privy Council system and as what the Catholics wanted as a general governmental policy. Gainsford strongly urged Catholics to take advantage of the legislation to establish their own reformatories, and he noted the progress already underway--at Brock Green, in Yorkshire, and in the Midlands.

---

[42]Ibid., pp. 314-315.

[43]Ibid., pp. 318-320, 327-328.

This progress had been made possible by organized regional efforts which, he said, showed that Catholics could improve the local basis of political and educational activity. He urged that these newly established organizations be expanded and made applicable to primary school systems in the same localities, and he suggested that the Catholic Poor School Committee develop regular communications with these regional organizations for further promoting education.[44]

Throughout 1856 the Weekly Register (formerly the Catholic Standard) reported the progress of the Catholic reformatories movement. The new reformatories were widely publicized and Catholics were encouraged to avail themselves of state funds, but there was little in the way of talk about basic church-state problems. Then in 1857 two additional measures were introduced which generated much concern within the small circle of Catholics concerned over this important pastoral problem. During the year bills by Sir Charles Adderley and Sir George Grey were discussed in the Weekly Register, the Tablet, and the Dublin Review. Grey's reformatories measure would have empowered town councils and county magistrates to establish and maintain reformatories. R. J. Gainsford wrote to the editor of the Weekly Register expressing fear that the measure would ruin institutions built on a voluntary basis and would thus threaten the Catholic movement; the editor of the Weekly concurred.[45]

---

[44]Ibid., pp. 316-320, 327-328.

[45]Weekly Register (February 14, 1857, p. 4; ibid., February 28, 1857, pp. 6, 8.

In March 1857 Cardinal Wiseman contributed a lengthy article in the Dublin Review, "The State of Catholic Affairs," which discussed Adderley's Industrial Schools Bill in detail. This important article revealed the Cardinal's detailed interest in social legislation in particular and in social-political questions in general. In addition to describing the progress of certain parliamentary struggles affecting Catholics, the Cardinal raised the question of the political responsibilities of Catholic Members of Parliament as well as Catholic electors. He virtually appealed to the Irish Catholic members to safeguard English Catholic interests, stressing the need for great attention to subtle riders and amendments which were so often tacked onto measures to damage Catholic rights. The Cardinal even touched on the disestablishment of the Church of Ireland and treated the explosive question of tenant rights.[46]

In these pages the Adderley (industrial schools) measure was described as a twofold threat to Catholics. It neutralized the religious safeguards achieved earlier,[47] and it made detention of children in reformatory institutions even more arbitrary by permitting the confinement of children not convicted of any crime or misdemeanor. By this act the police would be empowered to take custody of children found wandering, begging, or sleeping in the

---

[46][Nicholas Cardinal Wiseman], "The State of Catholic Affairs," Dublin Review 42 (March 1857): 211-230.

[47]Ibid., p. 221. Balfour, op, cit., is the only general study which covered these details concerning industrial and reformatory schools; on p. 5 Balfour claimed that an act was passed in 1856 (19 and 20 Vict. c. 109) providing religious protection for children in these schools.

streets, to put them in the workhouse for up to forty-eight hours and then to send them to an industrial school.[48] If their parents provided certain "security"--money--the sentence was not to exceed six months, otherwise it could be extended at the discretion of government officials. Parents could object on grounds of religion if they did so within fourteen days and if they could pay the expenses involved in having the children transferred. As Wiseman observed,

> Let any one, acquainted with the feelings and habits of the destitute poor, in London, for instance, imagine how many of them will have leisure or courage to go before that object of his awe, a police magistrate, to complain of the policeman of his beat . . .[49]

Wiseman stressed that the parents had to ascertain where the child could be sent, obtain proof that said institution was duly certified, and pay for the transfer. "Is this even a possibility for a poor hard-working man?" he asked. "No--The child´s fate is sealed," he answered, and he noted that unless experienced assistance was offered the children of the Irish poor would be threatened by such a law en masse.[50]

The Tablet discussed the May Parliamentary debates making similar observations about the Protestant character of the scheme and its dangerous conferring of arbitrary power on police magistrates. The editor said that two Catholic members had attempted to divide the house on the measure but had failed.[51] In July the

---

[48][Wiseman], op. cit., p. 219.

[49]Ibid., pp. 220-221.

[50]Ibid.

[51]Tablet, May 16, 1857, p. 305.

Tablet reported passage of both the industrial schools measure and the reformatories bill and said that the only hope for Catholic children lay in a great extension of the Catholic reformatories and industrial schools movement.[52]

The most striking characteristic of this coverage is its incompleteness; all that is made clear is that there were provisions here that were detrimental to Catholics and that it was believed the bills were aimed, at least in part, at the masses of Irish Catholic children in the slums. In addition this coverage reveals that prominent Catholics believed the reformatories and industrial school measures were part of the wider educational movement of the time. There seemed to be only a fine distinction between children committed to industrial schools and those sent to voluntary day schools--all were children of the poorest classes. That the state had the arbitrary power forcibly to commit non-criminal children to certain institutions suggests a dimension of the state's authority in education seldom discussed. Certainly further study of the industrial schools movement as it related to the broader movement is called for. More will be said about this when the Newcastle Commission report of 1861 is discussed. At this point it is necessary to return to the general educational legislation proposed during this period as it was seen by the Catholic publications of the day.

It was anticipated that Parliament would act on the education question in 1854, and the Tablet's awareness of the likelihood of

---

[52]Ibid., July 25, 1857, p. 472.

such a development was particularly acute. Early in the year the
editor predicted that if war did not disrupt domestic politics the
education question would be hotly debated. He observed that the
"shock of reform politics had been bridged in 1832, but that of
educational politics yet awaited such a test." The editor's greatest concern had to do with the increasing influence of secularism
in education. The pragmatic English had already discovered, he
said, that the lack of religious education was "no hindrance to
business." He believed this fact would have increasing appeal in a
nation which was already abandoning public worship--among a people
ever less willing to equate "respectability" with institutional
religion.[53] Save for such general editorial commentary, however,
the Tablet hardly touched on proposed education bills.

Although this was true of most other publications as well
during 1854, the Catholic Standard issued an editorial in February
which should be mentioned. Reminding readers how the Tories had
been responsible for the Irish education scheme, the editor observed that it was indeed remarkable that Sir Charles Adderley and
Sir John Pakington had introduced a supposedly liberal education
measure for Manchester; this was all the more remarkable because
Manchester had its own competent representatives who opposed the
Adderley-Pakington scheme. The editor suggested that the affair
had been contrived to win favors in behalf of Anglican education in
Ireland. Certainly this is a subject only indirectly related to
this study, but it suggests a contemporary awareness of the

---

[53]Ibid., January 28, 1854, p. 57.

relationship between the two educational questions of the day--in England and Ireland--which calls for further study. The editor also commented on the problem of local taxation included in the scheme, saying that it would become a perennial source of discord at the local level and would produce the tyranny of the majority in school matters. Accordingly an extension of the voluntary, denominational system was called for as the only feasible plan for a society characterized by religious pluralism. The editor acknowledged the influence of the Manchester movement but pronounced against its basic tenets: local rates and local political control.[54]

During 1855 four measures were introduced in Parliament, but only two of them received any serious attention in the Catholic press. One was a Tory bill, the other a Government measure.

The earliest discussion of 1855 education schemes appeared in the March issue of the Dublin Review. An article by Gainsford treated Lord John Russell's education bill and called it the "worst" scheme yet to appear. The bill proposed to give town councils and parish vestries authority to establish, control and maintain schools independent of existing denominational institutions. The religious instruction given in such schools was to be determined by the council or vestry. Gainsford was extremely critical of the way the measure permitted secular without religious education and of the provision for civic management committees. Because of Russell's earlier commitment to the denominational system he was condemned for a complete about-face; ironically the

[54]Catholic Standard, February 25, 1854, p. 8.

article implied Catholic support for Russell's 1853 proposal which certainly aroused no widespread support at the time. Again it was said that the whole operation of local government would be distorted if the school question were thrust upon the existing machinery. A disproportionate amount of time and talent would be devoted to the education question and municipal matters would become of secondary importance.[55] This line of discussion appears with sufficient frequency as to suggest that the desire for local political control over schools may have been less widespread than many historians have indicated.[56]

One observation found in these pages deserves special mention. Russell's 1853 bill recognized the existing pluralistic educational system and supported it without imposing unnecessary political interference. Gainsford said that this was the only feasible approach to the existing situation. His reasoning was straightforward: "The state cannot originate in this country a uniform religious system of its own," and so it should work with the existing system.[57] It was his view that the only alternative was politically controlled secular education, and that he believed was both wrong and unwanted. The historical accuracy of that statement about affairs in 1855 hardly seems questionable; yet the momentum of the unwanted alternative was already gaining.

The same article also discussed Pakington's proposal and the

---

[55][Gainsford], "Lord John Russell's Education Bill," Dublin Review 38 (March 1855): 213, 216-217.

[56]See also the Catholic Standard, March 31, 1855, p. 9.

[57][Gainsford], "Russell's Bill," p. 224.

National Public School Association scheme. The latter's secularist provisions Gainsford dismissed as being unsuitable for human beings having a soul. The Pakington scheme was condemned for providing for local political control of schools, which Gainsford said was wholly unacceptable to Catholics and would be both unnecessary and injurious to England.

The Tablet approached the subject of Pakington's scheme in March with a three-column editorial, but that editorial was more a discussion of what Protestantism had done to bring about the ruin of England than a treatment of actual measures proposed in Parliament.[58] Later in March the Catholic Standard published a substantial editorial about Pakington's bill, characterizing it as an attempt to extend Anglican education. This it said was a grave blunder because the time had long since passed when the Establishment could succeed in such a policy. Pakington would have given control over education to the same constituencies which elected the notoriously Anglican Poor Law Guardians in the counties and to town councils elsewhere. On this point the Catholic Standard reiterated the theme about school politics ruining local government. The editor claimed that the measure was supported only because it included the widely demanded local-rates financing of education. The ultimate outcome of local-rate-schools would be secularism, it was predicted, because local bodies would find themselves as unable to settle religious disputes as Parliament had proved itself to be, and the local bodies would give in to secularization. It was the editor's view, then, that the Pakington scheme

---

[58]Tablet, March 24, 1855, p. 185.

was proposed as a plan for Anglican extension but supported as a means whereby eventual secularization might be secured. The Standard editor pleaded with the Established Church to wake up to the fact that "the time for an exclusive education system had passed." He urged churchmen to join with all others who still desired religious education in a campaign to "get a system religious and yet fair to all parties."[59] This was believed to be possible if the local rate funds were distributed on a capitation basis among existing and extended denominational schools. But the Catholic Standard did not expect Anglicans to give up their obstructionist policy:

> What it can and what we fear it will do, is to resist and overcome, as unfavorable to itself, every proposal for religious schools, till the country is at least prepared to acquiesce in a merely secular system. Then the gentlemen will be glad enough to accept what we now propose, when neither they nor we together are strong enough to obtain it; for practical men of business feel more strongly day by day, that more than half the population of England has no education at all; it is neither taught at school nor trained at home, but simply left to ruin in the streets. Something might be done by secular schools; little enough we know; but as they hope much, and if the demand for religious education means that nothing is to be done at all, the very word will soon lose its hold upon the convictions of practical men.[60]

This constituted one of the strongest indictments of Anglican obstructionism found in the Catholic press during this period.

On April 28 the Catholic Standard published another editorial describing certain details of Pakington's bill and their capacity to secure Anglican control over the schools. Again the editor

---

[59]Catholic Standard, March 31, 1855, p. 9.

[60]Ibid.

stated his belief that any rate-based system would eventually be secularized. Similarly, the Tablet condemned the scheme and stressed that it would be ruinous to Catholic interests.[61] It was said the separation of religious and secular education on the ground that parents would teach religion at home was absurd, a "pure delusion."

While neither the Tablet nor the Catholic Standard provided any serious editorial coverage of Russell's proposal, both papers published reflective articles more or less prompted by the general thrust of the educational proposals discussed at Westminster during the year. In June a Weekly Register (formerly Catholic Standard) article entitled "Make Hay While the Sun Shines" insisted that Catholics should be more aware of the probability that a legislative educational settlement was to be expected soon. Catholics should thus be ready, it was said, and therefore they should take advantage of Privy Council money while it was available to build and staff as many schools as possible, before the new system was established on terms unfavorable to and unacceptable by Catholics.[62] During the summer the Tablet published a series of articles by Henry Formby defining certain fundamental principles of Catholic education and appealing to Catholics to sharpen their understanding of the situation in preparation for the inevitable legislative changes.[63]

---

[61]Tablet, May 12, 1855, p. 296.

[62]Weekly Register, June 30, 1855, p. 8.

[63]Formby's articles appeared in the following issues of the 1855 Tablet: June 9, pp. 362-363; June 16, p. 377; June 23, p. 394; June 30, pp. 410-411; July 7, p. 426; and July 14, p. 422.

Perhaps it is appropriate to mention here that after Wilberforce assumed editorial management of the Catholic Standard its coverage of social and political problems in England increased rather noticeably.[64] Despite this, little attention was given to general educational proposals in either Wilberforce´s paper or the Tablet during the 1856-1858 period. There was some mention of Russell´s 1856 scheme in both the Tablet and the Weekly Register, but no new themes were developed. Even so it became increasingly clear that the editors expected one of these bills to pass sooner or later. On the whole the remainder of this period was marked by disputes having to do either with the reformatories and industrial schools bill or with problems unrelated to proposed legislation. But before turning to other characteristics of the press coverage of church-state-education questions during these years some mention should be made of the Rambler´s posture with respect to legislative questions.

Throughout the 1853-1858 period the Rambler published no articles whatever dealing with the many educational proposals discussed in Parliament. It seldom discussed legislation as such, though there were articles treating the ´nunneries inspection´ controversy and the Maynooth grant.[65] Otherwise this journal only treated contemporary politics in a general way either offering historical perspectives or developing theoretical interpretations.

---

[64]A similar change took place in mid-1853 as well.

[65][Robert Ornsby], "Inspection of Convents," Rambler 12 (July 1853): 1-11; [Capes and Richard Simpson], "Education: the Maynooth Report," Rambler, 2nd ser., 3 (May 1855): 366-385.

Two or three of these general articles revealed the editor's views on certain questions vaguely related to the education problem.

In his "Catholic Politics and Catholic M. P.'s" (February 1855) Capes vigorously attacked the way Lucas mixed up his defense of Catholic interests with "certain political demands" supported by politicians whose character and speech merely strengthened prejudices against Catholicism. Capes was clearly referring to the Irish faction in Parliament and their policies concerning the union and tenant rights. Capes dismissed the tenancy question as one which was terribly "dry" to all save farmers and landlords.[66] Again in May 1857 he attacked Irish Catholic politicians for making tenancy appear to be a Catholic question when it was clearly a "purely economic and local question."[67] Capes expressed particular concern that this faction's claim to Catholic allegiance imparted an "ill odour" to English Catholicism. The editor was clearly pleading that such awkward political arguments be entirely dissociated from Catholicism.

With regard to what he called "other semi-political matters which have a peculiar interest for Catholics"--such as disabilities of Catholic soldiers, workhouse and hospital inmates--he insisted it was "perfectly useless to raise a disturbance on the general question." Instead he recommended that "civilly expressed" requests for redress be submitted to the proper authorities in individual cases. He urged Catholic Members of Parliament to "acquit

---

[66][Capes], "Catholic Politics and Catholic M. P.'s," Rambler, 2nd ser., 3 (February 1855): 91, 93.

[67]Idem, "The Political Future," Rambler, 2nd ser., 7 (May 1857): 331.

themselves of their duties with becoming sobriety and modesty, and a very moderate amount of speech-making.[68]

Capes' position was very much in line with that urged by the most 'respectable' members of old Catholic society, and the Rambler's position was not highly regarded in certain quarters as a result. All that need be said here of Capes' views on the Irish question is that hundreds of Protestant commissioners who had investigated conditions in Ireland during the nineteenth century knew very well that the tenancy question was anything but a local problem of interest only to a few farmers and landlords; and it is hardly likely that the Irish Catholics--bishops, clergy and laity combined--would have agreed that the tenancy question was totally divorced from Catholicism. It had been so thoroughly bound up with Protestant ascendancy and Protestant ascendancy was so bound up with the work of Parliament that Capes' conclusions appear naive at best; more probably they merely reflected the English Catholics' desire to avoid embarrassing political alliances which might ignite English 'no-popery' sentiments. Capes' judgment concerning the uselessness of treating English Catholic grievances as general political questions is even more problematic, for most of those grievances were somehow the result of legislation.

If these questions seem remote from the education question one need only be reminded that the vast population of Catholic poor children was Irish, and that the Rambler's stand on these Irish problems would not have been overlooked by the Irish in England.

---

[68]Ibid.

If the Rambler editor thought otherwise there is evidence in the pages of the contemporary Tablet that the Irish in England had been alienated by this journal, at least to some extent.[69] And so long as English Catholics were almost totally dependent upon the Irish Catholics in Parliament for the defense of Catholic interests, the protection of English Catholic poor schools was related to the Irish faction in Parliament.

That the basic tension between the Rambler and its opponents within the episcopacy was theological cannot be denied, but it is unfortunate that no attempt has been made to characterize the way social and political questions affected such tensions. For example, it will be seen in the following pages that the Rambler's treatment of the school question fitted into a much larger political controversy. And within the same period the article by Capes just cited followed and was in fundamental opposition to the social and political positions propounded by Wiseman in a March 1857 Dublin Review article.[70] Wiseman's concern with the social and political dimensions of the enormous pastoral problems posed by the presence of masses of poor Irish Catholics in England has not been

---

[69]Tablet, May 16, 1857, p. 314. There is also coverage in the 1854 Catholic Standard concerning a dispute between an Irish theologian, Dr. D. W. Cahill, and the Rambler, which disturbed the Irish in England; see Cahill's Works of the Rev. D. W. Cahill (New York: A. Franchi, 1854), pp. 108-122. The Rambler's 1855 obituary on Lucas, condemning his Irish policies, similarly angered many; see Capes, "Frederick Lucas," pp. 450-460. This question of the possible opposition to the Rambler among the Irish deserves further attention.

[70][Wiseman], "The Present Catholic Dangers," Dublin Review 41 (December 1856): 441-471, and ibid., 42 (March 1857): 245-248.

duly treated by his biographers,[71] so this dimension of his quarrels with contemporaries has been missed. Similarly this dimension of his alliance with Manning has been underplayed; both men were zealous pastors who expended extraordinary time and energy in behalf of the Irish poor whether in the cause of the poor schools, industrial schools, reformatories, missions, workhouses or hospitals. These were causes dear to both men, and overemphasis on the problem of theology and the Papacy has obscured an important part of this history. While the present study examines only one aspect of the question--that involving popular education--it is clear that wider study is needed.

Catholic Conflicts Over the State Grants

While editors speculated on the probable terms of the expected Parliamentary settlement of the education question, a dispute arose among Catholics over the terms of government grants to Catholic schools. Concern centered on the conditions of the trust deed and the power of the government inspectors, but the dispute was also aggravated by an underlying opposition to cooperation with a government which had so faithfully demonstrated hostility to Catholicism. The press controversy--for in fact the dispute was carried on in the columns of the press over a twelve-month period-- reveals deep divisions within the Catholic body. The controversy reached its peak during 1856 and 1857, but it was in the making

---

[71]Of course W. Ward, op. cit., remains the standard biography, but Brian Fothergill, Nicholas Wiseman (London: Faber and Faber, 1963) leaves this matter untreated. Similarly that by Denis Gwynn, Cardinal Wiseman (Dublin 1950), does not emphasize the Cardinal's interest in such matters to any great extent.

long before that time. It has been seen that the work of the
Catholic Poor School Committee was not universally approved by
Catholics and that Catholic relations with the government had
aroused widespread suspicion as soon as the inspectors began
issuing their official reports. In approaching the 1856-1857 disputes it will be helpful to review the formative period, 1853-1855,
and to begin that review by examining what the weekly press had to
say about the work of the Poor School Committee, its relations with
the state, and general aspects of state policy.

The _Tablet_'s appraisal of the work of the Poor School
Committee was critical long before 1853; that did not change during
the remainder of Lucas' life. But during 1853 the _Tablet_ attended
little to the committee's work. The articles that appeared had to
do primarily with legislation or with the Irish national education
system. But an editorial published in November touched on the
church-state-education problem and deserves mention. The editor
predicted that Parliament would legislate radical changes in the
education system and urged Catholics to prepare for battle by
clarifying their understanding of the situation. Lucas said that
the English idea of education as it related to religion was undergoing profound change. Protestants who had always insisted that
religion was the foundation of education were increasingly influenced by talk about the possibilities of secular education or the
separation of religion and secular subjects. The religious concern
was being pushed into a secondary position and becoming a matter of
private opinion, private judgment. Historically, Lucas observed,
attitudes about the state's responsibilities toward education were
changing, and at the same time the state was abandoning its duty to

enforce Protestantism it was assuming the function of teacher.

The Tablet editor viewed these trends with grave concern, for his understanding of the functions of government was traditional and conservative. Until lately learning was considered something distinct from civil government, but that notion was changing. The state was taking upon itself the duty of teaching at precisely the time when it was discarding its duty to enforce any religious doctrine; this meant that the state could not teach any kind of religion--nor could it teach anything upon which doubt could be cast. Lucas said this meant that the sphere of what the state could teach was both highly questionable and ever changing.

But the main problem arose from the fact that the state had "no knowledge or authority to settle disputes, and therefore the more those multiply on all subjects not immediately connected with law, the more circumscribed becomes the extent of its teaching." Considering the character of the state, its power to enforce its will--its capacity to compel obedience--Lucas argued that acquiescence in the theory that "it is a function of government to give even secular education" implied acceptance of the state's right "to enforce its own opinion in all the arts and sciences." This he concluded was nothing less than the power to "tyrannise over the intellect."[72]

Although these editorial comments were not specifically related to Catholic-state relations, Lucas' concern about the state's assumption of the teaching function was not altogether remote. The

---

[72]Tablet, November 12, 1853, p. 730.

examining power of inspectors had a direct influence--if not a controlling influence--on school curriculum, and that power was not limited by any agreements whatever. It remained for Ullathorne to develop this aspect of the question fully, but much of what was said in the _Tablet_ helped shape the thinking of many people on this subject.

During 1853 the _Catholic Standard_ reported on the progress of school building or on other educational developments, but there was little said about church-state-education questions. Still, it is worth noting that one finds here considerable coverage of general social and political questions affecting the Catholic poor, particularly after June 1853 when a change of editors was announced.[73]

During 1854 interest in the work of the Poor School Committee seemed to increase. Early in that year the _Tablet_ published two more editorials on the problem of secular education, reiterating views already discussed. In one of these, however, Lucas developed his thoughts on the dilemma posed by having the state provide secular education as a means of safeguarding freedom of conscience. "Liberty of conscience is a general principle of the grandest value in the eyes of educationalists, and they think that they save it when they propound their doctrine of secular education," Lucas observed; but he insisted that this scheme was an illustration of the "truth" that "Liberals are only despots in disguise." That despotism consisted in their desire to impose upon the majority a secular education which excludes all religious doctrine--merely to

---

[73]It has not yet been possible to identify the new editor who then assumed control.

preserve freedom of conscience for those who object to being taxed for the purpose of teaching religious views which they do not hold. According to Lucas the problem lay in the fact that "no account is taken of the conscience of those who object to establishing secular schools and paying for them." So while the Baptist's conscientious objections to paying for the Congregationalist doctrine taught with tax funds was to be respected, the conscience of the man who objected to secular education was to be coerced. Lucas concluded:

> Liberty is, as usual, one-sided . . . If it be unjust to spend the public revenue in teaching the religion of a minority, it is equally unjust to spend it for teaching what a minority only requires to be taught.[74]

In the spring of 1854 there was an exchange between Lord Edward G. Howard (a son of the Duke of Norfolk) and Charles Langdale concerning the failure of Catholics to support the Catholic Poor School Committee. Both the Tablet and the Catholic Standard published this correspondence.[75] On the surface this problem appeared to be only internal, having little to do with church-state relations; but the reason that the church-state question became so critical was directly related to the Poor School Committee's inability to raise sufficient funds. Howard's letter blamed English Catholics for a major failure resulting from apathy. This was no new accusation, and the financial needs of the committee were not new either. Both had been reported in the press from the first, but during the mid-1850s the committee's appeals for support revealed a growing anxiety over Catholic educational

---

[74]Tablet, February 4, 1854, p. 74.

[75]Catholic Standard, May 13, 1854, pp. 4-5; ibid., May 20, 1854, p. 7.

needs; this was complemented by an inclination on the part of those who wrote about the subject to locate the blame for the failure of the laity to support the committee's efforts.

One factor in this change had to do with the resignation of Scott Nasmyth Stokes who gave up his post as secretary to the committee to become a government inspector of Catholic schools.[76] He was succeeded by Thomas W. Allies, who served as the committee secretary for some thirty years after his appointment in August 1853. Stokes had been mildly outspoken as secretary and was to become even more so as an inspector, and Allies became extremely outspoken in ways which crystallized resentments against the committee. But in 1853 and 1854 these developments had not yet taken place. Allies' first major letter on education published in the weekly press appeared in 1854. It was not a controversial letter; it merely provided helpful details about the condition of Catholic poor schools. It is the first major letter on the subject of the poor schools stating explicitly that the education of the poor was fundamentally an Irish problem. The press coverage on the subject heretofore had made this eminently clear, but Allies was the first to say so openly.[77]

During the rest of 1854 the _Tablet_ published occasional letters on the committee's work, but only one suggestive of developing tensions. Written by a "town priest" and published on August 12, it suggested that the Poor School Committee efforts to

---

[76]_Tablet_, April 9, 1853, p. 229.

[77]_Ibid._, June 17, 1854, p. 379.

arouse public opinion were not based on a sufficient understanding of the question--but this writer failed to say just what the understanding should have been.

Meanwhile the Catholic Standard published a letter in July condemning T. W. Marshall's official report as inspector.[78] This is perhaps the first genuinely hostile letter published in the Standard, and it is also the first to speak openly about there being a real division. That division was clearly between schools accepting government inspection and those refusing all connection with the state. Unfortunately the writer, "E. T." is not identified. This letter claimed that the inspector's reports were not representative of Catholic poor schools because inspectors were forbidden entry into "three schools in every ten." The writer insisted that "the best schools in the metropolis declined the government connection altogether." The same writer attacked Allies' June public letter, mentioned above, for overestimating what remained to be done and underestimating what had been achieved.

Allies' estimate of the number of children who should be in schools had been based on the assumption that all children between the ages of three and fifteen should be in school; E. T. claimed this was altogether unrealistic because children over twelve almost invariably sought employment and children under six were hardly ready for school. Allies' statistics were also attacked on other grounds. It is not possible to go into the details of these statistical disputes except to say that they may reflect the difference

---

[78]Catholic Standard, July 22, 1854, p. 4.

between a willingness to accept government estimates and the desire
to calculate Catholic efforts independently. It is no great exaggeration to suggest that Victorian statistical analysis bordered on
being shoddy, so the dispute hardly seems worth attending to, yet
these details will have to be looked into if the numerical significance of the minority of schools opposed to the Poor School
Committee's efforts is to be evaluated.[79] The remainder of this
letter consisted of a description of one segment of the London
slums and its schools. Of twenty-nine schools described the writer
said only eight or nine were under government inspection.

Until this time no such detailed information about schools
refusing to cooperate with the government had been published in the
Catholic press, so in a sense this might be considered the first
letter in the controversy that became so acute in 1856.

On December 9, 1854 the Catholic Standard announced another
change in editorial management; it was at this time that Henry
Wilberforce acquired the paper.[80] In terms of comparative coverage
of the education question in 1855 there was a marked change, for
Frederick Lucas became more and more involved in his efforts to
form a Catholic party in Ireland and traveled to Rome in hopes of
securing papal support for that plan, the Tablet tended to cover
English questions less attentively. Then of course Lucas' journey

---

[79]The real problem in obtaining accurate data has to do with
determining the number of schools not related to the Poor School
Committee or the government; diocesan records would have to be
checked against other statistics in an effort to find discrep-
ancies.

[80]Gillow, op. cit., 5:584. See LD 16:227, Newman's letter of
August 16 saying that Wilberforce became editor in August.

to Rome destroyed his health, and his long illness and death followed in October. The decline of Tablet attention to English educational problems was offset by the Catholic Standard's increased attention to such questions; still, that shift in the balance was not thoroughly noticeable until 1856.

Despite a noticeable reduction in the Tablet's attention to English questions during 1855 it published a series of six articles by Henry Formby who treated church-state problems in depth and argued against all state interference in education. Since Formby became one of the chief opponents of all Catholic connection with government grants a brief summary of the position he expressed in the Tablet between June 9 and July 14 1855 should be given.

Formby's writing was laborious and much of what he said was repetitious, but two or three points should be mentioned here. In discussing the state's right to educate he insisted that the family had a prior authority over the education of children. God, he said, had given that authority over the education of children to the head of the family. The state's efforts to take that authority from the family was wrong in principle and would be ruinous in practice. Since the authority of the family was the foundation of all civil obedience, that authority was as necessary to the stability of the civil government as to the survival of religion. Formby insisted that state education would tend to lessen the child's dependence upon his parents and this in turn would eventually lead to a lessening of all sense of obedience. Thus state education, by encouraging independence of family authority, would lead eventually to independence of all authority, including that of the state.[81]

Formby treated the education question in historical perspective, claiming that Protestantism had deteriorated to a point where it was "impotent" to solve the problem. In exasperation Englishmen turned to the state for the answer. Instead, he said, they should look in the opposite direction for the solution--to the family. The authority of the family should be further encouraged--instead politicians were trying to find a substitute for it.[82] The implication of the argument, of course, is that there is no such substitute.

Formby also reiterated the often-stated argument that state funding for secular instruction would reduce the significance of the religious element in education; he further suggested that there was a fundamental logical error in the state's argument that religious and secular instruction could be divided because there was nothing wrong with the principle of the division of labor. All divisions of labor, he said, presupposed a "ruling mind that has the power to judge the qualities of the workmen" and to apportion the work appropriately. Such a division of power precluded one power intruding into a sphere belonging to another; but the state's idea of the division of power derived from an incorrect assessment of where authority over education resided.[83]

Formby's articles were general and philosophical and did not so much as mention the Privy Council grants, but the line of argu-

---

[81]Tablet, June 16, 1855, p. 377.

[82]Ibid.

[83]Ibid., June 23, 1855, p. 394.

ment presented here was clearly in opposition to the state's activities and implied opposition to the Catholic connection with the government. As it proved, Formby was very much opposed to the government grants to Catholic schools, on the terms offered, but his earlier writings failed to trigger any major controversy.

In 1855 the Catholic Standard (after May the Weekly Register) published several articles by Gainsford, who took issue with government policies and suggested that Catholics received too small a proportion of state funds as a result. At the same time Gainsford attacked the Poor School Committee for its general apathy and failure to win broader support among Catholics.[84] In July Gainsford made several suggestions for improving the committee's organizational structure and for winning a broader clerical base of support for its efforts. He urged parish canvassing by laity and clergy and called for the formation of diocesan and parochial organizations similar to those characteristic of Protestant efforts.

Again in September Gainsford pressed his views concerning the need for Catholic Poor School Committee reform. He expressed disgust with the Catholic addiction to the "habit of divergence" and suggested that perhaps if Lord John Russell would write "another Durham letter denouncing Catholic poor schools as aggressive and unconstitutional, or if Parliament would but (as they well might) . . . pass an act declaring all Catholic poor

---

[84]Weekly Register, May 19, 1855, p. 3; ibid., July 7, 1855, p. 5; ibid., September 22, 1855, p. 5; ibid., November 24, 1855, p. 10.

schools illegal, and visiting the subscribers, managers, and promoters of them with fines and imprisonment, the English Catholics
would then perhaps be thoroughly roused . . ." Although Gainsford
was not unduly sympathetic with the Poor School Committee, his
writings were hardly a direct assault on the committee's policies;
yet they appeared to have had the cumulative effect of putting
committee spokesmen on the defensive.

Meanwhile the Weekly Register (Catholic Standard) published
two editorials more or less encouraging Catholic poor schools to
take advantage of state aid. A June 23 editorial urged schools to
acquire more pupil-teachers, and an August 25 editorial broached
the subject of the building grants. The editor regretted the great
reluctance of Catholics to accept building grants and admitted that
"almost every Catholic school is erected without a grant." This
reluctance was attributed to a "general belief" that the government
conditions would interfere with the liberty of the school. That
fear was dismissed as groundless, since the bishops and the
Catholic Poor School Committee had declared it so and had expressed
"their wish to see the building grants received by Catholic
schools." The writer went on to specify the reluctance as stemming
from some general impression that the government required school
deeds to "be conveyed to the government officials so as to become
legally their property." Arguing that this was a misapprehension,
the editor explained that the government only "required that the
school be conveyed to the trustees in trust for the permanent
maintenance of a Catholic school." The writer admitted having got

this information from the Poor School Committee.[85] That it represented only part of the picture need hardly be stressed.

The same editorial advanced two additional arguments in defense of the Privy Council grants. It was claimed that money not spent by Catholics would be spent by Protestants to build schools which would compete with Catholic schools; and since the Privy Council system would eventually be replaced by a local rating system from which Catholics could not expect fair treatment, they should build all the schools they could with Privy Council funds.

Until 1855 neither the Dublin Review nor the Rambler contributed to this general discussion, though we have mentioned the Dublin Review's contribution to legislative questions prominent during this period. In August 1855 the Rambler published an article criticizing Catholics for their failure to take advantage of state assistance, particularly support for teacher training.[86] The main topic of the article was the whole problem of teacher training and the need for an increased number of lay school teachers. Taken in isolation the article might not have been controversial, but amid the growing discussion over the question of state funding it must be seen as a strong statement favoring the extension of the government connection.

During the early months of 1856 the tone of the general press coverage of the poor school questions remained pretty much the same. Beginning in January the Tablet published another series of

---

[85]Ibid., June 23, 1855, p. 9; and ibid., August 25, 1855, p. 8.

[86][Capes], "The Poor School Question," Rambler, 2nd ser., 4 (August 1855): 89.

articles by Henry Formby, nine in all, on the "resources of the nineteenth century for the work of instructing the ignorant multitudes." These articles were more specifically directed against the work of the English government than the earlier series, but Formby's comments still remained more or less theoretical. Regardless, viewed in the context of Lucas' earlier criticism of the government policy's effect on Catholic education, the Tablet's publication of Formby's views constituted a degree of editorial endorsement.

Wallis announced his official assumption of editorial responsibility in March,[87] and his attitude toward the question of government grants represented a departure from that maintained by Lucas. Still, the fact remained that the Tablet had been more critical than supportive of the government connection.

By the spring of 1856 the occasional attacks on the Poor School Committee and the opposition expressed against its relations with the state had become much more pronounced. The public controversy was carried on by a small circle involved in educational politics. The chief proponents of the government connection were Allies, Stokes and Marshall. At one time or another all three suggested that the government connection should be made compulsory for all schools applying to the Catholic Poor School Committee for aid. Since both Stokes and Marshall were government inspectors their pronouncements were particularly resented by those predisposed to oppose government influence. Allies, a salaried secretary

---

[87]Tablet, March 22, 1856, pp. 184-185.

of the Poor School Committee, was criticized for being a government partisan rather than a true representative of Catholic interests.

Allies was an Oxford convert (1850) while Marshall and Stokes were both Cambridge men who had converted earlier, Stokes in 1842 and Marshall in 1845.[88] Of their Catholic lives we know little, although Allies´ daughter has left some biographical material on her father.[89]

Following his conversion Allies faced social and material impoverishment which lasted until his appointment to the committee was settled in the summer of 1853. In the meantime he had taken his family to dingy lodgings in London where he took in students. It is difficult to say how he viewed the committee post, but he was known to chafe "at a routine which robbed him of his time."[90] Allies apparently had mixed feelings about this position, but his preference was for intellectual work--study and writing--and he admitted to suffering from a "malady" stemming from the belief that he had a mind and education above his station. As the years passed he seemed to grow increasingly devoted to aspects of the work, particularly that having to do with the establishment of teacher-training programs.[91] In any event, he remained with the committee until 1890 and there is no doubt that his contributions were substantial. Yet he seemed to resent his station in life and to long

---

[88]W. Gordon Gorman, Converts to Rome (London: Sands & Co., 1910), pp. 4, 185, 261.

[89]M. Allies, op. cit.,

[90]Ibid., p. 68.

[91]Ibid., pp. 79, 84.

for intellectual recognition. How these dispositions affected his relations with members of the committee or his dealings with the parochial or slum mission clergy is not known, but common sense would suggest that some of his confrontations with the opposition clergy stemmed from social and intellectual discontent.

Among the most outspoken opponents of the Catholic dealings with the government were Henry Formby and Bishop Ullathorne. The other major figure in the press disputes was Gainsford, about whom little is known except that he was a Sheffield attorney who wrote for the Dublin Review in addition to publishing voluminous correspondence in the Weekly Register.

Gainsford's attacks against the inadequacy of the Catholic Poor School Committee's efforts to win support among the Catholic population as a whole appears to have brought the controversy to a head, despite the fact that he never attacked the Catholic connection with the government as such. Rather, he accused the Poor School Committee of doing too little, and blamed the Catholic population for faults it refused to correct internally. At the same time Gainsford attacked the government's education policy--not for imposing unfair or dangerous conditions on Catholics but for failing to provide aid according to need. He opposed the principle of distributing the grant on the basis of local subscriptions and urged the adoption of a capitation grant generally. This was a rather commonplace complaint about government policy, and Gainsford's suggested alternative was similarly commonplace.

Allies, Stokes and Marshall reacted by defending both the Poor School Committee and the government against Gainsford's accusations. Had they been content to defend the committee they would have aroused fewer hostilities, for their defense of the Privy Council and its policies crystallized opposition to the very idea of Catholic cooperation with the English government.

At first the proponents of the government connection merely belittled all objections to their policies, claiming that the bishops had sanctioned and the Holy See approved the Poor School Committee's agreements with the Privy Council Committee on Education. The Weekly Register and the Rambler tended to go along with this line of argument, as did the Tablet, though to a much lesser extent. Wiseman, in the Dublin Review called for moderation, and Bishop Ullathorne stepped in with a powerful statement clarifying the bases for opposition to the government-imposed conditions. Ullathorne's move clearly heightened the dispute and angered the Cardinal, but it served to force fundamental facts into the open: (1) the objections to government conditions were not merely absurd, (2) they were embraced by a substantial minority, and (3) the whole question was bound up with the sentiments of and about the Irish poor.

This is the broad outline of the controversy. Now something must be said about characteristics of the press coverage. From May 1856 until the spring of the following year the Catholic Standard, and to a lesser extent the Tablet, published controversial correspondence and editorials on the question of whether the Catholic relations with the state were compatible with principles of Catholic education. The volume of articles published over this period is quite impressive; if all of it were put into a single volume it would make a substantial book. For the dispute was not limited to the two weeklies but extended into the pages of the Rambler, the Dublin Review and even Liverpool's Catholic Institute Magazine. It is important to note that there were no major articles on this controversy in the Poor School Committee's Catholic School. Its prominence declined substantially during this period, and the Catholic School ceased publication in September 1856. It would be interesting to know whether this had anything to do with the disputes over the committee's operations and the government grants, but that information is not available. The committee's views, however, were adequately represented in the weekly papers, which published a number of articles by Allies.

A May 17 editorial in the Weekly Register occasioned by the appearance of a Privy Council Blue Book itemizing the distribution of educational funds, claimed that some 193 Catholic poor schools were receiving state money. This the editor commended, urging more schools to partake of this aid. The article concluded by saying there was "no obstacle but apathy" to the increase of state assistance.[92] The following week an answer was forthcoming from "One involved in the charge of 'apathy' but who pleads 'Not Guilty.'" "Not Guilty" claimed he was far from alone, that many canons, rectors and priests must be included among those who refused the grant and were thus subject to the charge of apathy. Here was a straightforward statement of the opposition party. The writer insisted that the bishops tolerated the apprehensions of those who feared the grant or objected to its conditions; the clear implica-

---

[92]Weekly Register, May 17, 1856, p. 6.

tion was that the press should be equally tolerant.[93]

Until this time the editorials in the Weekly Register had implied that there were no solid reasons for refusing the grant, and since the death of Frederick Lucas it seemed there was no one in the ranks of Catholic journalism to defend those who had reservations about dealing with the state. "Not Guilty" specified the conditions he found objectionable, stressing particularly the trouble he had encountered in locating and keeping certified teachers. They were, he said, "hard to catch and harder still to keep." "Not Guilty" had hired one such creature at a high salary and found his commitments to recommended scheduling and subject matter totally incompatible with the needs of his mission. This "trained master" had insisted on teaching "the system" which was geared to the questions inspectors asked on their visits; moreover, the teacher refused to hold school when the children in his parish could come. So he hired a more flexible teacher who met the needs of his parish, and the schools thrived. The writer implied that priests of Bradford, Birkenhead, Halifax, Leeds, Bury and other towns had similar views on the subject.[94]

Things were relatively quiet until September when Gainsford wrote on the subject of the school inspectors' annual reports. He said the government grant was not applied in the best way and recommended general capitation grants, from which he predicted Catholics would obtain greater benefits.[95] Allies took offense and

[93]Ibid., May 24, 1856, p. 6.

[94]Ibid.

[95]Ibid., September 20, 1856, p. 5.

answered Gainsford the following week. His reply was undoubtedly what brought the dispute into focus. Allies presented a strong defense of the government policy saying, "I cannot consider that there is any grievance at all to Catholics in the administration of the education grant." Allies always maintained that the government dealt fairly with Catholics, and he was certainly in a position to know; but under the circumstances this was probably the least politic statement he could have made. Part of the resistance to the government connection centered upon the Irish Christian Brothers, and it seems clear that much of the general resistance came from Irish communities. Allies' unqualified praise of the government could not have been better calculated to stiffen resistance among that segment of the Catholic population already hostile to all things related to the English government. It was a blunder of no small proportion insofar as it hardened lines of division. Otherwise Allies' response was substantial. He showed that the government was already making capitation grants.[96] It should be noted that such grants had been extended to rural areas in 1853; this was intended as a supplement to Russell's borough bill. The bill was dropped but the supplementary Minutes went through.[97] It seems clear from the correspondence published in the press that this fact was not widely discussed or understood by Catholics.

Allies also explained that the government system was intended not only to supplement local funds but to encourage a general improvement in teacher competence. He said it was particularly

---

[96]Ibid., September 27, 1856, p. 4.

[97]Sturt, op. cit., pp. 207-209.

important for Catholics to take advantage of teacher-training aid because they were in danger of being "robbed" of their children "by Protestant zeal" in this respect. Catholic parents, he insisted, could not be expected to send their children to inferior schools forever, and so long as Protestants availed themselves of teacher training funds the problem of Protestant competition would continue to be an important consideration. But Allies was not content to defend government policy; he went a step further and blamed Catholics entirely for receiving so small a share of the government grant. Even if he was technically accurate, his tone was unnecessarily provocative.[98]

That same week, September 27, the Weekly Register published a letter by Stokes who explained that an increase in the Catholics' share of the government grant would depend upon their making greater efforts to establish teacher training programs. Stokes praised the extent to which Catholics had partaken of state monies, but he denied that there was any basis to the supposedly popular claim that Catholic poverty was a substantial factor in explaining the comparatively small percentage of the grant received by Catholics. He implied that the combination of refusal to accept government conditions and the need for greater teacher training efforts explained why Catholics received so small a share of the grant. He

---

[98]The problem of determining whether the Privy Council policy was in fact entirely equitable toward Catholics would of course involve a full comparative analysis. That the government policies consistently favored Protestantism, at least until Catholics exerted pressure for exceptional revisions, is clear--but Allies' contention that the Privy Council was fair to the Poor School Committee cannot be readily questioned.

suggested a plan for overcoming resistance to the acceptance of the building grants calling for the controversial trust deed: subscribers should require schools to accept the deed. That was clearly tantamount to a threat.[99]

The next week Allies published a letter describing the details of the capitation grant, which was clearly intended to be informative,[100] but the same issue included an editorial praising the government's generosity and stressing that acceptance of state funds "only required" inspection, and that the conditions were guaranteed safe by the bishops.[101]

An October editorial urged Catholic schools to accept government funds and went even further to say Catholics should pursue this as a national policy. At this point it was admitted that of some sixty Catholic schools built since 1847 only seven received the state grant.[102] Up to this time Stokes and Allies had hinted that the resistance to the building grants had been fairly sizable--but this editorial suggests that those reluctant to apply for building grants were clearly in the majority.

The same issue published a detailed letter written by Allies describing the trust deed problem. Allies more or less dismissed the deed as a document which would assure that school buildings would be "legally settled for a school, and nothing but a school." With regard to the stand taken by those who refused the grant

---

[99]Weekly Register, September 27, 1856, p. 4.

[100]Ibid., October 4, 1856, p. 4.

[101]Ibid., p. 8.

[102]Ibid., October 11, 1856, p. 9.

Allies said the propriety of using the deed had "been removed from the individual judgment of the applicants and settled by competent authority"--the bishops. After presenting in simplified, and conveniently distorted, terms what he believed were the reasons for opposition (suspicion of the state, dislike of complicated forms, etc.), Allies took up the line Stokes had hinted at in his earlier letter: subscribers should insist on the deed. What he meant by this was not left open to question, for he emphasized that the biggest subscriber to all Catholic schools was the Poor School Committee.[103] This was nothing short of a threat to make the government conditions compulsory for all who would apply for Poor School Committee assistance. That this threat was understood to be just that was verified by the publication in this very issue of the Weekly of a letter by "a priest" who protested against the virtual threat contained in Stokes' letter mentioned above. This writer was apparently not opposed to the grant in principle but said his jurisdiction was too poor to qualify for the state funds.[104]

The correspondence continued along pretty much the same lines until mid-November, with Gainsford blaming the Poor School Committee for its inadequate efforts to improve Catholic financing and Allies blaming the Catholic public for its apathy and priests for their refusal to cooperate, all the while praising the government for its generosity and wisdom. The fundamental cause of the tension was plain to see: demands upon the Poor School Committee's

---

[103]Ibid., p. 12.

[104]Ibid., pp. 12-13.

funds were fast exceeding that agency´s capacity to provide aid,
and the Catholic public had failed to increase its support; in fact
public support was actually declining.[105] Gainsford believed that
the Poor School Committee should improve its fund-raising activities, while Allies believed that Catholics should accept readily
available state money. Both were undoubtedly correct. On the
surface Allies´ position might seem the more reasonable, but when
one remembers the Irish suspicion of the English government this
seems less clear. Whether it was more difficult to overcome resistance or to raise more money among a poor population was the
dilemma.

The important historical question is whether Allies, and even
Stokes and Marshall, understood the full dimensions of the problem.
Their casual dismissal of the questions raised suggests otherwise.
The objections which they struck down in their published correspondence were merely straw men; nobody minded deeds because they
legally secured school buildings as school buildings, and there is
little evidence to suggest that Catholics believed the school deeds
conveyed title to the government. Thus the proponents of state
aid--deliberately or otherwise--misrepresented the opposite position. Since that is a characteristic of public debate which
Victorians had well mastered the importance of this aspect of the
dispute should not be overemphasized. But the letters of Allies
and Stokes failed altogether to treat the management clauses which
were the real source of the trouble. Such de-emphasis of the real

---

[105]Throughout the post-1854-1858 period Catholic Poor School
officials complained, via the press, of the inadequacy of financial
support; thus the problem spanned the entire period of this study.

difficulty was reminiscent of the line taken by the Privy Council; so Allies and Stokes opened themselves to the accusation of government partisanship.

As Allies' defense of the government grew bolder Gainsford's attack on the Poor School Committee became more pointed, as did his accusations against the government policy. On October 25 Gainsford openly challenged Allies' claims about the government's impartial generosity. Repeating his argument that the state should provide aid more in proportion to the size of the population in need-- namely the Catholic population--Gainsford insisted that there was every reason to suspect the government of having anti-Catholic motives. The English government's policies in England and Ireland were different, he said, and the differences were specifically calculated to aid Protestantism in each country.[106] He continued this theme in subsequent letters, citing specific policies, but also demanding that Catholics be given special consideration because of their having been denied all aid for so long.[107]

The whole character of these discussions was changing. Gainsford really began by putting forth commonly held views, recommending the general capitation grant and suggesting improvements in the Catholic Poor School Committee's fund-raising policies. He ended by accusing the government of anti-Catholic motives and the Poor School Committee of apathy and a general lack of under-

---

[106]Weekly Register, October 25, 1856, p. 3.

[107]Ibid., November 8, 1856, pp. 9-10; ibid., November 15, 1856, p. 4; ibid., December 13, 1856, p. 5; and ibid., December 27, 1856, p. 6.

standing.

In November Formby's letters began to appear in the Weekly Register. While his articles in the Tablet had been general, he now became explicit and accused Allies of acting as though he had a right to investigate the conduct of the clergy with regard to the government grant. He set out to defend the views of the opposition, particularly against what he construed to be Allies' accusation that priests who refused the grant were remiss in their duty. Formby expressed particular annoyance with the way Allies had become a "partisan of the Privy Council" and anger with the threat to withdraw Poor School Committee aid to all schools not accepting government-imposed conditions. In one sense Formby was demanding that priests' rights of conscience be respected in this matter, but he also implied that those who accepted the government's conditions were wrong in principle and were somehow undermining the integrity of Catholic education.

It is not easy to identify the aggressors. The threat to make the acceptance of the state conditions compulsory for all Catholic schools applying to the Poor School Committee for aid preceded the most outspoken attacks against the grant. But those outspoken attacks represented a block of solid resistance to state aid which had been developing over a long period--long before Allies began to challenge the resistance. Given the dire financial straits in which the committee found itself there was perhaps little choice but to encourage schools to accept state money--and to attempt to overcome resistance to that policy. Gainsford clearly believed otherwise. He insisted that the committee had failed to make full use of Catholic resources, and that so long as the Catholic Poor

School Committee failed in this regard it should not be so ready to blame the Catholic public and priests for their failures.

This situation is reminiscent of the troubles the Catholic Institute had encountered in 1847 when Lucas accused that body of failing to reach the total Catholic population—including the Irish poor. Gainsford was not equal to Lucas in literary force or organizational zeal, but his complaints about committee policies were similar to those put forth by Lucas. Gainsford underscored the need for parish canvassing, regional and parochial organizations, and political cooperation. The Catholic Poor School Committee had a twofold problem: general apathy among the English Catholics and unwillingness or inability to reach out to the Irish poor. If this was not explicitly stated by Gainsford and other correspondents it is clearly implied by the suggestion that the Poor School Committee lacked the full confidence of the Catholic population.

Allies constantly defended his position by an appeal to authority; this was the main line of defense taken by the Weekly Register editor through most of 1856. The fact that the Poor School Committee activities were sanctioned by the bishops and the Pope was sufficient; all objections were therefore inconsequential. Interestingly enough, specific references to episcopal support usually mentioned by name only Bishop Gillis of Edinburgh and Bishop Turner of Salford. The main problem with these appeals to authority was that they were never elaborated. No bishops were defending the trust deeds in particular answer to the questions raised, and as it proved, that episcopal unity on the matter so often appealed to was not an altogether reliable source of support.

Before turning to Ullathorne's intervention and the other developments of 1857, however, the Tablet's coverage of events in 1856 should be examined and the way the Rambler and the Dublin Review were drawn into the fray should be discussed. The Tablet did not begin publishing correspondence relative to the controversy being carried on in the Weekly Register until November 1856 when it published a letter by H. Constable Maxwell.[108] Maxwell said that the letters published by the Catholic inspectors--Stokes and Marshall--made it evident that inspection should go no further. He claimed that the failure of Catholics to support the system was proof of extensive distrust of both the Catholic Poor School Committee and the government. Citing not only three centuries of persecution in England but also the government's contemporary efforts to "reduce and buy over the Irish poor" in Ireland, he argued that there were more than sufficient grounds for such distrust. Maxwell commended the Christian Brothers for setting a fine example, and he asked: "What has the Catholic Poor School Committee done to keep our education free and independent?" "Absolutely nothing!" was his reply. Instead of encouraging those who worked hard to maintain independence the committee seemed more anxious to "force upon them the Kemerton or model deed." Maxwell suggested that the Catholic Poor School Committee should reform itself and "work for Catholics who decline as well as for those who accept government assistance."[109]

The Tablet editor, Wallis, hastened to dissociate the paper

---

[108]Tablet, November 1, 1856, p. 693.

[109]Ibid.

from Maxwell's views while at the same time attempting to introduce some moderation into the discussion. Acknowledging that there were reasons for concern about state interference, he maintained that the Poor School Committee had secured independence for Catholic schools. What must be guarded against, he warned, were the two extreme positions:

> The adherents of one would give money only to schools which refuse government assistance; the adherents of the other would give to those only who accepted it.

It was said that a certain amount of rivalry was healthy but that care should be taken to see that support for the School Committee was not thereby diminished.[110]

Allies answered Maxwell's letter by describing the origin of the Poor School Committee and explaining how its agreements with the government secured episcopal control over the appointment of school inspectors and over all religious dimensions of education. He further explained that a new system of ecclesiastical inspection of religious instruction had been adopted to prevent overemphasis on secular instruction. Finally, he insisted that the committee had always worked for schools which declined as well as for those which accepted government funding. In support of this statement he cited statistics which not only proved the contention but suggested that the vast majority of schools aided by the committee did in fact decline the building and maintenance grants.[111] This letter was written in a much less hostile tone than previous letters.

---

[110]Ibid., p. 697.

[111]Ibid., November 15, 1856, p. 723.

Maxwell submitted another letter in answer to the _Tablet_'s editorial on his first letter; this appeared in the same issue as the above-referenced Allies letter.[112] He defended his description of the Poor School Committee as the "creature of the State" by saying that it was created specifically at the request of the government and for the purpose of dealing with the Privy Council Committee; moreover, he argued that the composition of the committee, particularly its domination by laity, had been the direct result of government policy demands. He continued:

> We have already often seen the committee disunited in its councils, lax in its tendencies—on one side its connection with the Priesthood completely ignored, and on the other frequently distrusted by Catholics, and in quarters where religion is seen in its most angelic form.

These "evil tendencies" should be publicized, Maxwell stated, so that solutions could be worked out.[113]

On December 27 the _Tablet_ published a long letter by Formby. In it he agreed with Maxwell that the matter should be more openly discussed rather than left to "rankle in our minds." Formby summarized the case of the opposition minority, repeating many arguments already discussed. He stressed that dependence upon Privy Council funds was "unreliable" because the government's intentions could not be altogether trusted in the present and safeguards against gradual encroachments were even more difficult to provide. Inspection was held to involve the separation of reli-

---

[112]_Ibid._, p. 723.

[113]_Ibid._ It would be interesting to know what Maxwell meant by referring to those "in quarters where religion is seen in its most angelic form." Unfortunately Maxwell remains an unknown, so his allies or favorites cannot be easily identified.

gious and secular education in principle. Formby pointed out that episcopal authority over the appointment of inspectors did not extend to their dismissal and that this flaw was an indication of the inadequacy of the securities supposedly provided against state interference. Formby belittled the way the Poor School Committee officials overrated the benefits of state funds, saying, in so many words, that their argument could be reduced to "money, money, money," and that a Catholic priest had every right to depend upon God and His Providence as a reasonable alternative to depending upon government money. Moreover, he contended that too much dependence upon public tax funds would undermine private charity and would lead to the deterioration of the "educational spirit, and render trainees of youth mercenary functionaries." Finally he admitted that his views were held by a minority but insisted that they should at least be respected rather than coerced.[114]

The Rambler's entry into school politics produced an unprecedented move on the part of Cardinal Wiseman. The November 1856 Rambler contained an article by J. G. Wenham, a Southwark priest who represented that diocese on the Poor School Committee. Entitled "The Rising Generations: Our Poor Schools," the article did not specifically address the ongoing controversy; nevertheless, it urged the acceptance of the government system, particularly inspection.[115]

Wenham's article began by comparing the "croakers" who were

---

[114]Ibid., December 27, 1856, p. 822.

[115][J. G. Wenham], "The Rising Generations: Our Poor Schools," Rambler, 2nd ser., 6 (November 1856): 321-341.

pessimistic about the difficulties faced by Catholics with the "couleur-de-rose man" who lived in a "poetical atmosphere of his own." Both perspectives on Catholic affairs were said to contribute to the understanding of the poor school situation.[116] The tone of the paragraphs that followed was more pessimistic and critical than "couleur-de-rose," however, and Wenham clearly believed the poor schools were in a bad way--primarily because Catholics lacked the will to deal with the problem.

On the whole the article might not have given offense, but its treatment of the government grant question was decidedly partisan in the context of the dispute being carried on in the weekly Catholic press. In fact the writer dismissed the controversy as having been settled by the authority of the bishops in favor of government inspection. Since the bishops had decided there was "nothing wrong or bad in inspection" it was argued that there was no reason for dispute. Further, it was suggested that government funds should be accepted by Catholics "uniformly as a body," and that there was something wrong with having "each private foot soldier acting on his own." As if this were not sufficient, the author praised the Privy Council Committee and said,

> Those managers who take most interest in their schools seem to have no difficulty about accepting government grants, whereas the "safe people" very often display a manifest want of interest in the whole subject.

In short, Wenham clearly sided with the proponents of the compulsory acceptance of state conditions by Catholic schools.[117]

---

[116]Ibid., pp. 321-322.

[117]Ibid., pp. 329-331.

Ironically Wenham's discussion of the question of who should manage Catholic schools made absolutely no reference to the state's policy, for he insisted that schools should be entirely managed by clerics.[118] The fact that he did not treat this as a church-state issue raises the question of Wenham's familiarity with the trust deeds controversy, which concerned the government's insistence that schools be managed by lay committees.[119]

It is not altogether clear why Wiseman took offense at this article in particular when so many offensive things were being said in the course of the schools dispute. Altholz contends that the Cardinal's anger had been aroused by Simpson's theological writings and was further irritated by the Rambler's intrusion into the subject of education which he believed to be beyond the province of the laity.[120] Unfortunately this is not very helpful, for Wenham was a priest who really advocated the exercise of episcopal authority. Most likely the Cardinal was exasperated by the way the controversy threatened to undermine public confidence in the Poor School Committee. The tone of the Dublin Review article of December 1856 tends to support this hypothesis, but this fails to explain why the Cardinal singled out the Rambler when much more provocative things were being said in the Tablet and the Weekly Register--and by men like Allies over whom he presumably had some

---

[118]Ibid., p. 332.

[119]Wenham was a member of the Poor School Committee, however, and should have been familiar with these details.

[120]Altholz, op. cit., p. 36.

direct authority.[121] For one thing Wiseman seemed to have assumed that the "couleur-de-rose man" was himself, and he was already angry with the Rambler over Simpson's theological writings, so the Wenham article probably served as a pretext for a double attack: against the Rambler per se and against the extremist position that would coerce all Catholic schools into accepting the government grant.

Much of Wiseman's attack focused on matters not related to the school question,[122] but the Cardinal also made important statements concerning the government grants controversy. In the opening pages Wiseman made it clear that he feared the Rambler's contribution to a spirit of disunion, especially with regard to the question of popular education. Since the Poor School Committee was dependent upon public opinion for financial support, quite as much as it was dependent upon episcopal authority, he urged that Catholic suspicions of the government be tolerated as reasonable and understandable. Moreover, he cited English relations with Ireland as grounds for such suspicions and fears. These fears, it was said, had been alleviated by the confidence placed in the committee organized by the bishops, but the Cardinal feared that a party might spring up

> intent on augmenting, to the utmost, government influence
> and government interference, ridiculing apprehensions
> which ought to be respected, desiring to force every
> school under the reach of the state patronage, increasing

---

[121]Although Wiseman was not officially head of the Poor School Committee, its headquarters were located in London, and it is difficult to believe that he did not exert greater influence over its deliberations—and employees—than other bishops.

[122]He discussed the divisions between Old Catholics and Converts, the tendency of the Rambler toward an elitism which many found offensive, and other matters.

the preponderance of secular instruction.

Wiseman predicted that if these apprehensions were disregarded they would "ripen into alarm," schools would be withdrawn from inspection, subscriptions would decline, and the Poor School Committee would be paralyzed. Thus would new dangers be introduced:

> . . . one day or other, a compulsory system may be introduced, justified on the very grounds of our withdrawal from state assistance, without our having any responsible organizational body to fight the battle of religious education.

He pleaded that everyone avoid turning the question into a "war cry" and asked, "Why taunt and goad those who are repugnant, to enter into a system which no competent authority has made compulsory?"[123]

There were follow-up notices of this exchange between the Rambler and the Dublin Review, but these significantly omitted all further reference to the school controversy, as did the Weekly Register's review of the matter.[124] The most important aspect of the whole affair, insofar as the education question was concerned, was Wiseman's plea for moderation and his insistence that episcopal authority had not demanded--and therefore would not demand--a uniform policy. The irony is that the Rambler, usually the jealous

---

[123][Wiseman], "Present Catholic Dangers," pp. 443-446.

[124]This is a puzzling aspect of the controversy and might be taken to suggest that the other aspects of the matter greatly overshadowed the importance of the school question. But the exchange was determined circumstantially by the Rambler's reply to the Cardinal, "The Rambler and the Dublin Review," Rambler, 2nd ser., 7 (February 1857): 140-144, in which Simpson and Capes, to whom the article has been attributed, made no reference whatever to the education question. This only indicates that Simpson and Capes had little interest in the question or were not ready to take issue with Wiseman over it. Wiseman's reply (see n. 70 above) only answered points raised in the Rambler article.

guardian of the rights of conscience, had called for the exercise of episcopal authority while the Cardinal, more often the champion of that authority, claimed its application to be neither necessary nor politic.

Although the Dublin Review had come out in virtual defense of those who had "apprehensions" about accepting state funds, Allies, Stokes and Marshall continued to champion the government system aggressively. Since the defenders of the grant always appealed to the fact that their position had episcopal sanction the implication was that those who resisted such terms were going against episcopal authority.

At this point it is necessary to insert a few words concerning a little publication issued in Liverpool, the Catholic Institute Magazine, which appeared under that title from October 1855 through December 1857, and was continued as the Institute from January through September 1858. As the title indicates, the magazine was the publication of the local Catholic Institute, but it was intended to reach the Young Men's Societies throughout England.[125] These societies--like the Catholic Institute--were intended to provide an intellectual and social meeting ground for the middle classes. The magazine's aim was to serve the Liverpool Catholic community and also reach beyond it with articles touching on religion and literature.

In the beginning the magazine pronounced itself "ultramontane in the broadest sense of the word," and the editors advised those

---

[125]"The Very Rev. Dr. O'Brien and the Catholic Institute Magazine," Catholic Institute Magazine (November 1857), p. 96.

who considered such views "illiberal" to "throw us aside in disgust at once."[126] Whether the Catholic Institute Magazine really had anything significant to contribute to the tensions between liberals and ultramontanes might provide an interesting topic for investigation, but the magazine's social posture had greater significance at the moment. Liverpool was such an important center of Catholicity, with its fifty some priests and heavily concentrated Irish Catholic population, that any periodical issuing from this immigrants' port of entry should contain important social commentary. The magazine contains valuable social material, but on the subject of church-state-education coverage was quite limited. A few articles on the reformatories movement, one or two on the relationship between education and crime, and one or two miscellaneous articles on schools constitute the extent of this publication's coverage of the present topic.

There is, however, one article on the press controversy of 1856-1857 which must at least be mentioned. Appearing in March 1857, "Our Educational Squabbles" came out strongly in favor of the government grants, citing Liverpool's extensive and favorable experience with the Privy Council. It was said that Liverpool was receiving ₤20,000 yearly. That the chief advantage of the government connection was money was hardly a new argument--but the issuance of such a statement from a community so predominantly Irish was important. The writer said that the Privy Council policies toward Catholics were exceptionally fair, especially when

---

[126]"Editor's Address," Catholic Institute Magazine (October 1855), p. 2.

compared with those of the Army, the Poor Law Unions or other agencies. With so much work to be done in these other areas where Catholics were discriminated against the writer wondered why so much abuse was being lavished upon the one department of government which treated Catholics well. This article cannot be called a major contribution to the controversy, but it certainly provided interesting testimony from a community which claimed to have a right to its pro-government opinion.[127]

During January and February 1857 there were numerous articles in both the weeklies and another in the Rambler,[128] but no substantially new positions were presented. The complexion of the controversy changed in February, however, when Bishop Ullathorne published a seventy-five-page pamphlet, "Notes on the Education Question," analyzing the Catholics´ relations with the Privy Council Committee. Ullathorne expressed cautious approval of the inspection system, so long as it remained confined to the letter of the official agreement.[129] Then he defined in the clearest terms the reasons why refusal to accept the trust deed was not only justified but commendable. This pamphlet was not written in polemical terms, but in the context of the ongoing controversy it caused a sensation and shattered the claim that the prelates uniformly

---

[127]"Our Educational Squabbles," Catholic Institute Magazine (March 1857), pp. 253-258.

[128][Wenham], "Principles of Education," Rambler, 2nd ser., 7 (January 1857): 37-52.

[129]William B. Ullathorne, "Notes on the Education Question," (London: Richardson & Son, 1857), pp. 15-27.

approved all the conditions of the government connection.

The Tablet was first to review the pamphlet. Wallis prefaced his analysis with a restatement of his opinion that acceptance of government funds was the lesser of two evils--the danger of government interference and the danger of Protestant competition in education. He said that if good schools could be established independently of government aid, well and good, but that if not, state aid should be accepted.[130] This was not a new position for the Tablet, but the editor's emphasis upon the desirability of maintaining independence if possible was much stronger than it had been in recent months.

In March the Weekly Register reviewed the pamphlet and respectfully took issue with the bishop's "bias" against the government grants. The paper had not altered its stand, but the tone had undergone a drastic change. Formerly the Weekly had dismissed all objections as groundless; now it displayed a serious respect for them. The editor developed the view, already hinted at by Wiseman, that the danger of arbitrary government interference in Catholic schools was increased rather than lessened by Catholic isolation from all government-financed systems. If Catholic schools were party to official contracts with the government, contracts similar to those maintained with all other denominational schools, the government could not change its policy without a "distinct breach of public faith" which would constitute an attack on all other denominations as well and would therefore not be

---

[130]Tablet, February 21, 1857, p. 122.

tolerated.[131] This argument was further elaborated in a number of later editorials wherein the writer, presumably Wilberforce, insisted that the trust deeds bound the government by stringent agreements which "rendered any state interference with our schools a flagrant breach of public faith." Wilberforce well understood the British political regard for public faith and said, "Public faith may be violated, but of all possible securities it is the greatest."[132]

The Weekly Register editorials between the publication of Ullathorne's pamphlet and the issuance of a later statement by Wiseman steered an exceptionally diplomatic course. While expressing apparently sincere regard for the suspicions and concerns of those who resisted dealings with the government the editor stressed the political dangers of isolation. All the time there was careful avoidance of any extreme statements calling for coerced uniformity. This policy of non-coercive encouragement of the government connection was clearly the policy Wiseman wished to pursue, and it seems fair to conclude that Wilberforce was deliberately supporting the Cardinal's policies.

In the meantime Ullathorne added more fuel to the fire by answering hostile reviews of his pamphlet in a letter published on April 4 in both weeklies. Since this letter also referred to the Rambler's review it is appropriate to mention that here. In March Capes wrote a very brief review of the bishop's pamphlet; the

---

[131]Weekly Register, March 21, 1857, p. 10.

[132]Ibid., April 4, 1857, p. 9; April 11, 1857, p. 9; and April 18, 1857, p. 9.

article was undeniably hostile to Ullathorne's position and was especially critical of his demand that school inspectors adhere to the letter of their instructions calling for complete silence on all matters religious. "Why insist on the inspectors being Catholic," Capes asked, "if their religion is to be entirely forgotten during the inspection?"[133] The context of the problem had to do with the fact that both Stokes and Marshall had been known to include comments about religious instruction in their official reports. Usually these were simple statements of praise, but they served to prove to those wary of inspection that government representatives could not be kept from interfering in religious affairs. As Lucas had phrased the problem much earlier, 'the right to praise implied the right to blame.'

Ullathorne's public letter turned the Rambler's comments into an advocacy of "the right of Her Majesty's Inspectors to instruct the managers of our poor schools on the religious teaching of those schools through the medium of documents addressed to the secular government."[134] He cited this bold position as more proof of "what will ultimately result from making the lay element preponderate in the management of the schools."

Ullathorne went on to attack the claim that the government connection had been fully approved by the bishops and the Holy See. He said the bishops had never voted on the matter as such, though they had discussed various aspects of the trust deed informally,

---

[133][Capes], "Short Notices," Rambler, 2nd ser., 7 (March 1857): 236-237.

[134]Tablet, April 4, 1857, pp. 218-219.

and he insisted that the Pope's granting of an indulgence to Poor School Committee subscribers was not approval of specific agreements. He then went over other arguments against the trust deed and concluded that the contracts in question could easily be construed against Catholic interests.

The *Tablet* replied to Ullathorne's latest letter with great reserve, saying that his claims changed the whole character of the debate.[135] But the editor also observed that the grants had been admitted in all dioceses and implied that the long period of unprotested acceptance represented de facto approval.

At this point the *Weekly Register* attended to the specific problem of whether a school committee rebelling against the Church's authority could destroy the bishop's authority as written into the trust deed. The editor said that the possibility of this happening was dependent upon having a majority of committee members in rebellion, which possibility he said was slim; moreover such a development would affect not the whole system but simply a single school. Ullathorne had argued that a challenge to episcopal authority by the committee could force a bishop to submit himself to a secular court decision, which would constitute submission to the secular jurisdiction in principle. On the contrary, Wilberforce said, the bishop could

> . . . never be required to prove before a secular court that his grounds were religious in order to obtain the legal enforcement of his decrees. Should he find it impossible to enforce his decision he had the obvious alternative of depriving the school of its Catholic character, requiring the priest to renounce his connection with it, warning the laity not to allow their children to

---

[135]*Ibid.*, p. 216.

attend it, and taking measures to supply a Catholic school in its place.136

Both arguments were powerfully and much more elaborately stated than this treatment can indicate, but it is clear that the balance of the controversy had shifted. Not only had the minority gained a public hearing over the months, but their position had been legitimated by an episcopal publication.

Wiseman, whose relations with Ullathorne were anything but smooth, was not long in rebuking his suffragan bishop. On May 2 both the Tablet and the Weekly Register published a copy of Wiseman's letter to Charles Langdale. The letter was an official statement of the bishops' support for the Catholic Poor School Committee and its relations with the government. There is no need to detail the arguments it put forth except to say that it was clearly intended as a rebuke against Ullathorne and it claimed that the bishops had indeed met and decided unanimously on the trust deed question.137 The Cardinal expressed anger that the faithful

---

136Weekly Register, April 18, 1857, p. 9.

137Ibid., May 2, 1857, p. 4. The specific answer to Ullathorne's claim that the bishops had not voted on the trust deed was the most important dimension of this letter, for Wiseman claimed that a meeting had been held at St. George's, Southwark, in November 1850, at which the question was voted on. Cuthbert Butler, The Life and Times of Bishop Ullathorne, 2 vols. (London: Burns, Oates and Washbourne, 1926), 1:180-182, cites the "unbusinesslike way" Wiseman conducted his business to suggest that Ullathorne had been correct in this matter, but Ullathorne acknowledged the Cardinal's position on this in a subsequent letter, published in the Weekly Register, May 16, 1857, p. 4, wherein Ullathorne acknowledged the meeting. This second Ullathorne letter also referred to an earlier communication he had received from the Cardinal complimenting him on the controversial pamphlet. In addition Ullathorne referred to another communication from the Cardinal denying that the letter of May 2 was intended as an attack against Ullathorne.

should be "harassed" over questions already decided. He admitted
that laws could be enacted which would so adversely affect the
present situation that Catholics would have to change their policy,
but he reminded Catholics that "such oppressive legislation could
be made to include and to molest schools without the building
grants or government inspection quite as much as those that have
accepted either . . ."

As if to put an end to the controversy the May _Rambler_ published an article by Stokes which was a further response to
Ullathorne´s stand. Stokes claimed that the bishop had "made no
trial of the dangers" which he dreaded, but since there is ample
proof that Ullathorne made no efforts to prevent priests in his
diocese from accepting grants if they were needed,[138] Stokes´
remarks can be seen as personal replies to certain accusations the
bishops made about the inspector´s reports.[139] This is undoubtedly
a minor point but illustrates the extent to which the whole matter
had become one of personalities. Stokes cited an "array of authorities" to show that acceptance of the grant had been widespread,
and he outlined the advantages and disadvantages of the government
connection as he saw them. These pages contained no new arguments.
Money, efficiency, security of property, independent management and
better teachers were cited as the typical advantages to be derived

---

[138]Ullathorne, _op. cit._, p. 26, states that Marshall inspected
schools in the Birmingham diocese, indicating that schools there
received government aid; there are frequent references throughout
the period to various diocesan activities involving government aid
showing that Ullathorne did not prohibit schools in his district
from dealing with the government.

[139]_Ibid._, pp. 24-25.

from the government scheme. Stokes even suggested that the lay school committee strengthened rather than weakened the security of the system against government interference, and he pictured committeemen as a body of defenders of Catholic independence.[140]

As a defense of the government system this article was as strong as any previously issued by the same author. As an answer to Ullathorne's objections it was weak. In the first place Stokes' characterization of Ullathorne's position was inaccurate. Stokes claimed, for example, that Ullathorne had argued that the "Government should not promote education."[141] In fact Ullathorne had argued that "teaching" was not the rightful occupation of the state. Teaching and promoting education are sufficiently distinct activities that such an erroneous characterization must be seen as deliberate, particularly since Ullathorne's pamphlet defined this very clearly. The bishop had presented a very careful statement of the government's scheme of examining pupil-teachers and teacher certification candidates, showing that this examination procedure had a profound influence on the curriculum of the schools--training schools and poor schools alike. He said that he was concerned not with the way the examination system was operating at the time but with the discretionary power which the government possessed in this area. Ullathorne expressed specific concern about the fact that there was nothing in any contracts or laws which prevented the

---

[140][Stokes], "The Controversy on the Poor School Grant," Rambler, 2nd ser., 7 (May 1857): 344.

[141]Ibid., p. 343.

government from changing its examination schemes at will.[142] As a matter of historical fact it was through the exercise of this discretionary power that the government brought about drastic policy revisions in 1861, which revisions will be discussed in the following chapter.

Stokes' other attacks against Ullathorne similarly misrepresented the bishop's position. Since there was nothing new in Stokes position, however, it need not be discussed in further detail here.[143]

In the larger context the Rambler articles on the school question were not exceptionally important,[144] but it seems very possible that at least part of Ullathorne's later hostility toward the Rambler might be explained by the publication of Stokes' article. Ullathorne's genuine interest in the education question is easily proved by the fact that he was the only bishop to publish any independent analyses of the education problems of the day; if

---

[142]Ullathorne, op. cit., pp. 40-42.

[143]One argument Stokes presented which is slightly different from some presented earlier was that the composition of private Catholic charities was "mixed"--laity and clergy combined--and he insisted that the bishops had not objected to that arrangement (see Stokes, "Controversy on the Poor School Grant," p. 343). He did not mention, however, that such arrangements were not bound by contracts to which the government was a party.

[144]Later in the year Stokes wrote another article for the Rambler ("Industrial Schools," Rambler, 2nd ser., 8 (July 1857): 12-24), but it had very little to do with church-state problems. In addition the Rambler published another article by Wenham, "What Books Shall We Use in Our Schools," in October 1857, pp. 245-258; this article provided a slight departure from earlier Rambler articles emphasizing the benefits of the government connection; in these pages Wenham expressed concern that too much emphasis on secular teaching might result in the deprecation of religious instruction. Ecclesiastical inspection was urged as the remedy for the system.

the bishop's 1850 pamphlet was not a major publishing event, the 1857 pamphlet was extremely important--in fact it remains one of the clearest statements of Catholic church-state relations with regard to education. The importance of Ullathorne's interest in this matter also derives from the fact that Birmingham was the city where the secular education movement of the 1860s developed; indications of future trends were readily discernible there during the 1850s. There is no doubt that Ullathorne's distrust of the laity influenced his hostility to the Rambler in general and to Stokes in particular. Equally important, however, was his demand that all aspects of the question be weighed. And in this instance the Rambler consistently presented only one side of the picture. In this its coverage of the question differed from all other publications of the period, save the Catholic School which, after all, was the official publication of the Poor School Committee.

Before turning to the Catholic press response to the work of the Newcastle Commission and the subsequent introduction of the 1861 Revised Code it is essential to mention that the controversies of the mid-1850s appear to have increased rather than decreased the number of schools applying for state aid.[145] An assessment of the long-term impact of these tensions must be reserved for the final chapter; for the moment it should suffice to suggest that this increase in the number of schools accepting the government connection was probably due more to the fact that extensive publicity clarified complex details than to any real diminution of the oppo-

---

[145]Weekly Register, April 11, 1857, p. 10.

sition to state policies.   The following chapter will demonstrate that these tensions continued to plague the Catholic Poor School Committee.

CHAPTER V

CATHOLICS, THE NEWCASTLE COMMISSION

AND THE REVISED CODE, 1859-1865

These were crucial years for the Catholic Church: the Pope's temporal dominion was threatened, divisions between Liberals and Ultramontanes upset internal peace, intellectual challenges to religion were on the rise, and the power of the Catholic press proved ever more difficult to reconcile with Church authority. English Catholic problems must be seen within this broader context. International political troubles also provided the framework for English politics: the American Civil War frustrated diplomats and caused distress in English manufacturing regions while the Franco-Austrian-Italian scenarios absorbed much of Viscount Palmerston's attention and concern. And as though international difficulties were not sufficiently distracting there were the ever-present Irish problems, manifested at this time by Fenianism, famine and agrarian unrest.

Historians generally agree that preoccupation with foreign policy accounted for much of the domestic equilibrium of the Palmerston years. Concern with international tensions directed political energies away from potentially troublesome questions at home, such as reform, education, Irish tenancy and disestablish-

274

ment. The Catholic press coverage of this period sustains this understanding. English Catholic interest in foreign policy was especially acute since the Pope was in peril from both physical illness and the combined exertions for Italian unification. The deep-seated anti-Catholicism of the English people surfaced during the crises of Italian unification, which kept Catholic journalists busy answering antipapal calumnies, despite the tendency of Liberal Catholics to question certain aspects of the Temporal Power. Because the problem of the Temporal Power was closely associated with the larger problem of papal authority, tensions between Ultramontanes and Liberals increased and could not be separated from international developments.

Given the dominant importance of foreign policy, educational questions might have been expected to take a back seat during this period. They did, but not altogether, for these were important years in the history of English education. The Newcastle Commission[1] made an extensive survey of the Privy Council system of education--the only official and comprehensive study made of that system as it operated from 1839 to 1862. And the Privy Council's Committee on Education, under Robert Lowe's direction, introduced the Revised Code which produced major and fundamental changes in that system. Certainly the Catholic press attended to these developments, but its coverage of the education question was more scanty than it had been earlier when pressing international questions were

---

[1]So named after its chairman, the Duke of Newcastle, the Commission was more accurately entitled "The Royal Commission Appointed to Inquire Into the State of Popular Education in England." Hereafter cited as the Newcastle Commission.

fewer. Another factor which may account for the relatively light coverage of the education question was undoubtedly the increasing attention given to the treatment of Catholics in prisons, jails and workhouses.[2]

In surveying the Catholic press coverage of educational policy during the 1859-1865 period one might ask whether Catholics would have been more attentive to educational policy had international crises not distracted them. This suggests a further question: could the Privy Council have maneuvered such changes through Parliament at any other time? As it was, the Revised Code caused a great stir in the popular press; had full attention been devoted to domestic policy one must wonder whether such a course would have been attempted.

Additional Publications During This Period

There were several additions to the ranks of Catholic journalism during these years. The Universe appeared in 1860, as did the Liverpool Northern Press. The Home and Foreign Review[3] began its

---

[2]Throughout these years press attention to these problems was particularly full due to the existence of a workhouse committee in the Westminster diocese and to the work of the Parliamentary committee inquiring into the administration of the English Poor Law; this committee sat from 1861 to 1864, and the Catholics exerted considerable efforts in behalf of Catholic inmates. The Poor Law problems related to the education question because there were over 10,000 Catholic children in workhouses. The Catholic interest in reformatories and industrial schools has been noted; though it has been this author's intention to stress the connections among all these aspects of popular education, the specialized structure of this particular study has not permitted full inquiry into the different areas.

[3]The Home and Foreign Review was published quarterly from July 1862 through April 1864 as the successor to the Rambler. See the Wellesley Index, 1:547-549, for a brief review of its history.

short-lived career as successor to the Rambler in 1862. The Month
was first issued in July 1864, and the Workman came out at the
beginning of 1865. In addition, another small publication, the
Workhouse Papers, appeared in 1860.

The Universe was established at the initiative of Cardinal
Wiseman, who contacted members of the Society of St. Vincent de
Paul about the possibility of operating a penny paper similar to
the famous Paris publication, L'Univers. Wiseman's main aim was to
issue a cheap paper which would counter attacks against the Papacy.
Although the Society of St. Vincent de Paul could not undertake the
venture itself, some of the brothers of the society joined to
launch the venture, including G. J. Wigley, the London correspondent for L'Univers. The paper got under way on December 8, 1860,
under the editorial leadership of Archibald Dunn. The editorial
history of this newspaper remains unchronicled, but apparently
Dunn's tenure was short-lived. At first the paper refused to print
controversial political articles; later, when that policy was dis-
continued Dunn and a large part of the editorial staff resigned.
At that point it appears that the printer, Denis Lane, took control; however, there are references to a series of editors including J. A. O'Shea, James O'Connor (M. P. for Wicklow), Prior
O'Gorman, and Father Alexius Mills.[4]

Editorial addresses published during the first year tell us
that The Universe Newspaper Company, Ltd. had been capitalized at
£2,000 during 1861; its directors included Henry Pace, Thomas J.

---

[4]Dwyer, op. cit., pp. 506-507.

Wilson, N. H. Westlake, John Ross, C. J. Brett, J. A. Henson, and Thomas Egan, Esquires, in addition to Wigley.[5] Circulation was reported to exceed 3,000.[6]. In March 1861 the editors provided a quarterly report in which they claimed to have a larger circulation than any other Catholic paper. Given the low price of the paper this might have been true, but Victorian editors' claims about their own circulation must be viewed with caution. It was also mentioned that the paper's circulation had been extended to Manchester, Preston and Birmingham. Despite these claims the paper was not paying its way and supporters were urged to help.

Given the paper's early policy of avoiding domestic politics it must be said that the Universe's contribution to educational debates was not overwhelmingly important, but the Cardinal's interest in establishing a penny paper--obviously aimed at the Irish readership in London--makes the publication important in itself. Its coverage of matters of social and economic concern to the Irish--including a great deal of Irish news--also has intrinsic importance.[7]

Liverpool's Northern Press and Catholic Weekly Times was published under that title from June 9, 1860 through September 10, 1870, as the Catholic Times from September 17, 1870 to March 3,

---

[5]Universe, January 12, 1861, p. 1.

[6]Ibid., July 20, 1861, p. 3.

[7]Fletcher, op. cit., pp. 307-308. He mentioned another Catholic paper begun at the same time and having a similar title, the Universal News. It has not been examined for this study, as files could not be located. See also Husenbeth, op. cit., p. 2.

1876, and as the Catholic Times and Catholic Opinion from March 10, 1876 to December 26, 1925. S. B. Harper[8] was founder and editor; he remained editor until 1876. Thomas Burke's history of Liverpool Catholicism reports that the editor was decidedly Ultramontane with respect to the question of the Temporal Power and that he quarreled with the Daily Post on this subject. Unfortunately, little more can be said about the paper or its editor.[9]

In its editorial column the paper boasted of a large circulation and mentioned the existence of the Northern Press Newspaper Company. Members of that company's provisional committee included Edward Challoner, D. Powell, J. Yates, J. Walton and J. Neale Lomax, Esquires, Provost Cookson, Canon O'Reilly and Rev. James Nugent.[10]

As a provincial paper for Northern England the Northern Press claimed to represent Liverpool, Manchester and other important towns. Given the region's heavy concentration of Catholics--most notably Irish Catholics--its importance should not be underestimated. Unfortunately this author did not have access to a complete

---

[8]Burke, op. cit., p. 144. Harper remains an obscure figure, though he is mentioned in Josef L. Altholz, Damian McElrath and James C. Holland, eds., The Correspondence of Lord Acton and Richard Simpson, 3 vols. (Cambridge: Cambridge University Press, 1971-1975), 1:68n; here it is noted that Harper discussed with Wiseman the possibility of editing the Dublin Review. This discussion is said to have taken place during 1858 when the Dublin was undergoing difficulties. The Acton-Simpson correspondence will be cited hereafter as Correspondence of Acton and Simpson.

[9]Presumably the Liverpool diocesan archives have information about this publication; these remain to be consulted for a fuller appreciation of the subject but were not examined by this author.

[10]Northern Press, June 22, 1861, pp. 1, 4.

run of the paper,[11] but issues examined contained some pertinent material on the education question.

A very small and short-lived periodical, also begun in 1860, was published in London by Burns and Lambert. This was the Workhouse Papers, which appeared monthly from May through November 1860. All issues are contained in one fifty-six-page volume. It is not absolutely certain that the Workhouse Papers never appeared after November 1860, but no evidence has been found to the contrary. This was the publication of the Workhouse Committee of the Westminster Diocese, formed in 1860 for the redress of Catholic grievances in workhouses. Because the scope of the committee's activities goes far beyond the scope of this study it has not been possible to study the connection between workhouse schools and other aspects of the Catholic education question, but it will be seen that pauper education was an integral part of popular education. The Workhouse Papers provide helpful data on the former subject.[12] Wiseman's secretary, Canon John Morris, was one of the

---

[11]Issues from June 1860 through April 1863 were examined. The British Museum Newspaper Library lacks issues for the 1864-1868 period.

[12]Published for less than a year, this little news-sheet which focused exclusively on a rather narrow question might be seen more as a committee report than a periodical, but it seemed wise to mention it in the text because of its relation to the pauper education problem. Material contained in these issues does not pertain directly to the so-called "general education questions" which were generally considered to define the scope of this study, and any effort to treat the material contained therein adequately would call for a thorough study of education in workhouses and under the auspices of the Poor Law. This is really a full study in itself—and as much as it needs to be done such a study clearly exceeds the originally defined scope of this dissertation. Still, it should be stressed that the Workhouse Papers contain valuable material on the subject of workhouse education and Catholic difficulties with re-

moving forces behind the Committee and served as its secretary. Though it is probable that he edited the Workhouse Papers this requires further verification.[13]

The Month came out in July 1864 under the guidance of Fanny Margaret Taylor, a convert who became Mother Magdalen Taylor of the Poor Servants of the Mother of God.[14] She had been connected with another Catholic periodical, the Lamp, during the early 1860s[15] and then through her association with the Jesuits of Farm Street founded the Month. Her specific role in the venture remains somewhat unclear, as she described Father Peter Gallway as the founder and credited Father Henry James Coleridge with an important part of the writing during the early months of its publication. Newman also took an interest in the magazine and contributed both his support and his writings.[16] The history of this still-published magazine has been well documented and requires little elaboration here, especially since it was only in operation for a few months before the period of this study came to a close with the death of Wiseman in February 1865. Moreover, the numbers which were published during these few months emphasized literary subjects rather than

---

gard to workhouse education.

[13]Workhouse Papers (May 1860), p. 5

[14]Dwyer, op. cit., p. 496.

[15]Francis Charles Devas, Mother Mary Magdalen of the Sacred Heart (Fanny Margaret Taylor), Founder of the Poor Servants of the Mother of God, 1832-1900 (London: Burns, Oates and Washbourne, 1927), p. 319.

[16]Dwyer, op. cit., p. 496; and Devas, op. cit., p. 320.

political or educational controversy, and no further reference to the _Month_ will be made in the following pages.

Mention must also be made of another small magazine entitled the _Workman,_ or _Life_ and _Leisure,_ sometimes called the _Literary Workman._ The magazine was conducted by Gertrude Parsons, a novelist and contributor to the _Lamp._[17] Its contents included a preponderance of light fiction, much of which was written by Mrs. Parsons, but it also extended to topics of political and social importance. During the first half of 1865 the magazine appeared under the title of the _Workman,_ but that title was given up at mid-year because it had been mistakenly assumed to imply that it was directed toward a working class readership. In order to remedy this class problem the title was changed to _Literary Workman,_ which was maintained until the periodical ceased publication at the close of the year.

The Newcastle Commission

Although it is essential to keep in mind the primacy of foreign affairs during the Palmerston years this fact cannot be allowed to obscure the importance of the fundamental changes brought about by Robert Lowe's Revised Code, nor should the work of the Newcastle Commission--which set the stage for Lowe's new policies--be overlooked. The Newcastle Commission's efforts had little effect upon Catholics, because they refused to participate, but

---

[17]Gorman, op. cit., p. 212. No further reference will be made to this periodical as it did not deal in any serious way with church-state-education questions. It is mentioned here only because it was one of the periodicals published during this period which was surveyed for this study.

that refusal caused an important press controversy during the early months of 1859.

This commission, properly called the Commission Appointed to Inquire into the State of Popular Education in England, was appointed by the Queen in 1858 at the request of Parliament. Sir John Pakington had moved for such an inquiry at the end of 1858, and appointments were made soon after the Queen gave her assent. The Commissioners included the Duke of Newcastle as chairman, Goldwin Smith, William Nassau Senior, Edward Miall, Sir John Taylor Coleridge, Rev. William Rogers, and Rev. William C. Lake. All were Protestant; all save Miall were Anglican.[18]

When the Catholic Poor School Committee was asked to cooperate with the investigation it was learned that the inquiry involved religious as well as secular aspects of the schools. The Poor School Committee asked that a Catholic commissioner be named; when that request was refused the bishops met to determine what course to follow. As it happened the bishops were also concerned about alterations in government policy affecting the inspection of Catholic reformatories. Authority over reformatory inspectors had been transferred from the Privy Council to the Home Office; this also involved certain revisions in the wording of instructions to those inspectors. Since the Home Office inspectors were generally Anglican clergymen their instructions were of great importance to

---

[18]It is worth noting that historians have not generally inquired into the religious views of the commissioners, which most certainly had a bearing on their conclusions. This author is now involved with preliminary research on the Commission and the commissioners.

Catholics, and at this time the Anglican inspectors were demanding the right to inspect religious as well as secular aspects of the Catholic reformatories.[19] The question was under negotiation, but the bishops were more suspicious of government intentions than usual. In the end they decided not to cooperate with the commission because they feared any precedent which might be used to sanction Protestant inspection of religion in Catholic schools.

Because of sensitivity about government interference in the schools--which had produced the disputes of 1856 and 1857--the bishops were probably eager to avoid arousing further opposition to the government connection. In any event the matter was decided officially at a November meeting of the English bishops, and the clergy was notified by official printed circulars, which fact was noticed in the Tablet on November 13, 1858.[20] When in January 1859 the Rambler published a long article strongly attacking the bishops' policy a dispute began which lasted nearly three months and reached into the columns of the Tablet and the Weekly Register.

This particular educational controversy is one of the few which has received the attention of several historians of English Catholicism.[21] This fact is not to be accounted for by any recog-

---

[19]See Ullathorne's pastoral on this subject, Weekly Register, March 12, 1859, p. 3; details were also provided in Canon O'Neal's letter to the editor of the Tablet, November 13, 1858, pp. 729-730.

[20]Tablet, November 13, 1858, p. 725. Here the Tablet published the Bishop of Salford's circular to the clergy of his diocese; there was nothing in the notice to indicate that a general episcopal decision had been reached on the Royal Commission question.

[21]Altholz, op. cit., pp. 89-91; Butler, op. cit., 1:310-311; McElrath, Simpson, p. 80; and Abbot Gasquet, Lord Acton and His Circle (London: Burns and Oates, 1906), xlviij-lj.

nition of the importance of the education question but rather by
the fact that it resulted in Simpson's being forced to give over
editorial control of the Rambler to John Henry Newman, a development of major significance.[22] Since neither Newman nor Simpson
took great interest in the details of the education controversy
itself[23] it is necessary to look to the positions taken by Stokes,
the bishops and other correspondents for an explanation of the
hostilities aroused. It has been suggested that the bishops,
intending to resist lay interference in educational policy, were
guilty of exerting episcopal authority when the question was merely
one of political expedience.[24] The full circumstances, however,
suggest that the question was not purely political and that the
bishops were rightly concerned about more than lay interference.
Still, their heavy handed response may have contributed to a decline in lay attention to policies which called for superintendence

---

[22]Of course it was not merely that Newman was made editor that
aroused interest but also the bishops' exercise of so-called cen-
sorial powers.

[23]Both Simpson and Acton had a general interest in larger
questions of education, as did Newman, but Newman admitted to
Allies in 1864 that he knew almost nothing about the work of the
Poor School Committee (see Dessain, Letters and Diaries of Newman,
21:65). Although Simpson discussed the details of the Royal
Commission crisis in an article published in the Correspondant (May
1859), pp. 167-171, under the title, "Lettre sur le Rôle des
Catholiques dans les Dernières Elections in Angleterre," the content of that article appears to have been based primarily upon
material presented by Stokes in his two Rambler articles ("The
Royal Commission on Education," Rambler, 2nd ser., 11 (January
1859): 17-30; and "The Royal Commission and the Tablet," Rambler,
2nd ser., 11 (February 1859): 104-113). For the English translation of the Simpson article see Richard Simpson, "The Catholic
Church in England," ed. D. McElrath, Downside Review 84 (April
1966): 171-192.

[24]Altholz, op. cit., p. 90.

by laity and hierarchy alike.

Stokes, in his unsigned article published in the January 1859 Rambler, attacked the decision against cooperating with the commission as one based on misinformation and likely to harm Catholic interests, and he accused those responsible for that policy of raising false issues. His opening paragraph set the tone:

> What henceforward is to be the attitude of English Catholics toward the Crown and Parliament of Britain? In the progress of civilization and the advance of popular liberty, shall we, by showing honour and respect to the civil magistrate within his legitimate sphere, prove ourselves fit inhabitants of a land of freedom? Or shall we, by adopting the principles of those "whose infirm and baby minds are gratified by mischief," strengthen the worst prejudices of our religious and political opponents?[25]

Stokes contended that the Catholic refusal to cooperate would stimulate hostile suspicions about Catholic schools, that the bishops and the Poor School Committee had only themselves to blame for the exclusion of Catholics from the commission, that there was nothing to fear from that body as constituted, and that Catholics had everything to gain by demonstrating through such an investigation the distinctive character of Catholic schools.[26]

It is not without significance that the writer of this article was no mere layman but also a government inspector of Catholic schools.[27] Stokes never admitted knowing that an official decision

---

[25][Stokes], "The Royal Commission on Education," p. 17.

[26]Ibid., pp. 17-20.

[27]None of the discussions focusing on this question note the significance of Stokes' position vis-à-vis the bishops. Butler, op. cit., p. 310, called Stokes the "principal authority on the subject," and Altholz, op. cit., p. 89, merely quotes Butler. Gasquet, op. cit., pp. 1-1j, describes Stokes' position more fully

had been reached and justified his commentary by saying that the public had already been "appealed to on one side," and that his purpose was merely to furnish further materials for a judgment on the question. At the same time he insisted that there was no religious principle at stake, which of course suggested the matter should not be deemed a conflict of authority. But there is another aspect to the question of authority which has not been noted. Since Stokes was a government-employed inspector of Catholic schools, his commentary touched not only on the authority of the bishops to decide such matters for Catholics but their authority vis-à-vis the government inspector. The authority of the government inspectors was a matter of some sensitivity at the time; inspectors were officially forbidden to discuss matters of religious authority in their reports to the government, and Stokes had been criticized on several occasions for violating those instructions. Now with respect to a broader area of sensitivity having to do with authority in the matter of education, it has been seen that there was much controversy over the trust deeds precisely because there was some question as to who had the power to determine what was and what was not a matter of religion.

Of course there was nothing in the Catholic school inspector's instructions which prevented him from publishing his views outside the context of his official reports to the government, but certainly there were implied difficulties in his doing so. The principal difficulty related to whether a government inspector should publish

---

but gives no indication that it had any impact on the views expressed concerning episcopal authority.

anything which appeared to contradict episcopal policy or to assume the authority to determine what was or was not a religious question. Although Stokes' article in the Rambler was unsigned, the correspondence published subsequently in the Tablet and the Weekly Register shows that his identity was hardly unsuspected.[28] With these background factors in mind it is possible to look more carefully at the Rambler article.

Two interdependent lines of argument were developed in the Rambler, one advocating cooperation with the commission, the other attacking the policy of non-cooperation. Had Stokes been content to advocate cooperation on the positive grounds he put forward his contention that he was unaware of an official episcopal decision to the contrary might have been less subject to question. As it was, his attack was formulated in language which must have undermined possible sources of support for the policies he favored. In the article itself there was a semblance of balance between attack and advocacy, but because the resulting controversy focused more on his lines of attack the conflict of authority came to be stressed over and above the question of whether it was prudent to find a means of cooperating with the commission.

Stokes said that Catholics had only themselves to blame for their non-representation on the commission; he also attacked the

---

[28]See the following issues of the Weekly Register: February 12, 1859, p. 3; and February 19, 1859, p. 5. George Montgomery's letter to the Tablet, February 11, 1859, p. 105, says: "Let us be certain that he is not a salaried official of 'the Government which cannot be thought friendly' to Catholics, or that if he is, he has some guarantees to give of his independence of thought . . . ."

choice of Charles Langdale as a possible commissioner. And, as if to add insult to injury, he claimed that Catholics were a minority too insignificant to demand such representation.[29] He was clearly motivated by the belief that Catholics had nothing to fear from the commission as already constituted, but his severe comments about Catholic bungling and Langdale's unsuitability for a seat on the commission tended to obscure the positive dimensions of his posi-tion. The claim that Catholics themselves were to blame for not being represented on the commission was never effectively refuted, nor was the claim that commission appointments had been sufficient-ly publicized to give the bishops and the Poor School Committee adequate notice to seek Catholic representation while there was still a chance to succeed. Other lines of discussion were more questionable. Stokes said that the fact that the Commission was bound to write a report favoring Protestant education would put a Catholic in an embarrassing spot when it came time to write the report. But what aroused strongest hostility in some quarters was the suggestion that Catholics had no one qualified to serve; Stokes recommended the Oratorian Father Anthony Hutchison but noted that he was not well enough known among the powers that be. His nega-tive remarks about Langdale provoked particular irritation.

The positive aspect of his position was based upon the view that Catholic education was endangered by the growth of forces hostile to the denominational system. Since the major obstacle to the destruction of that system was the existence of religious difference, those who were committed to the continuation of denomi-

---

[29][Stokes], "The Royal Commission on Education," pp. 20-21.

national education should use the commission's inquiry to demonstrate as powerfully as possible the strength of religious differences. Thus Stokes argued that the Newcastle investigation provided Catholics with a grand opportunity to prove "to impartial
witnesses" that Catholic schools were so distinct in their
religious teaching that a merger with other schools was an impossibility.[30]

While this view certainly had much to recommend it, it must
also be remembered that denominationalism was a Protestant phenomenon and its defense a Protestant cause. If a study of Catholic
schools had revealed that only Catholic schools were distinct in
their catechetical offerings, such a revelation would have contributed to their isolation as thoroughly as any policy of non-
participation. Of course some would say that Anglican schools were
also distinctively denominational. True, but they were also the
chief object of attack. It is hard to see that Catholics would
have benefited from a demonstration that only Anglican and Catholic
schools had anything to gain from the continuation of the denominational system. As events proved, Dissenters were willing, only a
few years later, to sacrifice their own denominational instruction
in order to undermine Anglican schools. It seems unlikely that
their policies would have been restrained by a clearer understanding of Catholic commitment to denominationalism. After all, one
reason why High Church exclusiveness in education was under attack
was that it was believed to be too Catholic. This line of thought

---

[30]Ibid., pp. 26-27.

was hinted at by one of the disputants in the controversy,[31] but its historical importance calls for careful understanding.

Stokes dealt with the Commission's instructions to investigate religious teaching in the schools in several ways, not all of which were compatible with one another. He distinguished between the inspectors who were subject to Privy Council arrangements and the Royal Commissioners, saying that the latter could not be bound by terms which applied only to that one office of government. It was his view that the commission's inquiry into religious teaching in no way violated Catholic agreements with the Privy Council. Failure to understand this distinction and its implication, he said, had produced some of the misunderstandings that led to the erroneous policy of non-cooperation.[32] Stokes did admit that there was some, but only minimal, risk involved in permitting the commission to look into the religious teaching in Catholic schools, but he insisted that the investigation was absolutely essential because the religious difficulty was "the chief obstacle" to the establishment of a national undenominational system. He dismissed the element of risk involved in having Protestants investigate Catholic doctrinal teaching by saying that the commissioners were not interested in making judgments about doctrine but only wanted to ascertain "simply as a matter of fact" what formularies were taught and whether they were taught "so as to be understood." He went on to explain that:

---

[31]Tablet, February 25, 1859, p. 139; and Weekly Register, February 26, 1859, p. 4.

[32][Stokes], "The Royal Commission on Education," pp. 24-25.

> They will inquire into the facts, and are not authorized
> to express any opinions . . . It is not conceivable that
> any disposition exists to censure the use of Catholic
> catechism in avowedly Catholic schools, or to report that
> religion is carried either too far or not far enough. Of
> all persons living, the commissioners are probably the
> most full alive to their incapacity to deal with such
> questions.33

To assume that Victorian Protestants could be so objective about Catholic teaching was somewhat naive; to press such an assumption upon the whole Catholic body was impolitic. And to say that the matter was one of political expediency involving no religious principle could not have been better calculated to stir up controversy.

Stokes concluded by stating that the whole question of the inspection of reformatories had been "very unnecessarily mixed up with the Royal Commission, with which it has no concern." Since he had argued that the authority of the commission was not bound by precedent, that indeed it was "an inquisition sui generis," he naturally believed the troubles with reformatory inspectors had nothing to do with the matter, but he failed to note that the reformatory inspection problem involved a definite religious problem--the right of Anglican clerics to inspect religious teaching in Catholic schools.34

The Tablet published several critical letters and an equally critical editorial in response to Stokes' article. The first to appear was the January 8, 1859 editorial expressing regret over the language used in the Rambler and over the existence of disunity on

---

33Ibid., p. 26.

34Ibid., pp. 25, 29.

so important a question. The writer said that the protest was particularly serious because it came after an official decision had been reached "by those with whom the decision rests." The editor asked, "Whose are the ´infirm and baby minds that are gratified by mischief´?" He went on to say, "The Rambler thinks it a subject of congratulations that no Catholic is on the Commission." This he described as a "miserable line for a Catholic writer."[35] It is clear that Wallis was as much offended by the tone of the Rambler article, which Simpson later characterized as "temperate,"[36] as by the content of its arguments. Wallis acknowledged that the only religious principle at stake was the "obedience due to Episcopal commands by those who have received them." Apart from that, the editor said the question was not one of religion or conscience. He admitted, in other words that it was not a matter of dogma or morals. Wallis also noted that the Rambler writer had displayed an unbecoming servility to government policy.[37] Stokes had been accused of this before.

During the remaining weeks of January the Tablet published numerous letters about the Rambler article focusing primarily on Stokes´ claim that Catholics had no right to be represented on the Newcastle Commission. In keeping with the traditional English understanding of representative interests one writer argued that the distinctiveness of Catholic schools afforded sufficient grounds

---

[35]Tablet, January 8, 1859, p. 24.

[36]Simpson, "Catholic Church in England," p. 182.

[37]Tablet, January 8, 1859, p. 24.

for their being represented, which argument he said would have been understood even by Parliament. It was also stressed that Protestants were not qualified to judge any aspects of Catholic religious teaching for the simple reason that Protestants did not understand such teaching themselves.[38] One correspondent translated this point into a spoof about what might have happened at a school being investigated by a Protestant commissioner.

The scene depicted took place in a Catholic boys' school. A few samples from the fictitious question-answer session suggest what the writer had in mind:

> Commissioner: What religion are you of?
> Boy: By the Grace of God, I am a Christian.
> Commissioner: True, but let me see that you understand
>   the meaning of your answer. You do not, of course,
>   mean that you are a Christian in any exclusive
>   sense?
> Boy: By the grace of God, I am a Christian.
> Commissioner: Well; but must you not define and limit
>   your answer? Your are a Christian, it is true, of
>   the Roman Catholic persuasion; but in this country
>   there are many other Christians, not of that per-
>   suasion. Wesleyan Christians, Independent
>   Christians, Christians of the Church of England.
>   You ought at least to know something of the sects
>   which, in common with your own, conscientiously
>   dissent from the Established Church. Who are the
>   Dissenters?
> Boy (puzzled): The Soupers.

There followed a discussion about Sunday observance; after the boy had said the way to keep the Sabbath holy was to attend Mass, the commissioner asked what must be avoided; when the child answered that servile work must be avoided the commissioner continued:

> Commissioner: Tell me, now, something which it would be
>   exceedingly wrong, or what you would call a "mortal
>   sin" to do on Sunday.
> Boy (after reflection): To go to a Protestant Church.

---

[38]*Ibid.*, January 15, 1859, pp. 41-42.

Finally the conversation turned to the problem of supremacy:

> Commissioner: Who is the head of your church?
> Boy: The Reverend Father Dempsey, Sir.

After intervening discussion between the commissioner and his assistant concerning the propriety of this line of questioning the commissioner went on to ask, "Is not the Pope the Head of your Church?" He was told that the Pope was "head of the Holy Catholic Church." Then the commissioner came to what he believed to be the key question:

> Commissioner: You have told me, my lad, that the Pope is regarded by you as the spiritual (the spiritual head, observe) of the Roman Catholic body? Again, I ask you, who is the head of the Established Church of this country? Of the Protestant Church, if you so like to call it?
> Boy (after a little hesitation, and somewhat confused): The Devil, Sir.39

In February the Rambler published a second article, this time in answer to the Tablet's criticism. It had now become clear that Stokes was aware that there was a problem of authority, for much of his discussion attempted to demonstrate that no authoritative decision had been communicated "to the laity for support." As part of his argument he submitted that respect for the hierarchy precluded his believing that a decision had been made, and he concluded that the rumored decision was "tentative and provisional."40 The problem here is that there is evidence that Stokes and Simpson discussed the bishops' circular before the first article was published

---

39Ibid., January 22, 1859, p. 58.

40[Stokes], "The Commission and the Tablet," pp. 104-113.

in January.[41]   Regardless, Stokes attempted to minimize the
impression that he was attacking the bishops, and in this article
he stressed condemnation of the Poor School Committee for its
failure to hold meetings to discuss the question as well as for its
general lack of communication with supporters.   For the most part,
however, the article repeated the position Stokes had developed
earlier calling for Catholics to cooperate with the Royal
Commission.

The controversy continued in the pages of the _Tablet_ and the
Weekly Register during February and March.   The _Rambler_ was attacked by Canon O'Neal of the Westminster diocese as well as by Charles
Langdale, George Montgomery, Bishop Ullathorne and an anonymous
writer.   Critical correspondents focused on the authority of the
bishops to decide the question and gave reasons why it was not
desirable to deal with the commission.   For their part Stokes and
Marshall contended that participation in the inquiry was not a
matter of episcopal authority, and they recited again the reasons
favoring cooperation.   It was clear by this time that there was
more at issue than Catholic participation in the commission's
educational inquiry; the whole scope of episcopal authority was in
question.   Therefore, some reference to other grounds on which that
authority was being tested would seem helpful.

These were years when episcopal relations with the Catholic
press were particularly troublesome, and in England the _Rambler_
gained a reputation for stirring up difficulties.   But the hier-

---

[41]Simpson to Acton, December 24, 1858, _Correspondence of Acton
and Simpson_, 1:112.

archy had its own problems of authority to contend with; there were Wiseman's disputes with his Chapter; there were disputes among certain bishops having to do with control over the seminaries; and there was widespread resentment outside the Westminster diocese over the Cardinal's understanding of the powers of a Metropolitan as they affected the powers of the suffragan bishops. In addition there was discontent among the clergy stemming from their disappointment at not receiving parochial privileges.[42] Several of these disputes made their way to Rome and were subject to the long and often misleading processes of Roman litigation.[43] Of course in the larger spectrum there were the debates between Liberal Catholics and Ultramontanes over the Temporal Power and papal authority. It is not easy to determine just what place the educational controversy had in this total picture, but it is certain that its significance has been underrated. A broad re-evaluation of many other factors is necessary to sustain that judgment; and while that larger effort is not possible in these pages it is essential to stress the capacity of the education question to arouse serious hostilities.

Keeping these background factors in mind it may be helpful to turn for a moment to an article written by Richard Simpson in 1859 for the Correspondant.[44] This article, a little over twenty pages

---

[42]Morgan V. Sweeney, "Diocesan Organization and Administration," in Beck, op. cit., p. 124ff. See also W. Ward, Wiseman, 2:253-288, 321-394; and Butler, op. cit., 1:197-256.

[43]The most readable account of this problem is that presented by Butler, ibid.,

[44]Bibliographic discussion of this Simpson article is given in n. 23, above.

in length, treats two "coups" by which the English hierarchy was said to have increased its despotic power over laity and clergy.[45] Simpson was roughly treated by the bishops in February 1859 when he was forced to give up editing the Rambler;[46] this explains why this particular article was more devastating than most. One of the coups described was the hierarchy's victory "not over its enemies but over its friends" in the matter of the education commission, and about half of the article was devoted to the Royal Commission question. Since there is little evidence that popular education was one of Simpson's major preoccupations, and since the positions stated here were substantially those developed by Stokes in the Rambler--with one or two important exceptions--it must be assumed that immediate circumstances prompted the preparation of this trenchant attack upon tyrannical bishops. Still, the article illustrates something about the Rambler's troubles which should be mentioned here.

The Rambler was forever being accused of a failure to present the "true position of Catholics," and its stance on the education problems of the day must be admitted to lack much by way of obvious concern for what many believed were essential "Catholic interests." If one were to make a superficial evaluation based upon quick reading and impressions it would not be difficult to argue that the Rambler published articles on education primarily when there was reason to take issue with episcopal policy, or when some particular

[45]Simpson, "Catholic Church in England," p. 171.

[46]McElrath, Simpson, pp. 80-82; Altholz, op. cit., pp. 91-97; and Correspondence of Acton and Simpson, 1:151ff.

aspect of Catholic educational sentiment was open to criticism.
Careful study would not sustain such a conclusion, at least not
without major qualifications, but the Rambler's avoidance of 'vulgarity, prejudice and ignorance'[47] resulted in certain distortions
in their coverage of the education question. It would seem that
the writers assumed their commitment to "true Catholicity" and
published their criticism of its distorted expressions. The result
was a balance which misled some to believe the Rambler was more
anxious to defend the Government than the Church.

The Simpson article under discussion here illustrates that
tendency. In discussing his views about religious education
Simpson mentioned having witnessed the "utter futility and hypo-
crisy of the pretended religious instruction" in an Anglican school
and expressed doubt as to whether young children should--or could
in fact--learn doctrine. In describing the secularist trend he
showed what were the points of appeal secularists were urging upon
the public. It seems clear that his purpose was to show that the
government's inquiry into religious teaching in English schools was
sensible and justified, even commendable. The government was paying dearly for religious education; religious education was coming
under heavy political attack; and therefore the government had a
right to find out whether that religious education was effective.
Simpson said that the question touched on religion and politics

---

[47]Simpson, "Catholic Church in England," p. 176. Here Simpson
used the terms "vulgarity, ignorance and prejudice" in another
context, but these terms appropriately describe the dislike both
Acton and Simpson evidenced for similar characteristics in
Catholicism.

simultaneously and that it was, therefore, the business of both the laity and the hierarchy. His point was that the bishops should not have acted as though it was their sole province and should certainly not have treated the Rambler so shabbily for its treatment of this question. He was merely pleading for sound political and religious judgment, yet his emphasis was upon the need for sound political judgment. When Simpson's kind words about aspects of secularist schemes are balanced against severe criticism about the content of religious education it is by no means clear that he would have defended religious education. It was partly because of this type of writing that some of Simpson's contemporaries questioned his Catholicity; in recent times the depth and sincerity of Simpson's Catholicity has been vindicated by the publication of his correspondence with Acton.

But to return to the question of authority; Simpson's plea for the rights of the laity should not be seen out of context. The bishops, school inspectors and members of the Poor School Committee were constantly expressing concern over the indifference of the laity toward the cause of popular education and the work of the Poor School Committee. It was said that advice was plentiful but contributions of labor and money and time were in short supply. The education question was much more than a problem of episcopal authority or political expedience. It was an enormous pastoral challenge. If Catholic press reporting is a fair indicator, Wiseman, Manning, Ullathorne and several other bishops gave an extraordinary amount of their time and energy to this problem which they seemed convinced was one of the major issues for English Catholics. There were many who believed the Catholic press had an obligation to provide supportive coverage. This the Rambler did to an extent, but the balance of its coverage did not seem to contemporaries to be on that side.

If the Rambler refused to give lip service to certain obvious statements of Catholic interests in education it is equally clear that the bishops refused to give lip service to the political analysis provided in the Rambler, which earned it a high reputation among Victorian periodicals. But these supposedly conflicting positions ran like parallel lines, and the bishops refused to tolerate criticism from a quarter whence no help appeared to emanate.

These were some of the factors relating to the controversy over authority. Happily, analysis of the question of whether it was wise, politic or safe to cooperate with the commission was less complex. As already suggested, Stokes' arguments evoked numerous responses; it is time to look briefly at some of the positions developed in the Weekly Register and the Tablet. George Montgomery, who was responsible for a poor mission in Wednesbury,[48] challenged Stokes' statement claiming that opening Catholic schools to commissioner' inspection would demonstrate that Catholic education "was not the hole-in-the-corner mixture of jugglery, immorality, and sedition which the ignorant imagine."[49] Montgomery said

---

[48]Biographical information on Montgomery is given in his signed letter to the editor; see "Correspondence: the Dublin Review and the Work of the Converts," Rambler, 2nd. ser., 7 (April 1857): 318-322.

[49]Tablet, February 11, 1859, pp. 105-106; and Weekly Register, February 12, 1859, p. 31.

Stokes´claim proved that it was not the kind of "purely factual" inquiry which Stokes wanted all to believe but involved serious judgments about the teaching of Catholic religion. Such a right of judgment, he said, touched on the question of jurisdiction, and the state´s jurisdiction could not be admitted to intrude that far upon religious matters.

In the Weekly Register of February 19, Canon O´Neal criticized the Rambler position from another perspective. O´Neal charged that the aim of the Royal Commission was the overthrow of the present system and implied that Catholic cooperation with it would serve that purpose--a purpose which was totally opposed to Catholic interests. O´Neal also criticized the way Stokes had tried to dismiss the reformatory matter as having nothing to do with the bishops´ decision:

> He knows well that the attempt of the Home Office to substitute Protestant for Catholic inspection in our Reformatories is at the present time a subject of grave discussion between the Bishops and the Home Office, which may ultimately lead to a severance of the existing Reformatory schools from the Government Grant; yet he flippantly takes it for granted that it is a settled matter. Were we to admit the Protestant Inspectors sent to us from the Royal Commission, and allow them to examine our children, not only in the elementary branches of the school teaching, but also to catechise them in their religious knowledge, upon what grounds could we ever after refuse admission to the Protestant Inspectors forced upon us by the Secretary of State? The very existence of the establishment mainly depends upon the will of the latter, whereas we can expect neither thanks or reward from the former.

Toward the close of his letter O´Neal offered the following observations:

> To conclude this letter . . . it is obvious that the Board of Education is now arraigned before the tribunal of this Royal Commission. The promoters of this commission have determined to introduce a new and difficultly organized system of education. They know that their

system must be built up on the ruins of the existing one. The natural inference is, that they will magnify every weak point which comes under their cognizance. Can we suppose that we are so immaculate and so perfect in the education of our poor children that their inspectors should not discover matter for censure? More especially as our opponent tells us that even if we had a Catholic on the Commission it is not likely that he could conscientiously affix his signature to their report. If such be the misgivings of the advocate of this commission, it appears obvious that its proceedings do not merit either Catholic co-operation or confidence.50

O'Neal's emphasis upon the political aims of the commission being hostile to denominationalism is historically important; this is a perspective which requires further investigation. Suffice to say here, however, that several members of the commission were anything but strong defenders of state aid to denominational education, despite their official status as Anglicans.51

On March 12 the Weekly Register published two pastoral letters which treated the Royal Commission question: Ullathorne's and Wiseman's. Ullathorne insisted that the Commission was a Protestant "tribunal" incapable of judging Catholic teachings in a way which would benefit Catholic schools. He also elaborated upon the circumstances which had led to the bishops' November decision, stressing the religious dimensions of the investigation as the main reason for their determination. This was not news, but his explanation of the way the reformatory inspection problem had influenced their thinking was not without significance. It was shown that

---

50Weekly Register, February 19, 1859, pp. 4-5.

51For information concerning the religious views of two commissioners see Samuel Leon Levy, Nassau W. Senior, 1790-1864 (New York: Augustus M. Kelley, 1970), pp. 56-59; and Elisabeth Wallace, Goldwin Smith, Victorian Liberal (Toronto: University of Toronto Press, 1957), pp. 211-214. See also the Weekly Register of January 11, 1862, p. 9.

exceptionally subtle policy changes threatened Catholic reformatories with religious inspection by Anglican clerics. Stokes had
implied that the bishops had simply confused the inspectors' role
with the commissioners' role, but Ullathorne made it clear that
what he feared was the precedent of permitting Protestant inspection of Catholic religious teaching.[52] In the same issue of the
Weekly Register Wiseman's pastoral similarly recounted the bishops'
decision, though the Cardinal's emphasis was more on the authority
of the bishops to decide than upon the basis for the decision. In
the context of all the controversies raging over the way Wiseman
used his authority, his plea, "Obey your prelates and be subject to
them" was hardly likely to encourage that spirit of reconciliation
the Cardinal so often described as his fondest hope for English
Catholicism.

What the foregoing discussion has attempted to show is that
there were substantive positions on both sides, that the bishops'
decision was not merely the result of ignorance and panic. But if
that is admitted it must also be admitted that their authority was
exerted with a heavy hand. McElrath has described the way the
bishops moved against the Rambler by depriving Simpson of editorial
control,[53] though without recourse to any canonical processes.
Newman was asked to be the instrument of their policy, and in the
course of his dealings with Ullathorne was told that Simpson

_____

[52]Weekly Register, March 12, 1859, p. 3

[53]McElrath, Simpson, pp. 72-73.

"plainly cannot judge what is and what is not sound language."[54]

Ignoring the merits of Ullathorne's statement it must be asked
whether that constituted sufficient or valid grounds for drastic
episcopal action. Many believed not, including Simpson, and of
course Acton, but perhaps more significantly including also Newman,
William George Ward and others.[55] The problem was well stated by
Charles Weld in a letter to Simpson in which he conveyed his views
that the private concessions made by Simpson were a mistake and
that the affair should have been aired publicly,

> . . . as a warning to all who by writing or public life
> of any kind wish to serve the cause of Religion as inde-
> pendent laymen, or in any other quality or office but
> that of Bishops--if no other is recognized in the Ch. let
> us have it so declared--If all Catholic literature is to
> be confined to Bps pastorals & politics merely to be
> their echo let it be known to all whom it may concern.
> If the Cardinal's alleged dictum, that "the only function
> of the laity is to pray" be really the law of this land,
> let us know it, that we may get out of it into some more
> Xtian country. If we are to have an Index without its
> rules, & an arbitrary literary dictatorship, let it be
> declared openly, & don't let us have a secret Inquisition
> too &c &c. There is no limit now to the clerical ambi-
> tion in England.56

Simpson, however, acquiesced, and the treatment meted out to
him was followed by a devastating attack against Newman who assumed
editorial control of the _Rambler_ and proceeded to defend its right
to publish Stokes' articles. It was Stokes' position that
questions of Catholic policy were open to discussion prior to

---

[54]Ullathorne to Newman, February 16, 1859, in Dessain, _Letters and Diaries of Newman_, 19:211-212.

[55]For information on Ward's response to this situation see Simpson to Acton, March 19, 1859, in _Correspondence of Acton and Simpson_, 1:158.

[56]Charles Weld to Simpson, n.d., cited in Simpson to Acton, March 22, 1859, in _Correspondence of Acton and Simpson_, 1:160.

authoritative and publicized pronouncements by the episcopacy. His first statement to this effect provoked an attack which Newman answered with his famous article on 'consulting the faithful.'[57] Here he elaborated the view that the laity had both the right and the duty to defend the faith and cited historical instances in which the laity had indeed been instrumental toward that end. The story of the troubles this brought upon Newman has been told elsewhere[58] and need not be retold here, but it must be noted that he was delated to Rome and subjected to a cloud of suspicion about his orthodoxy for several years. The whole affair reflected badly upon many individuals and was most unfortunate for the developing relations between the Catholic press and Church authority.

There is reason to conclude that the Rambler editors failed to grasp certain facets of the education question and equal reason to conclude that the bishops failed to understand what damage might be wrought by the overzealous exercise of authority. Acton, Simpson and Newman understood that times were approaching--had indeed arrived--when the defense of Catholicism called for the full efforts and talents of the laity and that the press could become an instrument for calling the laity to its task. The point must be made that much greater restraint was called for from both sides. The crux of Stokes' position would not have been sacrificed by the suppression of the most offensive elements of his articles, and certainly the bishops might have dealt with the Rambler more hon-

[57]Newman, "On Consulting the Faithful in Matters of Doctrine," Rambler, 3rd. ser., 1 (July 1859): 198-230.

[58]Altholz, op. cit., pp. 98-112.

estly, more openly, less arbitrarily, and less severely. But of course such speculations contribute little to our understanding of history. History must deal with what actually happened as a result of this controversy, and it will be seen that there was a noticeable decline in the Catholic press coverage of educational questions. Accounting for that decline is an important historical problem. Surely one can cite the obvious reasons why such coverage fell off--the ever increasing importance of foreign affairs, the confusion over the Revised Code, distractions having to do with Catholics in workhouses, and Irish questions--but Simpson's eviction as _Rambler_ editor cannot be eliminated as one of those reasons.

The decline of press discussion of this question was most unfortunate, for the developments of the 1860s were crucial to the future of denominational education, and the one policy least likely to contribute to the defense of denominationalism was silence. So one is forced to conclude that those who provoked and those who overreacted to the provocation must share responsibility for weakening the press's role in this struggle.

The Newcastle Commission's report appeared early in 1861, evoking no more than a mild response in the Catholic press. This report, which comprised six volumes of data and analysis, has received only the summary attention of historians. It must be admitted that the organization of material is such as to encourage historians to pick and choose from its contents, which helps explain why one finds such contradictory accounts of the commissioners' findings and recommendations. Two aspects of the report deserve special attention--those having to do with the religious question and those having to do with the way Victorians defined the scope of popular education. With respect to the latter it must be emphasized that the report treated popular education as a unit which included not only the weekday education of the independent poor who attended the so-called poor schools but also the education of children in workhouses, reformatories, industrial schools, military schools, and private schools. The commissioners' attention to private education is of particular significance, for it was estimated that at least one-third of the lower class pupils attended such schools.[59]

Increasingly historical studies of popular education have been highly specialized, which is understandable given the massive documentary evidence to be mastered; but what has resulted is a picture of education dominated by denominational day schools which tended to be given over to the board system after 1870 for a variety of reasons. If one thinks about what it meant to talk of the education of the poor at mid-century one cannot avoid recognizing that the distinctions between the factory poor, the workhouse poor, the vagrant non-convict poor, the vagrant convict poor and the children of poor soldiers and sailors in addition to the ordinary poor children who attended regular weekday and evening schools--these were fine distinctions indeed and were more bureaucratically useful than real. Yet bureaucratic divisions have a way of becoming real, and the temptation is to assume that divisions pre-existed the

---

[59]Newcastle Commission Report, 1:80-83.

bureaucracy's effort to structure them into governable subdivisions of a larger whole. One of the most important aspects of the Newcastle Commission report is that it makes it clear that Victorians understood educational problems to be 'one of a piece.' Now the factor common to all elements of the education problem was the religious factor.[60] This would lead one to expect that the Newcastle Commission's report might have attracted considerable attention to its conclusions regarding the religious dimensions of education; but few historians have paid much attention to that facet of the report. Thus even the relatively mild response of the Catholic press to this report has some historical significance.

Only the Dublin Review, the Rambler, and the Weekly Register published major articles about the report, though the Northern Press also made reference to it. The Weekly Register was first to notice the report, but its coverage was limited to a single issue—— that of April 6, 1861. This issue contained two articles on the subject——one an editorial, the other an excerpt from an Anglican source. The editorial stressed statistical returns which showed that Catholics constituted a larger minority of the school popula- tion than had been expected. This was cited as proof that Catholics should have been represented on the commission. The article also remarked on the commissioners' recommendation that aid to schools be more closely tied to student achievement. There was also discussion of numerous other details contained in the report,

---

[60]There is considerable evidence in the Catholic press indi- cating that the Church of England took advantage of bureaucratic divisions affecting education to establish religious monopolies in certain areas——particularly in workhouses, jails and prisons.

but all that need be noted here is that the report was not viewed as being hostile to the denominational system.[61]

The Weekly Register's interpretation is reinforced by a second article in the same issue, which was taken from the report prepared by the Establishment's Education Society. The first item in this report confirmed that the commission recommended the continuation of the denominational system. There followed a list of twenty-eight other recommendations. The Commission's decision against recommending the compulsory adoption of a conscience clause was high on the list, while many others had to do with technical changes proposed with a view to simplifying bureaucratic procedures, increasing local responsibilities (without introducing local political control over the schools) or with recommended changes in the teacher training curriculum.

Basically the recommendations were these: building grants were to remain the same while the annual grants (teacher and pupil-teacher salaries and stipends, maintenance and school improvement grants, books, maps and supplies grants etc.) were to be eliminated in their existing form. That complex of funding was to be replaced by a combination of local and Privy Council grants. The Privy Council grants were to be distributed on a per capita basis according to attendance and on the condition that schools met certain conditions--primarily the employment of certified teachers and the existence of a minimally approved facility; the local grants were to be paid out of local--county or borough--rates according to the results of student achievement tests to be administered by a newly

---

[61]Weekly Register, April 6, 1861, p. 9.

appointed body of county examiners. The general inspection was to remain intact and the duties of inspectors were to continue unchanged as well, although the effectiveness of the secular instruction was to be more closely tested at the local level.[62]

The details of these proposed arrangements need not be discussed here for they were never carried out as proposed, but it is necessary to emphasize that with respect to the church-state issue these suggestions would have left the denominational system intact--would most likely have strengthened it--with inspection remaining denominational as initially established. This is extremely important because inspection was one of the chief means whereby Anglican schools were secured for religious purposes. Of course this fact did not have a direct impact on Catholic schools, though Catholics insisted that denominational inspection was essential as a means of preventing government inspectors from inspecting religious aspects of Catholic education.

It may also be worth noting that the Weekly Register editor accepted the Anglican conclusion that the report posed no threat to denominational education. Certainly Wilberforce was acquainted with Anglicans active in the politics of education, so he may have understood the immediate intentions of the commissioners. Equally significant, he recognized that Catholics shared with Anglicans a long-term concern over the future of the denominational system.[63]

---

[62]Ibid., p. 11.

[63]See Newsome, op. cit., pp. 220-221, for discussion of Wilberforce's Anglican background.

The Commission recommendations summarized in the Weekly Register also touched on two aspects of the question which are too often neglected. In the first place both the local and the Privy Council grants were to be extended more liberally to the vast number of private schools heretofore outside the scope of government influence. Local grants were to be made available to all schools whether or not they employed certified teachers, assuming their facilities met minimal standards. Privy Council grants were to be distributed only to schools employing certified teachers, but provisions were to be introduced making it possible for private school teachers to obtain certificates without attending teacher-training colleges. These arrangements would have extended the benefits of public aid to schools on a much broader scale while preserving the character of private and denominational schools alike.

The second aspect of these recommendations requiring attention had to do with the connection between charities and endowments and popular education. It was proposed that the Charities Commission be joined with the Education Department and that action be taken to render educational charities and endowments more useful to the cause of education. By these measures it was assumed considerable funding would have been released to support education.[64]

The importance of both aspects of the commission's recommendations was this: they assumed that education should remain within the sphere of voluntary, private and denominational activity and

---

[64]Weekly Register, April 6, 1861, p. 11.

provided means for improving the private sector's capacity to support popular schools. This is exceedingly important because those calling for a national publicly funded system of schools claimed that voluntarism was inadequate to the task. That argument gained momentum during the 1860s. Significantly, that argument became more convincing only after the government refused to take those steps necessary to improve the capacities of private interests to do the job.

In May 1861 the Dublin Review published an article on the report which was written by Wiseman's secretary, Canon Morris. Although he expressed regret about the exclusion of Catholics from the commission it is clear that Morris believed that the commissioners favored the perpetuation of the existing denominational system.[65] In this regard Morris called attention to the Commission's finding that private subscriptions to the schools were over twice the amount spent by the government. Morris had high praise for the way the Privy Council had treated Catholics and expressed relief and approval that the commissioners believed the existing system to be "the only one by which it would be possible to secure the religious character of popular education."[66]

The Dublin Review contributor was not content to assert the report's support of denominationalism but quoted at length from the commissioners' conclusions concerning alternative proposals--undenominationalism and strict separation of religious and secular

---

[65][John Morris], "Popular Education in England," Dublin Review 50 (May 1861): 73-76.

[66]Ibid., pp. 72-73.

instruction. He showed that the Commissioners believed neither alternative was "suitable" for England; the writer also showed that the Commissioners believed that rate-supported and controlled schools would be unable to provide a harmonious basis for popular education.[67]

Morris discussed other dimensions of the education question at length--the pauper schools, the industrial schools and reformatories. This further verifies one of the arguments presented in these pages, that Victorians viewed the scope of popular education in broader terms than their twentieth-century historians. It remains for future historians to bring all these elements together into a much needed re-evaluation. But before leaving the Dublin Review's discussion of the report it may be beneficial to glance at Morris' summary of the statistical distribution of various kinds of schools aimed at the education of the poor. Over one and a half million students were said to be enrolled in religious week-day schools; in addition there were over a half-million students distributed among the following types of publicly supported institutions:[68]

---

[67]Ibid., pp. 75-76.

[68]For additional information see the Newcastle Commission Report, 1:80-83.

TABLE 3

NUMBER OF CHILDREN ATTENDING SCHOOLS
RECEIVING PUBLIC FUNDS, 1860

Type of School	Number of Students
Ragged, orphan and other philanthropic schools, and factory schools	43,098
Evening schools	80,966
Sunday schools	411,554
Workhouse, reformatory, naval and military schools	47,748
Collegiate and superior or richer endowed schools	35,000
Total	618,366

SOURCE: [John Morris], "Popular Education in England," Dublin Review 50 (May 1861): 89-91.

This, however, is far from the whole picture, for the report itself tells us there were over 860,000 pupils in private schools.[69] In short, the elementary education taking place under Privy Council supervision was important but much less dominant than historians have implied by virtue of the inordinate attention they have given to that system.

Catholics had particularly good reason to be concerned with other aspects of education because the Catholic poor constituted a significant minority in workhouses, because the Irish poor were particularly subject to vagrancy laws which propelled them into industrial schools and because Irish street children seemed to be vulnerable to convictions which subjected them to reformatory institutions. In addition the Catholics constituted about a third of the ranks in the armed forces, which accounted for their interest

---

[69]Ibid., 1:83.

in military and naval schools operated for the children of soldiers and sailors. These facts would explain why the Catholic press attended carefully to these seemingly peripheral aspects of popular education, yet Catholics were nowhere in the majority so one is left with the obvious conclusion that awareness of the scope of popular education was by no means a peculiarly Catholic concern.

Finally, it is appropriate to look briefly at the _Rambler_'s coverage of the commissioners' report, which was contained in two articles; as the second one focused primarily on the revised code, however, the first will be discussed here and the second will be discussed below. The first article appeared in November 1861; it was written by Stokes who pointed out that the report put Catholic schools in an unnecessarily bad light, which he blamed on the Catholic refusal to cooperate with the commission.[70] Stokes seemed more concerned with vindicating the _Rambler_'s earlier position than with the content of the report, and he failed to treat the commissioners' comments about the future of denominationalism. This is particularly interesting since he had argued that the fate of denominationalism was crucial to the Catholic interest and that the Catholic refusal to participate in the investigation would undermine that system.

Stokes also raised a question about the conscience clause by calling attention to Marshall's testimony before the commission.[71] Marshall had reported that Protestant children attended Catholic

---

[70][Stokes], "The Education Commission," _Rambler_, 3rd ser., 6 (November 1861): 63-64, 66ff.

[71]_Ibid_., p. 84.

schools rather extensively, and Stokes made an issue of pointing out that Catholic schools were obligated to see that Protestant children be exempted from catechetical instruction if their parents so desired. He cited part of the agreement made between the Poor School Committee and the bishops back in 1847 and argued that adherence to this 'conscience clause' was important. As Marshall's testimony had indicated that the policies of the Catholic schools in this regard were quite varied, Stokes' remarks were intended to be critical. This may seem to be a minor point, but Stokes' position concerning the conscience clause was much more closely allied with the position taken by secularists and those favoring undenominationalism in education than with the position maintained by most denominationalists. It may also have reflected the government's increasing interest in imposing a conscience clause uniformly on state-aided schools. Strict enforcement of any kind of conscience clause would have entailed absolute separation of religious and secular subjects, which denominationalists wanted to avoid, almost above all. For Stokes to come out strongly in favor of such a policy at this point could not have failed further to convince many that his views were a better barometer of Whig educational policy than a reflection of Catholic interests.

The only other paper which noted the commission report was the Northern Press, which issued an editorial on the subject in June 1861. The editor took particular note of the commissioners' criticism of the results of England's educational efforts. In addition, the editor observed that the report was likely to produce a serious re-evaluation of the state's role as educator. Asking how Catholics were likely to fare in the future should state policy undergo change, he predicted that there would be an increase in government interference in education. This he said could hardly be welcomed by Catholics. Finally, the editor urged readers to be on guard against new developments in state educational policy.[72]

The Revised Code and Its Aftermath

The Royal Commission report was followed within a few months by the famous Revised Code, surely one of the most tedious subjects in English educational history, yet perhaps one of the most important. The Education Department of the Privy Council had codified operative regulations as the Code of 1860. The Revised Code appeared in the summer of 1861. It introduced changes in the method of extending grants to public schools, eliminating old annual grants based on the functions they were intended to serve (e.g. to pay for books, teacher salaries, building and maintenance costs, etc.) and introduced in their stead per capita grants to be based primarily upon student achievement, which was to be tested by inspectors. The system thus introduced has generally been called the system of payment by results and historians of English education have attended quite carefully to the financial details of that system and to its educational merits or defects.[73] Certainly the Revised Code revolutionized the financing of state-aided schools,

---

[72]Northern Press, June 22, 1861, p. 4. Admittedly this editorial was not of great consequence in the context of the general press coverage of the Newcastle report, but the fact that this provincial paper noticed the matter at all is worth recording.

[73]For a cross-section of historical discussion about the Revised Code see Sturt, op. cit., pp. 248-282; Hurt, op. cit., pp. 186-229; and Kay-Shuttleworth, Memorandum on Popular Education (New York: Augustus M. Kelley, 1969).

but the Catholic press discussion of it, though not noteworthy for its volume or depth, suggests that the Code was viewed as revolutionary for other reasons which have received too little notice. While John Hurt has described the disputes produced by the introduction of this plan as "one of the major political storms of the century" there has been little effort made by Hurt or others to identify the roots of the controversy or to define its dimensions. Hurt claims that the Revised Code "constituted a significant victory for the state in its struggle with the Churches for control over education" but he emphasizes the state's position without explaining much about the struggle with the religious bodies. In short, he tells only one side of the story.[74] Of course the Catholic press does not say a great deal about the state's struggle with the Church of England, but it does suggest the scope of that struggle and identify important elements of it.

Before turning to the Catholic press itself one or two remarks are in order concerning the problem of analyzing the press coverage of this particular question. There was a substantial Catholic press response to the Revised Code, but so major a part of that response was restricted to discussions of the financial details of the Code rather than to underlying church-state questions that it is not easy to determine whether Catholic journalists fully appreciated the impact of the scheme upon the denominational system. Because the financial details themselves were not necessarily important to church-state questions it is impossible to dwell on

---

[74]Hurt, op. cit., pp. 200-202.

discussion of them except to note that great dissatisfaction was expressed from many quarters, especially from teachers who stood to suffer pecuniary loss. There was a considerable body of correspondence treating this aspect of the problem--money--but there is little to be gained from statistical analysis of the Code's impact upon school managers' budgets.[75] The cumulative effects of these financial provisions will, however, be noted at the close of this chapter.

The publications which attended to the problems raised by the new code included the Rambler, the Dublin Review, the Tablet, the Weekly Register and the Northern Press. It should be noted here that while the Universe was examined for this period under study, 1859-1865, its pages contained no substantial coverage of the educational questions being discussed. The Dublin and the Rambler both published major articles on the code, and both weeklies, the Tablet and the Weekly Register, contained numerous columns--letters and/or editorials--on the subject; while the Tablet's coverage focused heavily upon financial details, the Weekly Register addressed more basic questions concerning the Code's impact upon the denominational system. The Northern Press coverage cannot be fully analyzed here because the files surveyed were incomplete, but it will be seen that this paper recognized the significance of the code.

The Weekly Register was the first Catholic publication to respond to the appearance of the Revised Code in its editorial

---

[75]Correspondence concerning the financial details of the code was particularly numerous in the Tablet during the first half of 1862.

columns. On August 13 the Register remarked that the Code brought
about fundamental changes calling for careful attention on the part
of Catholics. At this time the editor was concerned only with the
financial effects.[76] On September 21 the Register noted the
general controversy which the Code had started, centering at this
point upon the wrath of certified teachers whose incomes were
threatened. At the same time the editor claimed that the Code
reflected deep-seated constitutional changes taking place; the fact
that an official holding so minor a post as Robert Lowe's was able
to introduce such vast changes on his own authority was cited as
proof that the central government had accumulated unprecedented
power. This, it was said, was nothing less than a revolution in
the balance of power wherein the central bureaucracy had gained a
"degree of power after which the most absolute Monarch of former
ages could never have ventured to aspire." But this increase in
the power of the bureaucracy was not condemned; rather it was
viewed as the "inescapable result of a higher state of civilization, of increased wealth, of more general education, and more easy
communications . . ."[77]

In this context it is appropriate to mention Simpson's article
on "Bureaucracy," which appeared in the February 1859 Rambler.
Simpson commented on the same phenomenon but exhibited concern
rather than delight over the growth of bureaucratic power. The
appointment of the Newcastle Commission apparently prompted this

---

[76]Weekly Register, August 31, 1861, p. 8.

[77]Ibid., September 21, 1861, p. 8.

article which began by noting that the general inquiry into education reflected a growth of bureaucracy which Simpson viewed as a
dangerous trend. The "idea of a bureaucracy," he said, was incomplete so long as it lacked the "pedantic element of a pretence to
direct our life, to know what is best for us, to measure our
labour, to superintend our studies, to prescribe our opinions." He
saw bureaucracy as the tendency toward what would be called totali-
tarianism today; its chief characteristic was its increasing
attempt to treat the "whole area of human life and thought." As
that characteristic became more clearly developed and defined the
bureaucracy became a "kind of tutorship." And Simpson concluded:
"Its whole type is pedagogic; its symbol is the school master."[78]

This article is an excellent statement of opposition to centralization in education, not only because of its impact upon
education but because of its impact upon the growth of bureaucracy
which Simpson viewed as disastrous and revolutionary in character.
According to Simpson bureaucracy was revolutionary because it was
logical and therefore led to the introduction of "changes inconsistent with the habits of the people." He advised that the best
means of avoiding such developments was to restrain the "meddle-
someness of government," and to encourage patience "under the
unreadiness and slowness of an independent system . . . and to
oppose consistently every great attempt at centralization." He saw
aspects of the system of popular education tending in this direc-

---

[78][Simpson], "Bureaucracy," Rambler, 2nd ser., 11 (February
1859): 113-116.

tion, which he lamented.[79]

It seems somewhat ironic that, considering the views just summarized, Simpson stoutly defended and encouraged Stokes' views on education, since Stokes was one of the few outstanding defenders of the government's centralizing policies.

The Weekly Register continued to report on the educational controversy during the fall of 1861. In September implementation of the Code was postponed because of opposition expressed from all sides, and the Register described that opposition as having both financial and religious bases. Reference was made to the Protestant journals' complaints that the new emphasis the Code placed upon secular learning would undermine religious teaching. From this the Register editor concluded that Catholics had been right to refuse to allow the government to tamper with religious teaching in Catholic schools--to prevent inspectors from examining religious instruction. It was stressed that while Anglicans were faced with a diminution of the religious character of their schools the Catholics were safe from any such encroachment. In short, Wilberforce concluded that the religious objections to the Revised Code affected only the Protestant Schools, though he admitted that Catholics would share the general financial results of the scheme.[80]

The view that Catholic schools were isolated from the religious impact of this scheme, if technically correct for the time, was precisely the kind of narrow outlook Lucas had warned against

---

[79] Ibid., pp. 123-125.

[80] Weekly Register, September 28, 1861, p. 8.

in 1849 when Catholics were ready to rejoice over the National Society's defeat in the trust deeds controversy.[81] It was Lucas' view that anything which could be imposed upon the Anglicans would eventually have an impact upon all religious schools--that the weakening of Anglicanism in the schools would ultimately mean the weakening of religion in other schools. It should be recalled that Wilberforce had predicted that a policy of religious isolation would ultimately prove harmful to Catholics; his failure to apply that view to the Revised Code, certainly one of the most important policy developments in education over the 1833-1870 period, cannot be accounted for except by a narrowness of perspective.

The Register occasionally reported on the Anglican complaints about the Code, which always warned that the policy of paying only for results achieved in secular subjects would ensure the decline of religious teaching.[82] As coverage of this and other publications indicates, however, the complexity of the Code prompted such a variety of complaints that opponents seemed unable to concentrate their opposition on any one aspect of the government's policies. This was no small advantage for the government and may have been a crucial disadvantage for the Church of England.[83]

The Revised Code continued to receive sporadic attention in the Register through 1862; after that it remained a prominent

---

[81]Tablet, June 16, 1849, p. 376.

[82]Typical citations from the Weekly Register include October 26, 1861, p. 9; January 25, 1862, p. 1; and February 15, 1862, p. 1.

[83]This aspect of the Code controversy is seldom stressed, but it was clearly of considerable tactical importance.

subject for discussion as modifications were introduced and corollary policies established. The one fact which this coverage makes extremely clear is that there was an extensive, major Anglican response consisting of massive petitioning of the government, public meetings, press controversy and the like. Anglicans charged that the Code was a breach of faith, a violation of the 1840 Concordat guaranteeing that inspectors would attend equally to religious and secular elements of education.[84] Historians have noted this response only briefly; it would seem to deserve much closer study.

Anglicans also used the controversy over the code to voice their objections to other state policies, one having to do with the conscience clause, the other having to do with subtle alterations in the conditions under which the Privy Council approved building grants for denominational schools. The Weekly Register's coverage of these primarily Anglican questions was minor, but it hints at a general trend in government policy which must be noted. Neither the conscience clause policy nor changes in building grants policies were strictly related to the Revised Code, but they must be seen in connection with the totality of changes wrought by Lowe and his secretary, Ralph Lingen.[85]

The government's increasing insistence upon the conscience clause permitting children to be withdrawn from religious instruc-

[84]Weekly Register, January 25, 1862, p. 1.

[85]For biographical information on Lingen see A. S. Bishop, "Ralph Lingen, Secretary to the Education Department, 1847-1870," Journal of British Educational Studies 16 (June 1968): 138-163.

tion at parental requests suggests a definite trend away from denominationalism. Carried to its logical conclusion the conscience clause required strict separation of religious and secular education, while the integration of the two elements was the key to denominational education. What was at stake was not so much the clearly defined catechetical teaching--to which the conscience clause could easily be applied--but rather the whole question of interpretative teaching. The right to apply religious perspectives to all subjects was at stake. The 1840 Concordat protected that right for Anglicans by securing the inspection of religious and secular subjects together. The redefinition of inspectors´ responsibilities achieved by the Revised Code did undermine that fundamental principle, and increased insistence on the conscience clause did the same. And government policies concerning building grants appear to have gone a step further. It had been customary for the Privy Council Committee to acknowledge that a denominational school was justified where there was a reasonable number of students whose parents wished them to have denominational education; apparently definition of what constituted a sufficient number had been fairly arbitrary. During the 1860s the government began to refuse building grants to denominational applicants--particularly Anglicans--on grounds that places were available for students in existing schools operated by other denominations.[86] Regulations provided for a certain amount of leeway with regard to such factors, but Anglican complaints made it clear that the principle of denominationalism

---

[86]Extensive documentation on the Anglican problem in this regard can be found among the Parliamentary Papers of this period; see (1862), 43:268; (1864), 44:487, and (1865), 43:331.

was being gradually undermined at the operative level.

The Weekly Register also referred to another minor aspect of denominationalism which came under subtle attack. Denominational inspection was an important element in the system, but it prompted considerable criticism because it was wasteful of inspectors´ time and efforts and prevented the development of uniform efficiency. In the course of the spring of 1862 debates in Parliament treating the Revised Code, Charles Adderley attacked denominational inspection and specifically cited Roman Catholic inspectors for never reporting anything seriously wrong in Catholic schools.[87] The editor took up the question and defended the integrity of the Catholic inspectors out of fear that such unrefuted charges might induce the public to believe Catholics were "unworthy to retain the inspection of their schools." If that happened the editor feared the "days of the denominational system" would be numbered; he added that such a development would not only harm English Catholics but would furnish "an irrefragable argument against the demands of the Irish bishops" for the introduction of the denominational system in Ireland. So again the Irish question appears, and is it not appropriate that it should? Was it merely accidental that efforts to end denominationalism in England increased as Irish demands for that system also increased?

The Dublin Review also published in November 1862, an article relating to the Revised Code. The author, Myles O´Reilly, used the

---

[87]Weekly Register, April 5, 1862, pp. 9, 11; and ibid., April 12, 1862, p. 6.

subject of the code as a pretext for reviewing the general problem
of education in England and Ireland. O'Reilly elaborated his view
that two principles were at war with one another, the one based on
the notion that the state has the responsibility and the right to
educate the people, the other based on the notion that political
freedom must entail freedom of education.[88] Conditions in Ireland
and England had produced different results. Conditions in Ireland
had produced statism in Irish education, it was said, while conditions in England had promoted the development of free institutions
encouraged but not controlled by the state. Indirectly this
article also raises the question of how Irish Catholic demands for
denominationalism affected the educational views of English politicians, but O'Reilly was so concerned with theoretical and historical aspects of his subject that he never addressed specific problems related to the Code or to the politics of the day. There is
an implied hope that the English system might be applied in
Ireland; but given the growing opposition to denominationalism in
England we are forced to ask whether the impact might have worked
in the reverse.

The Rambler published two articles on the Code during 1862,
both by Stokes. In his first article he summarized the defects of
the denominational system as described by the Royal Commission
report, the most important being its tendency to become ever more
costly, with its inability to aid the poorest districts, with its
bureaucratic complexities and with certain shortcomings of its

---

[88][O'Reilly], "The Connection of the State of Education in
England and Ireland," Dublin Review 52 (November 1862): 121.

teacher training program. Stokes observed that these defects were "necessarily aggravated by the denominational system" and cited that system's wastefulness in support of this contention. He observed that the government entertained no proposal for doing away with the denominational system, which he took to be a good omen for Catholic education. Thus he concluded that no changes had been proposed which affected denominational arrangements.[89]

Most of the remainder of this article was devoted to the financial details of the scheme. While Stokes clearly objected to the Revised Code on the whole, that objection was based on financial rather than religious grounds; thus the article pertains only slightly to the present discussion, but it should be noted that Stokes seemed to take particular care to stress his concern over the way the Revised Code would harm Catholic schools financially.

A second Rambler article appeared in March which further criticized Lowe's schemes on technical bases.[90] Stokes was particularly concerned that the new scheme took no note of the achievements of backward children--an important problem considering the difficult backgrounds from which Victorian poor children came. Later in 1862 the Rambler commented on Parliamentary discussions of the Code, and when the Home and Foreign Review succeeded the Rambler it too noticed the debates, concluding that the effect of the code would be to "decentralize" the education system by increasing the responsibilities of local managers. As this was the

---

[89]Stokes, "The Commission on Education and the Revised Code," Rambler, 3rd ser., 6 (January 1862): 177-178.

[90]Idem, "The Revised Educational Code," Rambler, 3rd ser., 6 (March 1862): 293-300.

line taken by proponents of the measure it cannot be said to represent any particularly serious Catholic evaluation of the matter.[91]

The Tablet's coverage of the Revised Code was quite hostile. At first its revolutionary character was stressed and the government was attacked for failing to fulfill its promise that it would leave the former system intact.[92] But for the most part the paper dealt with the financial details and effects of the new system, publishing teachers' and managers' complaints, some answers to them, and related exchanges. In November 1862, however, there was a short article summarizing the grounds on which the Tablet said the Code had been and should be opposed:

> Some objected to it on the ground that it totally ignored religion, others that its fundamental principle was bad, a few disliked it because it emanated from the Liberals . . .

The writer concluded that the Code and its author were victorious despite the fact that concessions had been forced; he went on to speculate on the underlying causes which accounted for that victory:

> It is impossible for us to state the motives which guided the author of this code in tramping down things the use of which he was ignorant, and setting up his own idol to be worshipped. The spirit of materialism that pervades this Code sufficiently demonstrates that Christianity in High quarters instead of being in the ascendant, is on the wane. Their religion is secular; they are secularists in the treatment of education; and whether implied or not, one cannot help thinking that they wish secularism to predominate in the breasts of the rising genera-

---

[91]"Home Affairs," Rambler, 3rd ser., 6 (May 1862): 542-544; and "Current Events," Home and Foreign Review 1 (July 1862): 251-252.

[92]Tablet, September 21, 1861, p. 603.

tion. But they do not stop at the introduction of secularism, they go further, they cripple the resources of
those engaged in education.93

Oddly enough this was the only editorial published in the Tablet

treating the fundamental principles underlying the Revised Code;

its importance lies in the suggestion that Lowe--and by implication

Lingen--were moved by secularist aims with regard to education and

in the observation that the Revised Code was intended to cripple

the resources of religious educators.

While detailed discussion of the voluminous letters and

articles treating the financial aspects of the Revised Code has

been avoided here, one important factor about that discussion

should be noted. Educationalists understood that their system was

being put to a severe test by the government; that test resulted in

a substantial decline in state funds spent on denominational

schools. What did this mean with respect to the fate of the denom-

inational system of education jointly funded by state and private

funds? It meant that system was subjected to a critical test under

conditions deliberately formulated to demonstrate its supposed

inadequacy to meet the educational needs of the nation. There is

no other way to put it. It has been admitted that there was no

decline in the private funding of education--a fact of great im-

portance which modern historians hardly mention.94 The decline in

funding resulted from state policies intended to effect economies;

but there were indications that the policies of Lowe and Lingen

---

93Tablet, November 8, 1862, p. 712.

94For reference to this in a contemporary source, see Craik,
op. cit., p. 75.

were not only motivated by the desire to economize. Their increased efforts to impose the conscience clause--in direct opposition to the Royal Commission's recommendation to the contrary--and
their altered policies concerning building grants were aimed at
fundamental aspects of denominationalism. To these indications of
government hostility to the denominational system must be added
signs of opposition to denominational inspection. Suffice it to
say that the cumulative effect of the Revised Code and corollary
schemes was to weaken the underpinnings of the denominational
system. The extent to which this was intentional and deliberate
remains to be determined but certainly requires further study.

One last development reported in the Catholic press having to
do with church-state questions relates to the dismissal of J. R.
Morell, a government inspector of Catholic schools. Only three
inspectors were removed from office during the 1839-1864 period;[95]
two of them were Catholics. The Morell case combined elements of
anti-Catholicism with elements of hostility to the independent
power of school inspectors. Neither the press coverage of the case
nor the correspondence published in the Parliamentary Papers[96]
explains why Morell was dismissed. Prior to his dismissal in 1864
the Education Department was engaged in a concerted effort to
suppress inspectoral reports hostile to government policy. This
effort has been treated as an in-house struggle, but since the
inspectors were denominational, and since the government made no

---

[95]Hurt, op. cit., p. 54.

[96]Parliamentary Papers (1864), 44:215.

secret of its impatience with the wastefulness of the denominational inspection system, it would seem profitable to ask whether
aspects of this struggle might not have related to church-state
questions.[97]

Allies, generally a staunch defender of Privy Council fairness
to Catholics, admitted to Newman at the time that there had been
"three studied attempts of the Privy Council to prove Catholic
Inspectors guilty" of charges of disingenuousness and falsehood.[98]
The Catholic press coverage of the question touched only the surface and showed only that Morell had been judged on very narrow
grounds not applied to other inspectors.[99] To an extent the Privy
Council's harassment of Morell must be viewed as anti-Catholicism--
but given the general tendency of that body to treat Catholic
schools fairly one is prompted to ask whether this should be seen
as a sufficient explanation. One author notes that Morell had been
particularly resistant to the government's effort to censor inspectors' reports. This suggests the possibility that his dismissal might have been intended as an example.

The original agreements concerning the appointment and dismissal of inspectors involved joint authority over appointment, but
the authority over dismissal was left unclear. Ullathorne had
expressed concern that bishops lacked the authority to secure the
resignation of an inspector no longer acceptable to the Church; the

---

[97]Hurt, op. cit., pp. 66-67.

[98]Allies to Newman, n.d., in Dessain, Letters and Diaries of
Newman, 21:65n.

[99]Tablet, April 23, 1864, p. 265; ibid., April 20, 1864,
p. 285.

case at hand suggests that the Church also lacked authority to protect the position of a denominational inspector no longer acceptable to the government. At the very least the question related to the whole issue of bureaucratic--state--authority. If this examination of the Catholic press treatment of the matter fails to define the nature of the contest, it may at least prompt further inquiry. There are sufficient indications that the denominational system was being undermined from several directions to justify the hypothesis that the Morell case was somehow related to larger church-state questions than the details of his dismissal suggest.

Once the discussion of the effects of the Revised Code tapered off the Catholic press coverage of church-state-education questions declined. The _Tablet_ continued to publish occasional correspondence regarding financial details of the Revised Code, but as suggested above such correspondence was not related to church-state issues. Except for the slight mention of the Morell case it may be said that no further serious issues were given prominent attention in the publications analyzed for this study--that is, not until some time after Cardinal Wiseman's death in February 1865. During 1863 and 1864 the education question ceased to attract the level of interest which it had attracted during the preceding years. Thus the period under study ended quietly.

CHAPTER VI

CONCLUSION

The admission of Catholics to the education grant in 1847 represented a fundamental departure in Catholic relations with the state: for the first time there was regular and official cooperation between the Protestant government and its English Catholic subjects. Through analysis of the contemporary Catholic press this study has attempted to describe the evolution of that relationship as it was understood in its time. Every effort has been made to indicate how the Catholic press coverage of church-state-education questions reflected peculiarly Catholic perspectives and to relate them to the broad political and educational developments of the era.

Between 1847 and 1865 specific changes in perspective can be discerned. In the beginning journalists tended to treat the prospects of Catholic-state relations in theoretical terms, fearing considerable religious conflict, although some writers focused upon the need to imitate the politics of Dissent by developing constituent political power as a means of strengthening Catholic demands. In any event the traditional isolation of Catholics from the mainstream of English politics was reflected in the Catholic press. As a working relationship with the state progressed and

335

Catholics began to enjoy benefits from the state system their understanding of political realities seemed to crystallize. Notwithstanding, a minority of Catholics remained wary of all dealings with the state and continued to view educational politics from an isolated perspective.

Many severely criticized the minority's refusal to support the trend that would have made Catholic schools a more integral part of the state-supported denominational education system. There was validity in such criticism but it has been illustrated that elements in the minority view were rooted in an accurate understanding of contemporary trends. For example, Bishop Ullathorne's concern about the state's discretionary powers with regard to the examination of students and teachers proved to have been well founded when Lowe changed the whole grant system in 1861 and 1862 by merely changing the examination system as it related to funding. As the Bishop of Birmingham had warned, neither agreements nor laws bound the government to the previous system which had given schools much greater control over curriculum, which control was crucial to religious instruction.

This division over whether Catholics should work with the state and accept conditions which might ultimately prove to be incompatible with the Catholic philosophy of education appears, from press reporting over the years, to have contributed significantly to internal disunity. One reason for this was that education questions reached into all dimensions of religious and political life. In addition, there was a close connection between education and political parties, and there was much that was confusing in the Whig-Liberal position: their statements supportive of the denominational system were in contrast to the effects of the policies implemented by the Whig government. If the Whigs were the strongest promoters of popular education they were also loosely allied with the forces opposing denominational education. One of the significant results of this study has been to show that Whig policy was understood by many to be hostile to denominational education long before 1870, and that the introduction of the Revised Code and subsequent policies implemented by the Privy Council's Education Department represented the beginning of that party's official enforcement of policies which undermined the denominational system. It is one thing, however, to identify this perspective and quite another to demonstrate its accuracy.

While Catholics learned to understand the subtleties of Privy Council policies their journalists began to discuss educational problems in more conventional and less distinctly Catholic terms. At first they had expressed concern about all facets of state policy ranging from philosophical definitions of the meaning of education to the content of the reading books. This was particularly so during the early years. Although the Catholic press continued to treat the full spectrum of educational problems, those treated as important church-state questions were gradually reduced as Catholics began to see where the major tensions lay and as trends in church-state affairs became more clearly defined.

This change took place during the mid-1850s. Before then Catholic writers seemed unable to settle upon what constituted the most significant issues, so they wrote about everything--philosophical and theological values in education, inspection, trust deeds, curriculum, lay influence, episcopal and clerical authority, the encroaching power of the state, the need for greater Catholic efforts, the role of religious and many other matters. During 1855 and 1856 writers began to subordinate secondary questions to the two major issues of the day: the minority of Catholics who resisted all relations with the government's education system, and the increasing likelihood that some Parliamentary measure providing for politically controlled and rate-financed schools would be passed into law. Early in the 1860s fears concerning the work of the Newcastle Commission and the introduction of the Revised Code brought into sharper focus the attacks against the denominational system, and by 1865 the fate of that system had become the principal concern.

Despite this there was no serious attempt among Catholics to arouse opposition to the forces promoting undenominational or secular education. This was partly because there was no consensus as to where the real dangers existed. Other explanations have to do with the distractions of foreign policy and with the unwillingness of the denominations to cooperate with one another. On the whole, Catholics tended to shy away from political action unless they were faced with a bold onslaught such as the Ecclesiastical Titles Bill. One writer said that the only way to arouse Catholic interest in education would be to ask Lord Russell to outlaw Catholic schools. There were exceptions to the political timidity of Catholics, of course, but political respectability seemed to be the rule. Only once during this period was political action contemplated as a means of furthering Catholic educational interests; that was in 1847 when Lucas tried to promote a mass meeting to force Russell's government to recognize Catholic demands for state funds. That effort failed. If Catholics refused to exert political pressure when there was something tangible to be gained, there was little likelihood of their engaging in such behavior when there was but a vague if growing threat to the system which supported their schools.

Though Catholics gradually began to see their schools as an integral part of the English educational structure, they never lost their awareness of the way governmental policies favored specific Protestant educational principles; more importantly, they never ceased to attribute to the weaknesses inherent in Protestantism the nation's educational dilemmas. Catholic commentary on Protestant educational principles and schemes had the merit of being free from sectarian bitterness and from pervasive Victorian anti-clericalism. That is not to say that their views were free of pointed bias; it is merely to suggest that it is possible to gain valuable historical insights by reading Catholic assessments of Protestant problems.

This interest in Protestant education schemes was related to concern over the apostasy of the Irish poor as well as to fear of increased statist or secularist influence in national education. The connection between Irish apostasy and Protestant education was sometimes direct but more often indirect. Since religious education was viewed as the panacea to vagrancy, crime and poverty, Protestant philanthropists made extensive efforts to bring the Irish Catholic poor into their schools. As many of those schools received state funds, the competition for the souls of Irish street children became a prominent theme in church-state controversy.

Over the years the Catholic assessment of the Protestant danger changed substantially. Initially journalists focused on the work of Protestant schools as such and discussed the way they threatened Irish communities. But as the number of Catholic schools increased and the missions seemed better able to serve the needs of the poor, interest in Protestant schools declined and attention turned to the incapacity of Protestantism to defend the religious basis of national education. Protestant weakness was said to stem from its rejection of authority; this, it was said, accounted for the hopeless religious disunity of England which undercut the churches′ power to preserve the teaching of basic Christian doctrine in the schools. Thus was the failure of Protestantism seen as a crucial contribution to the rise of secularism. Protestants themselves often expressed an awareness of the way religious disunity hindered the cause of religious education, but the Catholic analysis went even further. Catholics saw the education question as a conflict of authority between the spiritual and the civil power; if the spiritual power abdicated its responsibilities the whole field would be left to the civil authority. And this was understood to be a distortion--an imbalance which would contribute to tyranny, not to mention the destruction of Christian education.

The initial purpose of this study was to ascertain whether Catholics appreciated the importance of the popular education movement in England. It has been shown that they did; moreover, it has been demonstrated that education was probably _the_ critical pastoral problem of the day. Prominent bishops and an impressive if not always well-known circle of Catholic laity devoted extraordinary energy and talent to educational and related social efforts. This survey has indicated that their work and its relationship to the other dimensions of Catholic conflict during the period calls for further study. In previous chapters it has been seen that several extended controversies were generated by educational questions, the most prominent among them being the Tablet's role in the initial development of church-state relations, the 1856-1857 quarrels over the work of the Poor School Committee and its acceptance of the government trust deeds, and the controversy over Catholic cooperation with the Newcastle Commission. The latter resulted in unfortunate episcopal action against one editor. All of this suggests that church-state-education questions were far more important to the history of Victorian Catholicism than the conventional bibliography suggests.

A second objective of this study was to determine the place of educational questions in the context of what might be called the Victorian settlement in church and state. That no clear-cut settlement was ever achieved seems certain; in fact there is considerable speculation as to just what happened to religion in the nineteenth century. Explanations abound, but the shift from the religious to the secular character of Victorian society remains largely unexplained. This study has examined but a very small aspect of the question, but the results indicate that many Victorians believed the struggle to preserve religious--doctrinal--education to be the pivotal church-state struggle of the era.

There is plentiful indication that the forces which favored undenominational or secular education were more powerful in the early 1860s than is generally understood to have been the case and that the Whig government's policy after the introduction of the Revised Code deliberately and steadfastly undermined the viability of state-supported denominational schools. Whether the perspectives so reported in the Catholic press were in fact accurate requires inquiry beyond the scope of this study.

It is usually argued that undenominational tax-funded education had to be introduced because denominational, voluntary efforts were inadequate to the task. The shortcoming of this argument is that the denominational system was state-supported and the funds which declined during the early 1860s were state funds, not voluntary funds. On that fact this research effort ends, but not without suggesting that answers to questions about the religious settlement in education may well be discovered in the Whig policies of the early 1860s

APPENDIX

MANAGEMENT CLAUSE APPROVED FOR TRUST DEEDS

OF ROMAN CATHOLIC POOR SCHOOLS

The following document was submitted to the Catholic Poor School Committee by the Lords of the Privy Council on October 26, 1850. It was formally accepted by the Poor School Committee on November 28, 1850, with the unanimous approbation of the bishops.

Management Clause

And it is hereby declared, that the said school shall be at all times open to the inspection of the Inspector or Inspectors of schools for the time being, appointed in conformity with the Minute of the Committee of Her Majesty's Most Honourable Privy Council on Education, relating to conditions of aid to Roman Catholic schools, and bearing date the 18th day of December, 1847. Provided always that such Inspector or Inspectors shall be in all things guided and limited in their duties by the instructions of the said Committee of Council to Her Majesty's Inspectors of schools, dated August, 1840, so far as such instructions are modified and limited by the said Minute of the 18th day of December, 1847, and are applicable to Roman Catholic schools, but not further or otherwise; and any departure from the terms of the said last-mentioned Minute on the part of Government, shall not oblige the Committee of Management of the said school either to submit to any inspection other than that mentioned in the said Minute of Council, or to refund the money advanced by Government, or any part thereof; and the said school and premises, and the funds and present endowments thereof, and such future endowments in respect whereof no other disposition shall be made by the donor thereof, shall be directed, controlled, governed, and managed in manner hereinafter specified; that is to say, the priest or priests for the time being having care of the congregation assembling for religious worship at the Roman Catholic Church or Chapel of St.   , in the parish of   , under or by virtue of faculties duly received from or confirmed by the Roman Catholic Bishop for the time being of the district or other ecclesiastical division in which the said parish is situate, so long as such faculties shall be subsisting and unrevoked, shall have the management and superintendence of the religious instruction of all the scholars attending the said school, with power on Sundays to use or direct the premises to be used for the purposes of such religious instruction exclusively. But in all other respects the management and superintendence of the school and premises, and of the funds and endowments thereof, and the selection, appointment, and dismissal of the schoolmaster and schoolmistress, and their assistants (except as hereinafter is excepted), shall be vested in and exercised by a Committee consisting of such priest or priests for the time being, holding faculties as aforesaid, and of other persons being Roman Catholics, of whom the following shall be the first appointed, that is to say,

and any vacancy which may occur in the number of persons last mentioned, by death, resignation, incapacity, or otherwise, shall be filled up by the election of a person (being a Roman Catholic), and the power of electing such person shall be vested in the remaining members of the said Committee until the Roman Catholic Bishop of the district or other ecclesiastical division, within which the said school shall be situated, shall, in writing, direct that the election shall be by the contributors to the funds of the said school; and thereupon and thenceforth such election shall be vested in such of the contributors during the then current year to the amount of ten shillings each, at the least, to the funds of the said school, being Roman Catholics, as shall be present at the meeting duly convened for the purpose of the election, or not being present thereat, shall vote by any paper or papers sent on or before the day of such meeting to the chairman thereof, and signed by any such contributor, in which shall be named the person or persons whom such contributor shall desire to elect, and each of the contributors qualified to vote shall be entitled at every such election to give one vote in respect of each such sum of ten shillings, so, however, that no person shall be entitled to give more than six votes in respect of any sum so contributed. Provided, nevertheless, that no default of election, nor any vacancy shall prevent the other members of the Committee from acting until the vacancy shall be filled up. And the said Committee shall annually select one of the members thereof to act as Secretary, who shall keep minutes of the proceedings at the meetings thereof in a book, which shall be provided for that purpose, and shall give due notice of all extraordinary meetings to each member of the Committee. The priest or senior priest for the time being of the Roman Catholic Church or Chapel of St.   aforesaid, shall be chairman of all meetings of the Committee when present thereat, and at any meetings from which he shall be absent the members attending the same shall appoint one of their number to be chairman thereof, and all matters which shall be brought before such meetings shall be decided by the majority of votes of the members attending the same and voting upon the question, and if upon any matters there shall be an equality of votes, the chairman shall have a second, being the casting vote. And it is hereby declared, that no priest shall be or continue a member of the said Committee, or exercise any control or interference whatsoever in the said school, who does not hold faculties duly received from or confirmed by the Roman Catholic Bishop for the time being of the district or other ecclesiastical division in which the said school is situated, subsisting and unrevoked, and that no person shall vote at any election for, or be appointed or continue a member of the said Committee, or be appointed or continue a master or mistress in the said school, or be employed therein in any capacity whatsoever, who is not a Roman Catholic. Provided always that the priest or senior priest for the time being of the Roman Catholic Church or Chapel of St.   aforesaid, shall have power to suspend any teacher from his office, or to exclude any book from use in the said school upon religious grounds, a written statement to that effect by the said priest or senior priest having first been laid before the Committee, and such suspension or exclusion shall endure until the decision of superior ecclesiastical authority thereon can with due diligence be obtained, and such decision shall, when obtained, and laid before the Committee in writing, under the hand of such superior ecclesiastic, be final and conclusive in the matter; and the Committee of Management for the time being is hereby expressly required to take all such steps as may be necessary for immediately carrying the said decision into complete effect. And it is hereby further declared, that if the said superior ecclesiastical authority, upon any such reference as aforesaid, shall direct or award that any master or mistress or teacher in the said school shall be dismissed, such direction or award, when a copy thereof shall have been served upon the said master, mistress or teacher personally, or by the same being left at his or her place of abode, or at the school aforesaid, addressed to the said master, mistress or teacher, as the case may require, shall operate as a dismissal of the said master, mistress, or teacher, so as to prevent him or her thenceforth from having any interest in his or her office, or in the said school or premises under or by virtue of this deed, and so as to disqualify him or her from holding thenceforth any right or interest under this deed by virtue of his or her previous or any future appointment. And the Committee may, from time to time, at a meeting to be held in the month of   , each year, elect and appoint a Committee of not more than   ladies, being Roman Catholics, to assist them in the visitation and management of the girls' and infants' schools, which Ladies' Committee shall remain in office until the end of the current year.

SOURCE: "The Management Clause," Catholic School 2 (January 1851): 92-94.

SELECTED BIBLIOGRAPHY

Newspapers and Periodicals

The dates given below indicate the period for which each publication was consulted for the purposes of this study.

Catholic Institute Magazine. October 1855-December 1858.

Catholic School. August 1848-September 1856.

Catholic Standard (subsequently Weekly Standard). October 1849-May 1855.

Catholic Vindicator and Irish Magazine. February 1851-August 1852.

Catholic Weekly Instructor (also titled the Catholic Instructor). August 1846-December 1847.

Dolman's Magazine. March 1845-June 1849.

Dublin Review. January 1847-January 1865.

Home and Foreign Review. July 1862-April 1864.

Month. July 1864-February 1865.

Northern Press and Catholic Weekly Times. June 1860-April 1863.

Rambler. January 1848-May 1862.

Tablet. January 1847-February 1865.

Universe. December 1860-February 1865.

Weekly and Monthly Orthodox, a Catholic Journal of Correspondence and Literature. January 1849-July 1849.

Weekly Register and Catholic Standard. May 1855-February 1865.

Workhouse Papers. May 1860-November 1860.

The Workman (subsequently the Literary Workman). January 1865–
   December 1865.

Official Documents

Catholic Directory. 1847-1865.

Catholic Poor School Committee, Annual Reports. 1847-1865.

Great Britain. Education Commission. Report of the Commission
   Appointed to Inquire into the State of Popular Education in
   England. 6 vols. 1861.

_____. Parliament. Parliamentary Papers (Commons), 1862, vol. 41.
   Cmd. 81, "Copies of All Memorials and Letters Addressed to the
   Lord President or Secretary of the Committee of Council on the
   Subject of the Revised Code."

_____. Parliamentary Papers (Commons), 1862, vol. 43. Cmd. 248,
   "Returns of All Industrial Schools Certified Under Act 24 & 25
   Vict. c. 113."

_____. Parliamentary Papers (Commons), 1864, vol. 44. Cmd. 215,
   "Copies of All Correspondence Relating to the Dismissal of
   Mr. Morell from the Office of Her Majesty's Roman Catholic
   Schools."

Contemporary Published Writings

Works published before the passage of the 1870 Education Act
are included in the following list.

Amphlett, J. The Newspaper Press in Part of the Last Century and
   Up to 1860, Recollections. London: n.p., 1860.

Andrews, Alexander. The History of British Journalism from the
   Foundation of the Newspaper Press to the Repeal of the Stamp
   Act in 1855. 2 vols. London: Richard Bentley, 1859.

Arundel and Surrey, Earl of. A Few Remarks on the Social and
   Political Condition of British Catholics. London: C. Dolman,
   1847.

Bowden, John Edward. The Life and Letters of Frederick William
   Faber. London: Richardson, 1869.

A Comprehensive View of National Education Schemes: Their Past
   Fallacies and Future Prospects. London: Wertheim and
   Macintosh, 1856.

Faber, Frederick William. Letter on the Acceptance of the Privy
   Council Grants to Catholic Education, 4 April 1857. London:
   n.p., 1857.

Gallwey, Peter B. How Some of the Poor Are Wisely Oppressed in Workhouses. London: n.p., 1861.

Hone, Richard Brindley. National Education and Other Objects of the Day, a Charge Delivered to the Clergy and the Church Wardens of the Archdeaconery of Worcester. London: J. W. Parker & Son, 1856.

Hunt, Frederick Knight. The Fourth Estate: Contributions towards a History of Newspapers and of the Liberty of the Press. London: D. Bogue, 1850.

Husenbeth, F. C. "History of the Catholic Periodicals," Catholic Opinion, January 30, 1857, pp. 1-2.

Kay-Shuttleworth, Sir James. Memorandum on Popular Education. London: n.p., 1868; reprint ed., New York: Augustus M. Kelley, 1969.

_____. Public Education as Affected by the Minutes of the Privy Council from 1846 to 1852. London: Longman, Brown, Green & Longmans, 1853.

O'Reilly, Myles W. P. Conservatives and Liberals Judged by Their Conduct to the Catholics of England and Ireland. Dublin: Browne & Nolan, 1867.

Reithmüller, Christopher James. Frederick Lucas, a Biography. London: Bell and Daldy, 1862.

Vaughan, Herbert. Popular Education: the Conscience Clauses and the Rating Clause. London: Longmans, Green, 1858.

Wiseman, Nicholas Cardinal. Home Education of the Poor. London: Royal Society for the Encouragement of Arts, Manufactures, and Commerce, 1854.

_____. The Religious and Social Position of Catholics in England: an Address Delivered by His Eminence Cardinal Wiseman. Dublin: James Duffy, 1864.

_____. The Social and Intellectual State of England, Compared with its Moral Condition. London: Derby, 1850.

Workhouse Education. London: Hatchard, 1862.

Later Published Writings

Adams, Francis. A History of the Elementary School Contest in England. London: Chapman & Hall, 1882.

Adamson, John William. English Education, 1789-1902. Cambridge: University Press, 1930.

Akenson, Donald H. The Irish Education Experiment: the National System of Education in the Nineteenth Century. London: Routledge & Kegan Paul, 1970.

Allies, Mary H. Thomas William Allies. London: Burns and Oates, 1907.

Altholz, Josef. The Liberal Catholic Movement in England: the "Rambler" and Its Contributors, 1848-1864. London: Burns and Oates, 1962.

_____. "The Political Behavior of English Catholics, 1850-1867." Journal of British Studies 4 (November 1964): 89-103.

Altholz, Josef, McElrath, Damian, and Holland, James C. The Correspondence of Lord Acton and Richard Simpson. 3 vols. Cambridge: University Press, 1971-1975,

Amherst, William J. "The Hon. Charles Langdale." Dublin Review 111 (October 1892): 395-425; 113 (July 1893): 515-531; 113 (October 1893): 859-873.

Armytage, W. G. H. The French Influence on English Education. London: Routledge & Kegan Paul, 1968.

Bagley, John J., and Bagley, A. J. The State and Education in England and Wales, 1833-1868. London: Macmillan, 1969.

Balfour, Graham. The Education Systems of Great Britain and Ireland. Oxford: Clarendon Press, 1903.

Barnard, H. C. A History of English Education from 1760. 2nd ed. London: University of London Press, 1961.

Beales, A. C. F. "The Beginnings of Catholic Elementary Education in the Second Spring." Dublin Review 205 (October 1939): 284-309.

_____. "The Struggle for the Schools." In The English Catholics, 1850-1950, pp. 365-409. Edited by George Andrew Beck. London: Burns and Oates, 1950.

Beck, George Andrew, ed. The English Catholics, 1850-1950. London: Burns and Oates, 1950.

Benn, Alfred William. The History of English Rationalism in the Nineteenth Century. 2 vols. London: n.p., 1906.

Bertrand, Claude Jean, ed. The British Press, an Historical Survey: an Anthology. Paris: O.C.D.L., 1969.

Best, G. F. A. "The Religious Difficulties of National Education in England, 1800-1870." Cambridge Historical Journal 12 (1956): 155-173.

Binns, Bryon Henry. A Century of Education. London: Dent, 1908.

Birchenough, Charles. History of Elementary Education in England and Wales. 3rd ed. London: University Tutorial Press, 1938.

Bishop, A. S. "Ralph Lingen, Secretary to the Education Department, 1849-1870." Journal of British Educational Studies 16 (June 1968): 138-163.

Bourne, Henry Richard Fox. English Newspapers: Chapters in the History of Journalism. London: n.p., 1887; reprint ed., New York: Russell & Russell, 1966.

Brady, L. W. "Penny-a-Liners and Politics: the growth of Journalistic Influence?" Victorian Periodicals Newsletter, no. 11 (February 1971), pp. 17-21.

Broderick, Mary John. "Catholic Schools in England." Ph.D. dissertation, Catholic University of America, 1936.

Brose, Olive J. Church and Parliament; the Reshaping of the Church of England, 1828-1860. Stanford, Calif.: Stanford University Press, 1959.

Brown, Charles Kenneth Francis. The Church's Part in Education, 1833-1941, with Special Reference to the Work of the National Society. London: National Society, 1942.

Brown, Stephen J. An Index of Catholic Biographies. Dublin: Central Catholic Library Association, 1930.

Burke, Thomas. Catholic History of Liverpool. Liverpool: Tingling & Co., 1910.

Butler, Cuthbert. Life and Times of Bishop Ullathorne. 2 vols. London: Burns, Oates and Washbourne, 1926.

Chadwick, Owen. The Victorian Church. 2 vols. New York: Oxford University Press, 1966-1970.

Cowherd, Raymond G. The Politics of English Dissent. New York: New York University Press, 1956.

Craik, Henry. The State in Its Relation to Education. London: Macmillan, 1884.

Cruickshank, Marjorie. Church and State in English Education, 1870 to the Present Day. New York: St. Martin's Press, 1963.

Curtis, Stanley James. An Introductory History of English Education Since 1800. London: University Tutorial Press, 1960.

Denison, George Anthony. Notes of My Life, 1805-1878. Oxford: James Parker & Co., 1878.

Dessain, Charles Stephen. The Letters and Diaries of John Henry
     Newman. Vols. 11-22. London: Thomas Nelson & Sons, 1961-
     1972; vols. 23- . Oxford: Clarendon Press, 1973-

Devas, Francis Charles. Mother Mary Magdalen of the Sacred Heart
     (Fanny Margaret Taylor) Foundress of the Poor Servants of the
     Mother of God. London: Burns and Oates, 1927.

Diamond, Marie Gertrude. "The Work of the Catholic Poor-School
     Committee, 1847-1905." Master's thesis, University of
     Liverpool, 1963.

Dowling, Frances. "The Liberalism of John Moore Capes (1812-
     1889)." Ph.D. dissertation, Catholic University of America,
     1974.

Duke, Christopher. "Robert Lowe--a Reappraisal." Journal of
     British Educational Studies 14 (November 1965): 19-35.

Dwyer, J. J. "The Catholic Press." In The English Catholics,
     1850-1950, pp. 475-514, Edited by George Andrew Beck.
     London: Burns and Oates, 1950.

Edmonds, E. L. "School Inspection: the Contribution of Religious
     Denominations." Journal of British Educational Studies 7
     (November 1858): 12-35.

_____. The School Inspector. London: Routledge & Kegan Paul,
     1962.

Edsall, Nichols. The Anti-Poor Law Movement, 1834-1844.
     Manchester: Manchester University Press, 1971.

Ellegard, Alvar. The Readership of the Periodical Press in Mid-
     Victorian Britain. Göteborg: Göteborgs Universitets
     Arsskrift, 1957.

Evenett, Henry Outramn. The Catholic Schools of England and Wales.
     Cambridge: University Press, 1944.

Fletcher, John R. "Early Catholic Periodicals in England." Dublin
     Review 198 (April 1936): 284-310.

Gilley, Sheridan Wayne. "English Catholic Charity and the Irish
     Poor in London, Part I, 1700-1840." Recusant History 11
     (January 1972): 179-195. "Part II, 1840-1870." Recusant
     History 11 (April 1972): 253-269.

_____. "Evangelical and Roman Catholic Missions to the Irish in
     London, 1830-1870." Ph.D. dissertation, Cambridge University,
     1970.

_____. "Heretic London, Holy Poverty and the Irish Poor, 1830-
     1860, Part I, 1830-1850." Recusant History 10 (January 1970):

210-230. "Part II, 1850-1860." Recusant History 11 (January 1971): 21-46.

_____. "The Roman Catholic Mission to the Irish in London, 1840-1860." Recusant History 10 (October 1969): 123-145.

Gillow, Joseph. "Early Catholic Periodicals." Tablet, February 19, 1881, p. 301; and February 26, 1881, pp. 341-342.

Goldstrom, J. M. Education: Elementary Education, 1780-1900. Newton Abbot: David & Charles, 1972.

Grant, A. Cameron. "A Note on ´Secular´ Education in the Nineteenth Century." Journal of British Educational Studies 16 (October 1968): 308-317.

Grant, James. The Newspaper Press: Its Origin, Progress and Present Position. 3 vols. London: Tinsley, 1871-1872.

Gregory, Robert. Elementary Education. London: National Society, 1905.

Grenouth, James Carruthers. The Evolution of the Elementary Schools of Great Britain. New York: D. Appleton, 1903.

Gwynn, Denis. Cardinal Wiseman. Dublin: Browne & Nolan, 1950.

_____. A Hundred Years of Catholic Emancipation (1829-1929). London: Longmans, Green, 1929.

Hickey, John Vincent. Urban Catholics: Urban Catholicism in England and Wales from 1829 to the Present Day. London: G. Chapman, 1967.

Hirst, Joseph. Father Lockhart of the Institute of Charity. London: Catholic Truth Society, 1912.

Holman, H. English National Education, a Sketch of the Rise of Elementary Schools in England. London: Blackie, 1898.

Horgan, J. W. Great Catholic Laymen. 2nd ed. Dublin: Catholic Truth Society of England, 1907.

Hourdin, Georges. La Presse Catholique. Paris: A. Fayard, 1957.

Howatt, J. R. Sketch of Fifty Years Work by the Ragged School Union. London: n.p., 1894.

Hulme, Anthony. School in Church and State. London: St. Paul Publications, 1960.

Hurt, John. Education in Evolution: Church, State, Society and Popular Education, 1800-1870. London: Hart-Davis, 1971.

Illing, M. J. "An Early H. M. I., Thomas William Marshall, in the

Light of New Evidence." _Journal of British Educational Studies_ 20 (February 1972): 58-69.

Inglis, K. S. _Churches and the Working Classes in Victorian England._ London: Routledge & Kegan Paul, 1963.

Jackson, John Archer. _The Irish in Britain._ London: Routledge & Kegan Paul, 1963.

Johnson, John Richard Bowman. "The Education Department, 1839-1864: a Study in Social Policy and Growth of Government." Ph.D. dissertation, Cambridge University, 1968.

Johnson, Richard. "Educational Policy and Social Growth in Early Victorian England." In _The Victorian Revolution: Government and Society in Victoria´s Britain._ Edited by Peter Stansky. New York: New Viewpoints, a Division of Franklin Watts, 1973.

Kekewich, George William. _The Education Department and After._ London: Constable, 1920.

Kilpurn, E. E. _Catholic Emancipation and the Second Spring: a Catholic´s Record from 1829-1929._ London, Burns & Oates, 1929.

King, John Patrick. "The Attitudes of the Roman Catholic Church toward Participation in State Systems of Education: the Irish Case." Ph.D. dissertation, University of Wisconsin, 1970.

Kitching, Jack. "Roman Catholic Education from 1700-1870." Ph.D. dissertation, University of Leeds, 1966.

Levy, Samuel Leon. _Nassau W. Senior 1790´-1864._ New York: Augustus M. Kelley Publishers, 1970.

Lucas, Edward. _The Life of Frederick Lucas, M. P._ 2 vols. London: Burns & Oates, 1886.

Lucas, Herbert. "The Catholic Institute and Frederick Lucas." _Month_ 51 (May 1884): 214-232; and 51 (June 1884): 334-345.

_____. "The Last Days of the Catholic Institute." _Month_ 51 (August 1884): 509-526.

McClelland, Vincent A. _Cardinal Manning, His Public Life and Influence, 1865-1892._ London: Oxford University Press, 1962.

McElrath, Damian. _Richard Simpson, 1820-1876, a Study in XIXth Century English Liberal Catholicism._ Louvain: Bibliothèque de l´Université, 1972.

McElrath, Damian, and Holland, James C. _Lord Acton: the Decisive Decade, 1864-1874, Essays and Documents._ Louvain: Bibliothèque de l´Université, 1972.

McEntee, Georgiana Putnam. The Social Catholic Movement in Great Britain. New York: Macmillan, 1927.

Maclure, J. Stuart. Educational Documents, England and Wales, 1816-1967. London: Chapman & Hall, 1968.

Maltby, Samuel Edwin. Manchester and the Movement for National Elementary Education, 1800-1870. Manchester: University Press, 1918.

Marshall, T. W. M. Protestant Journalism. London: Burns and Oates, 1874.

Mathew, David. Catholicism in England: the Portrait of a Minority: Its Culture and Tradition. 3rd ed. London: Eyre & Spottiswoode, 1955.

Montague, C. J. Sixty Years in Waifdom; or the Ragged School Movement. London: Charles & Murray, 1904.

Newsome, David. The Wilberforces and Henry Manning; the Parting of Friends. Cambridge, Mass.: Harvard University Press, Belknap Press, 1966.

Norman, E. R. Anti-Catholicism in Victorian England. New York: Barnes & Noble, 1968.

O'Conner, Kevin. The Irish in Britain. London: Sidgwick & Jackson, 1972.

Pugh, R. B. "Sources for the History of English Primary Schools." Journal of British Educational Studies 1 (November 1952): 43-51.

Purcell, Edmund Sheridan. The Life of Cardinal Manning. 2 vols. London: Macmillan, 1896.

Ramsay, Grace [Kathleen O'Meara]. Thomas Grant. London: n.p., 1874.

Read, Donald. Press and People, 1790-1850; Opinion in Three English Cities. London: E. Arnold, 1961.

Reid, T. Weymss. The Life of the Right Hon. William E. Forster. 2 vols. London: Chapman & Hall, 1888.

Rigg, James Harrison. National Education in Its Social Conditions and Aspects, and Public Elementary, English and Foreign. London: Straham & Co., 1873.

Roberts, F. David. "More Early Victorian Newspaper Editors." Victorian Periodicals Newsletter, no. 16 (June 1972), pp. 15-28.

Routley, Erik. English Religious Dissent. Cambridge: University Press, 1960.

Scott, P. G. "Richard Cope Morgan, Religious Periodicals and the Pontifex Factor." Victorian Periodicals Newsletter, no. 16 (June 1972), pp. 1-14.

Sider, Earl Morris. "Dissent and Religous Issues in British Politics, 1840-1868." Ph.D. dissertation, State University of New York at Buffalo, 1966.

Simon, Brian. Studies in the History of Education, 1780-1870. London: Lawrence & Wishart, 1960.

Smith, Frank. A History of Elementary Education, 1760-1902. London: University of London Press, 1931.

Sturt, Mary. The Education of the People: a History of Primary Education in England and Wales in the Nineteenth Century. London: Routledge & Kegan Paul, 1967.

Sutcliffe, Edmund F. Bibliography of the English Province of the Society of Jesus, 1773-1953. London: Manresa Press, 1957.

Sylvester, David William. Robert Lowe and Education. Cambridge: University Press, 1974.

Thureau-Dangin, Paul. The English Catholic Revival in the Nineteenth Century. Rev. ed. 2 vols. London: Simpkin, Marshall, Hamilton, Kent, 1914.

Ullathorne, William Bernard. Letters of Archbishop Ullathorne. London: Burns and Oates, n.d.

_____. Notes on the Education Question. London: Richardson & Son, 1857.

Wallace, Elisabeth. Goldwin Smith: Victorian Liberal. Toronto: University of Toronto Press, 1957.

Ward, Bernard. The Sequel to Catholic Emancipation. 2 vols. London: Longmans, Green, 1915.

Ward, Herbert. The Education System of England and Wales and Its Recent History. London: Cambridge University Press, 1935.

Ward, J. T., and Treble, J. H. "Religion and Education in 1843: Reaction to the Factory Bill." Journal of Ecclesiastical History 20 (April 1969): 79-110.

Ward, Wilfrid. The Life and Times of Cardinal Wiseman. 2 vols. London: Longmans, Green, 1897.

_____. William George Ward and the Catholic Revival. London: Macmillan, 1893.

Wardle, David. English Popular Education, 1780-1970. Cambridge: University Press, 1970.

Ware Cornish, Francis W. The English Church in the Nineteenth Century. New York: AMS Press, 1910.

Welch, Sylvia A. "The Role of the Birmingham Reformers in the Movement for Change in the Educational System of England, 1840-1877." Ph.D. dissertation, New York University, 1970.

Wilson, R. K. The First and Last Fight for the Voluntary Principle in Education, 1846-1858. London: Eastern Press, 1916.